INTERRACIAL MARRIAGE
IN HAWAII

PATTERSON SMITH REPRINT SERIES IN
CRIMINOLOGY, LAW ENFORCEMENT, AND SOCIAL PROBLEMS

A listing of publications in the SERIES *will be found at rear of volume*

PUBLICATION NO. 65: PATTERSON SMITH REPRINT SERIES IN
CRIMINOLOGY, LAW ENFORCEMENT, AND SOCIAL PROBLEMS

INTERRACIAL MARRIAGE IN HAWAII

*A Study of the Mutually Conditioned
Processes of Acculturation
and Amalgamation*

BY

ROMANZO ADAMS

Montclair, New Jersey
PATTERSON SMITH
1969

SBN 87585-065-0

Library of Congress Catalog Card Number: 69-14907

PREFACE

THE University of Hawaii through several of its departments is conducting studies relating to the character of the peoples of Hawaii and to their social relations. This volume is the outcome of one of these studies.

Hawaii presents an exceptional opportunity for the observation and study of a type of social process that has been going on in many parts of the world for a long time. As a result of migration, contacts are established between peoples who differ more or less in culture and in physical race traits. In the beginning the contacts tend to be mainly of an economic character and there is sentiment adverse to all relations of a more intimate character. At this stage the acculturation is almost wholly at the technological level and does not involve things greatly affected with sentiment. There is little tendency toward amalgamation if each group is made up of families. But gradually and without observation social relations of an increasingly intimate character come into existence, acculturation tends to take place at the level of the loyalties and, if the caste principle does not prevail, there is a more or less rapid amalgamation through intermarriage. That is, the two or more peoples become one people, one in blood relationship, one in culture and one in loyalty.

In relation to these processes Hawaii has some of the characteristics of a laboratory. Its population includes representatives of several European peoples and of several peoples of Asiatic origin. There are also the descendants of the native Polynesians and even a few thousand persons of African descent. The area and population of the Islands are not so large as to make the gathering of data an impossible task or to discourage one who seeks the insight that comes from a wide acquaintance with the people and their situations. Since Europeans and Asiatics began to come to Hawaii there has been sufficient time to permit of many interesting changes and some of the developments are at a sufficiently advanced stage that the student is able to see the relation of the earlier to the later.

For more than a century and a half there has been stimulus from the outside world and the historic developments may be seen as a response to such stimulus. Nevertheless, the Islands have enjoyed a measure of isolation so that outside influences have not been overwhelming. That is, Hawaiian life has had in it something that is distinctive, and at every stage of development the outcome has been determined largely by local interests and local traditions. There has been continuity. The data relating to these matters are the more readily available because of the doctrine and the ritual of racial equality which have prevailed in Hawaii. Because there has been an interest in these matters for a long time there is available to the student an exceptional amount of historical and statistical data.

It would be impossible in brief space to acknowledge properly the help received from others but the names of a few should be mentioned. The author owes much to Dr. Robert E. Park for his counsel relating to the project as a whole. Dr. A. W. Lind's still unpublished study relating to another aspect of the social situation in Hawaii has been helpful. Miss Margaret Lam performed a unique service in interviewing representatives of the various racial and mixed racial groups and in securing data relative to the family histories of several of the old mixed-blood families. To Miss Hester Lemon, head of the Territorial Bureau of Vital Statistics, is due much appreciation for her help in furnishing data as to births, deaths, and marriages. For the hundreds of University of Hawaii students and to school teachers, social workers, and others who have made their observations and experiences available for the use of the author there is grateful appreciation.

ROMANZO ADAMS

INTRODUCTION

It is no longer a secret, even to the layman, that there are not now and probably never have been—not at any rate, in the sense in which that term is ordinarily understood,—any pure races. What we sometimes refer to as historic races, that is to say, races that have actually existed and had a history, are merely peoples who have acquired distinctive and distinguishing racial traits through long periods of isolation and continued inbreeding.

Although it is now generally recognized that there are no pure races it is not generally known to what extent the surviving peoples are of diverse racial origins. There has, as a matter of fact, been until very recently, little scientific interest in human hybrids or in the natural history of races. Races are supposed to be pure; even if individual human beings are notoriously mixed.

Of all European peoples the Jews, because they have by pretty constant inbreeding, succeeded in preserving, such as it is, their racial integrity and their tribal religion are, in the popular estimation, the classic example of racial purity. It is curious, in view of this fact, that Jews are almost the only one of "historic races" that have been interested in investigating the extent and conditions under which their racial stock has, at different times, been contaminated with gentile blood.[1]

Although there has been so little interest in the study of human hybrids the subject is nevertheless of real importance. It is important not merely because, in the long run, it is the mixed rather than pure races that survive, but because race

[1] See Maurice Fishberg, "The Jew." A study of race and environment. London and New York, 1911.

relations have everywhere so largely determined the structure of human society.

It is probably not due to mere historical accident that society and civilization in India are everywhere dominated by the principle of caste, while in China, except perhaps between the Punte and Hakka peoples of South China, there is almost no trace of that institution. One explanation that suggests itself is this: In India the invading and conquering races were culturally as well as politically superior to the indigenous peoples. In China the reverse was the case. The result is that the Chinese have invariably absorbed and assimilated their conquerors, and race distinctions that might have once existed have disappeared. In India, on the other hand, the conquering peoples seem to have established a caste system, not merely to preserve their racial integrity, but to insure the permanence of a social order in which their dominance, having become customary, is now regarded as natural and right.

There is, however, another factor that invariably plays a role in race relations and that is visibility. In the case of India the invading races were of widely different physical types. They were so different, in fact, that even with all the miscegenation that has gone on since the earliest invasions the evidences of race mixture are everywhere evident to the most casual observer.

High visibility makes it easy to observe and to maintain race distinctions. On the other hand it is difficult,—particularly in a mobile society like our own, to maintain caste distinctions except—as in the case of the black man and the white—on the basis of obvious racial differences.

In China this situation did not exist. The Chinese empire and Chinese culture, partly by conquest and partly by the attraction which a higher civilization invariably exerts over less sophisticated peoples, have steadily extended their influence over the more primitive and tribal peoples on the margins of the Empire. Once these barbarians had acquired the Chinese language and Chinese customs, whether under the influence of Chinese merchants on the outer marches of the Empire, or, as in the case of the Mongols and Manchus, in the central cities, under the influence of Chinese officials with whose aid they ruled the Empire they had conquered, there were no very obvious racial marks to distinguish the foreign from the native peoples. Under these circumstances miscegenation, cultural assimilation and racial amalgamation, in a relatively short time, erased such racial and cultural differences as might otherwise have provided a basis for caste distinctions.

In any case whatever race problems the Chinese people may have encountered in the process of incorporating their tribal neighbors into the more complex matrix of a Chinese society, they were solved by the Chinese family system. The Chinese family seems to have included within the limits of its authority, at different times, a number of alien elements, including servants, slaves and concubines, and it is, apparently, under the influence of this familial authority that Chinese society has succeeded in assimilating the diverse racial elements of which, like every other higher civilization, it is composed.

If the caste system is characteristic of India, and the family system of China, then, in much the same fashion and to much the same extent, the territorial organization of society that we call the state, is characteristic of Europe. One of the functions of the state has been to provide a *modus vivendi* which would permit peoples of divergent races and cultures to live and work together within the limits of a single economy.

An examination of the population map of any European country today will reveal the existence of numerous little racial and cultural enclaves, where the language and tradition of some forgotten tribe or people, not yet wholly assimilated and absorbed, still persist in spite of the pressure imposed upon them by the enveloping economic and political order into which they are in process of being incorporated.

In this connection I am reminded of the fact that the Prussians, the most German of the German states, came into existence as the result of the imposition of a German upon a Slavic people. Prussia is, as a matter of fact, the name of Slavic people first subjugated and then assimilated by invading Germans.

One of the facts which is brought out into a clearer light by investigations of intermarriage in Hawaii, upon which this volume is based, is the intimate relations that exist here and elsewhere, between race and culture, and the extent to which in any society biological and social factors interact and influence one another.

If the diverse races of mankind are, so far as we can observe, the products of isolation and inbreeding, it is just as certain that human society and civilization are a consequence of the coming together of diverse races and peoples in intimate association and co-operation that we call society. Every society, every nation, and every civilization has been a kind of melting pot and has thus contributed to the intermingling of races by which new races and new cultures eventually emerge.

As I have said elsewhere:

Changes in race, inevitably follow, at some distance, changes in culture. The movements and mingling of peoples which bring rapid, sudden, and often catastrophic, changes in customs and habits are followed, in the course of time, as a result of interbreeding, by corresponding modifications in temperament and physique. There has probably never been an instance where races have lived together in the intimate contacts which a common economy enforces in which racial contiguity has not produced racial hybrids. However, changes in racial characteristics and in cultural traits proceed at very different rates, and it is notorious that cultural changes are not consolidated and transmitted biologically, or at least to only a very slight extent, if at all. Acquired characteristics are not biologically inherited.[2]

[2] Robert E. Park, "Human Migration and the Marginal Man," *The American Journal of Sociology*, Vol. XXXIII, May, 1928, No. 6.

These are very general statements, so general in fact that they will hardly serve, as I hoped they might, either to suggest the theoretic interest of the problems with which this volume is concerned, or to indicate the conceptual limits of the field in which this and similar studies of race relations may be said to lie. I have, however, ventured to repeat here, what has been more fully and better said elsewhere, because it has seemed to me that a volume, dealing as this does with a case study of race mixture and acculturation, under conditions that are relatively unique, would perhaps be more impressive and gain significance if it were read in connection with some larger and more general statement of the historical process, of which it is itself at once an example and an integal part.

If then it happens that in this study of intermarriage in Hawaii, we seem to be brought, so to speak, into the very presence of the historical process, where we may observe civilization as it evolves under something like laboratory conditions, this is due, in part at least, to the advantages of islands for the purpose of sociological investigation.

In Sir J. M. Barrie's comedy, "The Admirable Crichton," —a sort of whimsical version of the Swiss Family Robinson —the hero, who is the family butler, facing the prospect of an indefinite sojourn on a desert island, makes this prescient remark: "You can't tell what will happen on an island." As might be expected succeeding events more than justify this prediction.

All kinds of things can and do happen on islands. One has only to know what has happened in the Hawaiian Islands since Captain Cook landed there in 1778, or to become acquainted with the extraordinary diversity of conditions existing in the different islands of the archipelago today to realize the justice of this observation. It is a far cry from the little island of Niihau with its population of two hundred natives, living almost in a state of nature, at any rate in well nigh complete isolation from the world about them, to the bustling, modern city of Honolulu. Honolulu, situated on the island of Oahu, at the crossroads of the Pacific where East meets West, is the news center of the Pacific, a kind of international listening post, responsive to every sign and signal that indicates a change in the political weather, so far, at least as this weather reflects relations between the Orient and Occident.

There are six other inhabited islands in the Hawaiian Archipelago besides Niihau and Oahu, but every one, in respect to climate, geography, population and social structure, is marked by individual differences. Every island is, in fact, likely to enclose within the limits of its coast line not merely another community but a different world, each with its own local traditions and way of life, and each more or less self-sufficing and complete in itself. Possibly these differences are not actually as great as they seem but the effect of isolation, which life on an island imposes, is to intensify personal intimacies and by so doing promotes the growth of local customs in response to local conditions. Insularity, in short, encourages individuality and in this sense, it is true that one cannot tell what will happen on an island.

On the other hand, it is just on an island, particularly a small island—and most of the Hawaiian islands are small, —rather than elsewhere that one can know what does go on. In these little island worlds, where the populations are small and everyone is neighborly, there is likely to be very little of that mystery and sentiment in regard to race which so readily springs up in more populous communities where local and occupational segregation so easily becomes the basis for the formation of hereditary classes, or castes.

Countries which encourage immigration are usually tolerant in respect to miscegenation, and where intermarriage is tolerated, there is ordinarily very little race prejudice. Immigrants are notoriously not addicted to ancestor worship. They are too busy getting on in the country. It is only later, after the invading peoples have settled down and the disproportion in sex ratio has declined that race prejudice—the sort of prejudice that may be said to be normal or latent in any racially mixed community—tends to assert itself.

What are popularly referred to as race relations ordinarily involve some sort of race conflict. Race relations conceived in this way, may be said to arise as a result of an extensive movement or mass migration of peoples. In such migrations males invariably arrive first and it is only gradually that the normal balance of the sexes is achieved. It is never fully achieved, in fact, until some time after any movement that could be described as mass migration has ceased. It is the earlier years of these migrations, and on what has been described as the racial frontier, that miscegenation and inter-marriage goes on more rapidly. Later, as the disproportion in the sexes in the invading population is redressed, the pace at which intermarriage and race mixture proceeds will ordinarily decline.

The course of events, in such cases, is always more complicated than this statement of it indicates, and it is not possible to predict with any certainty the final outcome, except that one may expect, with a certain amount of assurance, that when stabilization is finally achieved race relations will assume one of three of configurations. They will take the form of a caste system, as in India; they will terminate in complete assimilation as in China; or the un-assimilated race will constitute a permanent racial minority within the limits of a national state, as is the case of the Jews in Europe.

What has been said suggests that race relations, like many if not most other relations among human beings, must be conceived as existing in three dimensions rather than, as we ordinarily conceive it, in two. Most human relations are a result of some sort of adjustment, and imply the existence, at any rate, of a *modus vivendi*, between individuals and between groups of individuals. But these adjustments are only partial and are themselves involved in a long term process of change, which frequently assumes, on closer examination, the form of an irreversible series or succession. Changes may be, or seem to be, merely fortuitous. At other times they assume a cyclical or secular form. All three types of change are involved in the processes of growth and all three are more or less involved in what we may describe as the "race relation cycle." This means that race relations, at least the sort of race relations with which we are concerned in this volume, can best be interpreted if what they seem to be at any time and place is regarded merely as a phase in a cycle of change which, once initiated, inevitably continues until it terminates in some predestined racial configuration, and one consistent with an established social order of which it is a part.

Race relations in Hawaii today seem to be approaching the terminus of such a cycle as here described. The population of the islands has risen from the lowest level in 1875 to what it was at the time Cook visited it. The demand for foreign labor for the sugar and pineapple plantations has, apparently, ceased.

This involves a drastic change in the policy which has, within a period of sixty-two years, repeopled the islands with alien races. However, the result of this experiment is still in doubt and probably will remain so, at least until the normal ratio of the sexes has been re-established in the islands. One reason why it has been as successful as it actually has is the fact that, owing to the control which the Hawaiian Planters' Association has exercised over its single important industry, Hawaii has had the advantage of a planned economy.

ROBERT E. PARK
University of Chicago

CONTENTS

ILLUSTRATIONS *

* The pictures are of high school pupils, nearly all of whom were found in one school in Honolulu. They are selected to represent a social type rather than racial types. Of diverse pure and mixed racial ancestry they are, with one possible exception, native born citizens of the United States. They share in common educational opportunities, participate in common social activities and approach a common standard of culture and refinement.

INTERRACIAL MARRIAGE
IN HAWAII

CHAPTER I

TREND OF POPULATION

AT the time of Captain Cook's second visit to Hawaii, 1778-9, Captain King estimated the population of the Islands at 400,000.[1] Mr. Bligh, master on Cook's ship, estimated it at 242,200.[2] On the basis of King's method and with more adequate information relative to the resources of the various islands and districts, it would appear that

[1] Captain King describes his method of estimate as follows: "The Bay of Karakakooa, in Owhyhee, is three miles in extent, and contains four villages of about eighty houses each; upon an average, in all three hundred and twenty; besides a number of straggling houses; which makes the whole amount to three hundred and fifty. From the frequent opportunities I had of informing myself on this head, I am convinced that six persons to a house is a very moderate allowance; so that, on this calculation, the country about the Bay contains two thousand one hundred souls. To these may be added fifty families, or three hundred persons, which I conceive to be nearly the number employed in the interior parts of the country amongst their plantations; making in all two thousand four hundred. If, therefore, this number be applied to the whole extent of the coast round the island, deducting a quarter for the uninhabited parts, it will be found to contain one hundred and fifty thousand. By the same mode of calculation, the rest of the islands will be found to contain the following numbers:

Owhyhee (Hawaii)	150,000
Mowee (Maui)	65,400
Woahoo (Oahu)	60,200
Atooi (Kauai)	54,000
Morotoi (Molokai)	36,000
Oneeheow (Niihau)	10,000
Ranai (Lanai)	20,400
Oreehoua (Lehua)	4,000
Total of inhabitants	400,000"

—A Voyage to the Pacific Ocean in the Years 1776–1780, Vols. I and II written by Captain James Cook; Vol. III by Captain James King, London, 1784. Vol. III, pp. 128–129.

[2] Bligh's estimate is published in the Mariners Mirror, London, October 1928, in an article entitled, "Bligh's Notes on Cook's Last Voyage," by Rupert T. Hughes. Bligh's estimate is penciled on the margin of page 129 of what was his personal copy of Volume III of the 1784 edition of Cook's Voyages. This volume is now in the possession of the Admiralty Library.

1

Bligh's estimate was the more nearly accurate. Probably there were about 300,000 people at that time.

The method used by King tended to exaggerate the population of the smaller islands since it proportioned the population, not to area but to periphery. These smaller islands not only had little back country proportionate to coast line, but being less elevated received less rainfall and hence were less productive. For example, Lehua, to which he assigned 4,000 people, is an almost barren rock 290 acres in area with no population of which there is knowledge, with no known supply of drinking water except in rainy weather and probably unpopulated in King's time. Molokai, Lanai, and Niihau all suffer from insufficiency of water and they do not at present have much more than a ninth of the population King calculated for them, and probably their population at that time was not a fifth as large as he estimated. The estimate for the larger islands was better, but in using the coast of Kealakekua Bay as a sample district and deducting a quarter for unpopulated parts he did not make a sufficient allowance for some thinly populated sections of the coast.

But whether the population was 300,000 or more, or less, it seems to have been large enough to occupy about all of the land capable of utilization under the conditions of a stone age culture. The journals of Captain Cook and of several officers and members of his crew furnish testimony as to the careful cultivation of the soil and as to the comparatively dense population on the better lands. Later explorers confirm these accounts, and even after the devastation of a long sanguinary war and of the pestilence of 1804, the drier and less fertile islands are known to have maintained a much larger population than they have had in recent years. Apparently the few hundred voyagers who came to Hawaii hundreds of years ago had multiplied by natural increase until they had reached numbers about as large as the islands were able to maintain, and then an approximate balance had been maintained. Factors related to this balance were:

1. A normal fertility of the women. Early explorers testify as to the abundance of children. Captain King, after making observations, thought that there were at least six people to the house on the average.

2. A favorable climate. The early white residents called it a salubrious climate.

3. The isolation of the islands. The mode of travel and the time required in the case of the original immigrants must have been such as to exclude many infectious diseases.

4. Occasional famines. When there was a deficient rainfall in some districts, the effect of crop failure was mitigated by the access of the people to the ocean with its fish and other sea foods.

5. Wars. Intermittent wars were sometimes very costly, not only in the lives of the fighting men but also, on account of the destruction of growing crops, in the lives of noncombatants.

6. Infanticide and abortion. Both boys and girls were the victims of infanticide, but the practice served chiefly to reduce the number of females. In this way the extra loss of life among males due to war was more or less balanced and the practice tended to bring about a numerical equality of the sexes. Because of the intermittent character of the warfare and the more constant practice of infanticide, it is probable that at some times males were in excess and, at others, females.

In 1823 the missionaries, who had lived in the Islands for three years, estimated the population of each island and of the whole archipelago, the total being 142,050. We know more about the resources of the various districts than did the missionaries of that date and we have the benefit of the data of the census taken nine years later. The missionary estimate was too high. I have estimated the population for 1823 at 134,750.

In 1832 a census was taken for each of the five more important islands by the missionaries assisted by the native school teachers who were, at this time, found in nearly all districts. Estimates were made for two of the smaller islands. Accepting the data of the census, revising the estimates on the basis of later and more adequate information and adding, I find the population in 1832 to have been 124,049. A second census was taken by the missionaries in 1836.

Later censuses taken under Hawaiian governmental authority are for the years 1849, 1850, 1853, 1860, 1866, 1872, 1878, 1884, 1890, 1896. Unted States Census data are available for 1900 and later census years. From the estimates and from the data of the censuses it is evident that there was a very important decrease of population in the century following the first visit of Captain Cook. The smallest population enumerated at any census was 56,897 in 1872, but, considering births, deaths and the passenger statistics, it appears that the actual minimum was in 1875, just before the larger importation of Chinese labor began. In the forty-five years, 1778–1823, it is probable that the population had decreased by more than half, and in the next fifty-two years, 1823–1875, it was reduced by about sixty per cent, so that in 1875 it was less than twenty per cent of the estimated number for 1778.

The economic basis for the maintenance of a resident foreign population in Hawaii was a matter of slow development. In the beginning the masters of ships engaged in the fur trade would round Cape Horn on the way to the Pacific Northwest and they would call at Hawaii for water, vegetables, fruits and fresh meat. After securing a cargo of furs by trading with the Indians of the American Northwest coast, they would return to Hawaii and again secure provisions before sailing for China where the furs were sold. But the furs did not make a full cargo. Sandalwood grew in the mountains of Hawaii and there was a market for the fragrant wood in China. Sandalwood was taken on to supplement the cargo of furs. Before 1820 it was the trade in foodstuffs and sandalwood, mainly, that called for a few foreign men in Hawaii. After 1820 Honolulu and other Island ports were visited by the vessels engaged in whaling in the North Pacific. They, too, needed foodstuffs and Honolulu became a center for the refitting of ships.

Almost immediately whaling assumed the leading role in relation to trade and held it for nearly a half century. On the side of the Hawaiians there was a steadily increasing demand for foreign clothing materials and other foreign goods and their agriculture was carried on more and more on a commercial basis.

In 1823 there was a foreign population estimated at 175 and among these were eight or ten American missionaries and their families. According to the census of 1850 there were 1,045 resident foreign men, 168 women and 359 children, 1,572 in all. Perhaps fifty to a hundred of these were Chinese, and there were about a score of Negroes. The rest were of American or European origin. As long as the economic relations between the Hawaiians and the foreigners were almost exclusively trade relations there was a demand for the services of only a few foreigners.[3] While there were always a few foreign men after 1790, there were no resident foreign women until the missionaries came in 1820. Among the foreigners, the sex ratios were always highly abnormal.

There were a few experiments with sugar production at a comparatively early date, but not until 1835 did any effort along this line meet with sufficient success to keep it going permanently. By 1852 there were seven little plantations which had been developed by native labor under foreign management.

[3] Some of the resident foreigners had no function in relation to trade. They were deserters from whaling ships and they lived with their Hawaiian wives largely after the manner of Hawaiians.

In the fifties there was a considerable development of agriculture under foreign control. Native labor was employed mainly but there were also a few hundred imported Chinese. In response to the.early demand of the California gold mining communities, there was, at first, a considerable diversification of production, but when demand conditions changed, the tendency was to specialize in sugar production. Land was available in the economic sense because the population had been so much reduced and in the legal sense its acquisition was facilitated by the recent changes in the land laws,—by the substitution of an allodial for a feudal system of land holding.

But the habits of the Hawaiians were not such as to dispose them favorably toward the steady labor that seemed to be necessary to the successful commercial production of any crop under foreign management. Since they had sufficient land for their own use, their needs were not such as to compel many of them to accept service under conditions they did not like. There was no thought of military compulsion. Hence, if there was to be any successful development of commercial agriculture with capital and control supplied by foreigners, it was necessary to secure laborers from outside. One may believe that there would have been no labor immigration had the native population been able to respond to the situation with a moderate rate of increase so that the Islands would have been populated at all times to a point approaching their carrying capacity. Such density of population would have meant a lack of unoccupied lands and an abundance of native laborers.

In 1850 a law providing for indentured labor was enacted. The purpose was to secure steadier work on the part of Hawaiians. But not many natives accepted service under its provisions. In 1852 a few Chinese were imported and, under indenture, were employed on the plantations. From 1852 to 1875 about 2,600 Chinese were imported. Most of them remained on the plantations for only a few years after which they found other opportunities more to their liking. But while the number of Chinese employed at any one time was small, a labor policy was worked out during these years and, when sugar production became more profitable, Chinese and other laborers were imported in much larger numbers.

Through the reciprocity treaty with the United States (1876), Hawaiian sugar gained free entry into a tariff protected market and this provided the profit incentive necessary to a marked enlargement of production. Mainly, the growth of population since 1876 has been due directly and indirectly to labor immigration. In 1850 about two per cent of the population was made up of non-Hawaiians; in 1872 about 10 per cent; in 1878, 18 per cent; in 1884, 45 per cent; and in 1930, 86 per cent.

The depopulation of the native people has conditioned the whole movement in Hawaii: There is the modern agricultural and commercial development, the importation of laborers, and the consequent interracial situation involving acculturation and the amalgamation of races. At this point a mere mention of the leading causes of depopulation will be sufficient.

1. There were the sanguinary wars which continued for seventeen years after Captain Cook's first visit.

2. Diseases new and highly fatal to the Hawaiians were introduced by foreigners.

3. There was much hardship and exposure incident to the new relations with foreigners such as the cutting and carrying of sandalwood, service on whaling ships, and the contributions of foodstuffs required for trade.

4. There was a serious disorganization of production due to trade and to contacts with foreigners.

5. There was a decadence of the old moral order.

6. A primitive people was unable to meet the requirements of a new situation promptly.

The following table shows the population as estimated

for certain dates and as reported for census purposes at
other dates. On the page following that, the movement of
population as estimated and enumerated is shown by means
of a curve.

TABLE I

Population of Hawaii*

	HAWAIIAN	PART-HAWAIIAN§	NON-HAWAIIAN	TOTAL
1778 (Estimate) .	300,000			300,000
1823 "	134,750		175 (Est.)	134,925
1832 (Census†) .	124,049		400 "	124,449
1836 (Census†) .	107,354		600 "	107,954
1850 (Census) . .	82,035	558	1,572 "	84,165
1853 "	71,019		2,119 "	73,138
1860 "	66,984		2,816 "	69,800
1866 "	57,125	1,640	4,194 "	62,959
1872 "	49,044	2,487	5,366 "	56,897
1875 (Estimate) .	46,400	2,900	6,047 "	55,347
1878 (Census) . .	44,088	3,420	10,477 "	57,985
1884 "	40,014	4,218	36,346 "	80,578
1890 "	34,436	6,186	49,368 "	89,990
1896 "	31,019	8,485	69,516 "	109,020
1900 (Census‡) .	28,718	9,536	115,747 "	154,001
1910 (Census) . .	26,041	12,506	153,362 "	191,909
1920 "	23,723	18,027	214,162 "	255,912
1930 "	22,636	28,224	317,476 "	368,336

* At most dates there were some native Hawaiians absent at sea and
hence not included in the above figures.

† There was a small element of estimate in the first two censuses—three
small islands—and these estimates have been revised on the basis of data
that became available later. All estimates are by the author.

‡ The first census taken under the United States governmental authority
was in 1900 and the attempt to use mainland racial classifications was not
successful. The Hawaiian and part-Hawaiian population for 1900 have been
revised by estimate based on data of the 1896 and the 1910 censuses.

§ The term "part-Hawaiian" was used as a classificatory term for census
purposes in 1896. Before that time the hybrid descendants of Hawaiians
and foreigners were classified as "half caste."

Before 1900 there were few women among the non-
Hawaiians and even in 1930 there were more than twice
as many men as women. Most of the few laborers who came
from Europe brought their wives and children. But the
Chinese, Japanese, Koreans, and Filipinos came mainly as

single young men. Some of the Chinese and Koreans and many more of the Japanese later secured wives from their native lands, and, in the more recent years, population has increased largely as a result of the birth of children to immigrants. More than half of the population of the Territory is now made up of the Hawaiian born children and

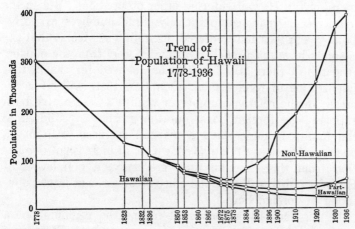

grandchildren of people who immigrated to Hawaii mainly after 1875.

What of the future? Will the population continue to grow in the next generation as rapidly as it has in the one just past and from the same causes? Will foreign laborers continue to be imported in large numbers? Will the racial situation be made more complex by the coming of people from still other countries?

The view here taken is that population growth will be much slower in the next generation than in the past. While some further agricultural development is possible, the rate of such development, limited as it is by market conditions and by the necessity of developing new techniques of production, will be slow. No mining can be expected and no further development of manufacture excepting for the working up of locally produced raw materials or for producing goods for the use of local consumers. Commerce and finance can increase in importance very little except in response to local needs.

In the past, the plantations have relied almost entirely on foreign born laborers for ordinary field work, the young men born in Hawaii entering other occupations. But in the very recent years comparatively large numbers of native born young men have entered plantation service so that the planters have not needed to bring laborers from the outside. Apparently there will be little or no need for the further importation of foreign men. Doubtless there will be an increase in the relative number of women as the native born supplant the foreign born, but the number of children to the family is undergoing a marked decrease. All in all, one may forecast a relatively low rate of increase of population from this time on and, gradually, a population of Hawaiian birth will take the place of the present large population of foreign born.[4]

If this forecast is correct it means the beginning of a new era in Hawaiian history. Common labor will be performed more and more by citizens and the foreign languages and other features of foreign culture will pass away. With immigration at an end, the further process of acculturation and amalgamation can be the better foreseen. While the new era will be one of important social developments, such developments will not be complicated by the introduction of a large new immigrant population. One may know what peoples and, approximately, what numbers of each are to have a part in the general process of acculturation and amalgamation. In the past hundred years there has been a constant and important change in the general social situation, due to the coming of immigrants from several sources.

[4] In 1930 the foreign born population of Hawaii, including those born in the Philippines, numbered 121,209, or 33 per cent of the total population. Over 90 per cent of these were adults and over 5 per cent were Filipinos, 17–20 years of age, who had come for plantation service.

Interest has centered in the adjustment of such immigrants to the situation in Hawaii and in the way their presence affected the people of earlier residence. But from now on it appears that interest will shift to the different sorts of native born citizens and to the social relations in which they are involved.

CHAPTER II

PRESENT RACIAL COMPOSITION OF
THE POPULATION

As a result of immigration from several countries of Europe and Asia and from the West Indies as well as the East Indies, Hawaii has acquired a population of much racial diversity. Through intermarriage among the various peoples there is coming to be an important number of mixed-bloods of several sorts.

Until about the beginning of the present century the amalgamation was almost wholly between the native Hawaiian people and the various immigrant peoples; that is, nearly all of the hybrids were part-Hawaiian, mainly the children of foreign men and Hawaiian women. More recently the immigrant groups have begun to intermarry and since the beginning of the century one group of fairly recent mixture, the Porto Rican, has been brought to the Territory.

The racial classification and definitions used for census and other statistical purposes are of such a character as to isolate those part-Hawaiians who claim their non-Hawaiian blood and to subdivide them into two classes, the Caucasian-Hawaiians and the Asiatic-Hawaiians, at least a third of the latter class having both Caucasion and Asiatic as well as Hawaiian blood. The other mixed-bloods are, for statistical purposes, classified as if they were of pure racial stock. For example, the Chinese-Caucasian mixture is counted as pure Chinese and the hybrid Chinese-Japanese is classified as pure Chinese or pure Japanese according to paternity. For census purposes the Caucasians are divided into four groups, the Portuguese, the Porto Rican, the Spanish and

12

the other Caucasian. By definition the Portuguese are those of all-Portuguese ancestry, and similarly in the case of the Porto Ricans and the Spanish. Hybrids such as Portuguese-Spanish are classified as "Other Caucasians." When the term "Other Caucasian" was first used (1910) it meant, with small exception, the people of white American or North European ancestry, but, on account of the inter-marriage among the Caucasian groups, it has come about that nearly a fourth of the civilian "Other Caucasians," children mainly, have some Portuguese, Spanish or Porto Rican ancestry. Porto Ricans, while classified for census purposes as Caucasians, are, commonly, of a Spanish-Negro-American Indian mixture.

In order to make an estimate as to the number of persons of pure and of mixed racial stocks in Hawaii it is necessary to use certain more or less arbitrary definitions. No one set of definitions is best for all purposes. The writer, there-fore, has decided for the sake of clarity to start with the census definitions and data and later to modify these in three ways, each for a special purpose.

TABLE II

Civilian Population as Racially Classified for Census Purposes (1930)

Race or People	Male	Female	Total
Hawaiian	11,311	11,325	22,636
Caucasian-Hawaiian	7,760	7,872	15,632
Asiatic-Hawaiian	6,282	6,310	12,592
Portuguese	13,870	13,718	27,588
Porto Rican	3,635	3,036	6,671
Spanish	631	588	1,219
Other Caucasian (est.) *	12,591	11,767	24,358
Chinese	16,561	10,618	27,179
Japanese	75,008	64,623	139,631
Korean	3,999	2,462	6,461
Filipino	52,566	10,486	63,052
Negro	322	241	563
All others	125	92	217
Total	204,661	143,138	347,799

* Estimated by subtracting from the total number of "Other Caucasians" the number of soldiers, sailors and marines and the estimated number of officers and members of families of officers.

For more than a hundred years there has been a passing over of part-Hawaiians into the Hawaiian group. That is, part-Hawaiians, especially the darker complexioned ones, frequently are ignorant of their possession of non-Hawaiian blood or they think that their little non-Hawaiian blood is of no practical importance and so they claim to be full blooded Hawaiians. It is estimated that, as a consequence of such passing and of further unrecognized intermixture, about 43 per cent of the so-called Hawaiians of today have a little of the blood of people who came after 1778. In making this estimate the historic situation covering over a century and a half has been considered. For example, there is evidence tending to show that there has been a continuous passing over into the Hawaiian group of part-Hawaiians,— mainly those of three quarters or more Hawaiian blood. It is probable that there was some living issue from the transient and irregular unions between sailors and native women of the fur trading and the whaling eras and weight has been given to evidence which tends to show that some of their later descendants were considered as Hawaiian, not as mixed. The number of such was, on account of abortion and infanticide, far smaller than it would have been if these practices had not existed.

The census definitions and classifications are such as to show the number of part-Hawaiians who know of and claim their non-Hawaiian blood, but all other persons of mixed blood, nearly equal in number, are classified as racially pure. The first modified classification of this chapter represents an attempt to measure the mixture that has taken place in Hawaii by regarding each immigrant people as a pure racial group and by segregating those descendants whose ancestry is not wholly within the group. Even the obviously mixed Porto Ricans are here treated as if they constituted a pure racial stock, and such related groups as Portuguese and Spanish are treated as if they were of different racial stocks. What the table aims to show is the amount of mixture that has taken place in Hawaii. Estimates relating to the number of non-Hawaiian hybrids are based on marriage and birth data.[1] For example, there were born in the two years ending June 30, 1933, 38 children of mixed Chinese-Portuguese parentage and all of these, according to the census classification, are pure Chinese. In the same two years 53 children of mixed Chinese-Japanese parentage were born and 26 of these are classified as pure Chinese because their fathers are Chinese, while the other 27 are counted as pure Japanese.

TABLE III

Civilian Population—First Modified Classification (1930)

(To show mixture that has taken place in Hawaii)

RACE OR PEOPLE	CENSUS CLASSIFICATION	AS RECLASSIFIED (ESTIMATES)	
		Pure Race	Hybrid
Hawaiian	22,636	12,856	9,780
Caucasian-Hawaiian . .	15,632		15,632
Asiatic-Hawaiian . . .	12,592		12,592
Portuguese*	27,588	27,588	
Porto Rican*	6,671	6,671	
Spanish*	1,219	1,219	
Other Caucasian . . .	24,358	18,516	5,842
Chinese	27,179	26,749	430
Japanese	139,631	139,131	500
Korean	6,461	6,301	160
Filipino	63,052	61,677	1,375
Negro	563	563	
All other	217	217	
Total	347,799	301,488	46,311

* The absence of mixed-bloods in Table III under the titles Portuguese, Spanish, and Porto Rican does not mean that there are no such mixtures but only that the mixtures are not, according to the arbitrary definitions of the census, counted in these respective classes. Ordinarily, the numbers in the third column do not indicate the number of mixed-bloods, but only the numbers classified in the census in a certain way. For example, 430 is the number of part-Chinese who are classified as Chinese. Thousands of part-Chinese are classified as Asiatic-Hawaiians and a few as Japanese.

[1] See Appendix, pp. 346–347.

The second modified classification is like the first excepting that some or all of the members of three immigrant groups of obvious and recent mixture are classified as hybrids: (1) the Porto Ricans, (2) the American Negroes, mainly, (3) a few of the Portuguese—those who came from the Cape Verde Islands or from Portuguese Guinea. The purpose is to show the total amount of race mixture that has taken place so recently that it is popularly recognized as such, whether it has taken place in Hawaii or in the regions from which the immigrants came.

TABLE IV

Civilian Population—Second Modified Classification (1930)

(Recent mixture whether originating in or outside of Hawaii)

RACE OR PEOPLE	RACIAL CLASSIFICATION CENSUS, 1930	RECLASSIFIED (ESTIMATED)	
		Pure Race	Hybrid
Hawaiian	22,636	12,856	9,780
Caucasian-Hawaiian . .	15,632		15,632
Asiatic-Hawaiian . . .	12,592		12,592
Portuguese	27,588	27,288	300
Porto Rican	6,671		6,671
Spanish	1,219	1,219	
Other Caucasian . . .	24,358	18,516	5,842
Chinese	27,179	26,749	430
Japanese	139,631	139,131	500
Korean	6,461	6,301	160
Filipino	63,052	61,677	1,375
Negro	563	100	463
All other	217	190	27
Total	347,799	294,027	53,772

The census computations designed to show the percentage of each racial group to the total population are based on the entire population including the military and on population data which are in some instances inaccurate on account of the arbitrary classification of hybrids. In the following table a comparison is made between the census distribution and a distribution of the civilian population only, the number of hybrids being estimated as in Table IV.

TABLE V

Percentage Distribution of Population (1930) with Racial and Mixed Racial Classifications

Of Pure Racial Descent	Total Population U. S. Census Classification Per Cent	Civilian Population Reclassified (Estimate) Per Cent
Hawaiian	6.1	3.7
Portuguese	7.5	7.9
Porto Rican. . . .	1.8	
Spanish	.3	.4
Other Caucasian . .	12.2	5.3
Chinese	7.4	7.7
Japanese	37.9	40.0
Korean	1.8	1.8
Filipino	17.1	17.7
All other	.3	.1
Total pure . . .	92.4	84.6
Hybrid		
Caucasian-Hawaiian .	4.2⎫	10.9
Asiatic-Hawaiian . .	3.4⎭	
Porto Rican. . . .		1.9
All other hybrid . .		2.6
Total hybrid . .	7.6	15.4
Total	100.0	100.0

In regarding the Portuguese, the Spanish and the "Other Caucasians" as three races, one does violence to conventional ideas as to race according to which all are to be classified as Caucasian or white. A similar statement could be made concerning the Chinese, Japanese, and Koreans. The third modified classification conforms to the more common ideas as to race, the unmixed population being classified into five racial groups as follows: Caucasian, Mongolian, Negro, Malay, and Polynesian. By reclassifying as pure Caucasian 5,842 persons of a mixture involving ancestry wholly within the Caucasian groups (Portuguese, Spanish and other Caucasian), and similarly, by classifying as pure Mongolian 375 persons of a mixture involving only the Chinese, Japanese and Koreans, the number of mixed-bloods is reduced from 53,772 to 47,560.

TABLE VI

Civilian Population—Third Modified Classification (1930)

	Five Races	Estimates
I. Polynesian	Hawaiians / South Sea Islanders	12,946
II. Caucasian	Europeans and their colonials / White Americans	52,865
III. Mongolian	Chinese / Japanese / Korean	172,651
IV. Malay—The Filipino		61,677
V. Negro		100
	Total of pure racial stock	300,239
	Hybrid	47,560
	Total	347,799

The preceding tables show the number of people of mixed racial ancestry as estimated for 1930, but they do not show the importance of the contribution of the various racial groups to the growth of the hybrid population in Hawaii. Table VII aims to do this. Considering only the hybridiza-

TABLE VII

Race Mixture—Contribution by Race (1930)

	Hybrids with Ancestry in the Specified Race (Estimates)
Hawaiian	38,004
White Portuguese	7,648
Spanish	486
"Other Caucasian"	30,360
Chinese	11,507
Japanese	1,685
Korean	545
Filipino	3,007
Porto Rican	1,320
Negro Portuguese	3,000
All other	100
Total	97,662
Twice the number of hybrids of Hawaiian origin	92,622
Extra counts due to ancestry in more than two races	5,040

tion that has taken place in Hawaii, it shows the number of mixed-bloods who have ancestry in each of the racial groups. Each hybrid is counted two or more times, once for each race in which he has ancestry. To the extent that the total exceeds twice the total number of hybrids of Hawaiian origin, it serves to show something as to the number of persons of a more complex mixture. The majority of these hybrids of more complex mixture are classified for census purposes as Asiatic-Hawaiians but they have Caucasian blood also.

1. According to the classifications of the 1930 census the only hybrids revealed as such were the part-Hawaiians and they numbered 28,224 or 8.1 per cent of the civilian population.
2. If we include the other sorts of mixture, if we consider such peoples as the Chinese and the Japanese or as the Portuguese and other Caucasians, as separate races, and if consideration is given only to the mixture that has taken place in Hawaii, about 13.2 per cent of the population was racially mixed in 1930.
3. If, with the above mentioned hybrids, we include the Porto Ricans and a few other persons of obvious and recent mixture originating outside of Hawaii, 15.4 per cent of the population was hybrid.
4. If the people are reclassified into the five racial groups there were 13.7 per cent instead of 15.4 per cent who were of mixed ancestry.
5. The racial groups that have been in contact for the longest period of time are the ones that have made the greatest contribution to race mixture. If two groups of more recent residence, the Japanese and the Filipinos, are excluded from consideration, nearly 40 per cent of the remaining population is of mixed racial ancestry.
6. Of the total civilian population in 1930, 49.7 per cent were Mongolian; 17.7 per cent, Malay; 15.2 per cent, Caucasian; 3.7 per cent Hawaiian; and 13.7, hybrid.

CHAPTER III

RACE MIXTURE

IN Hawaii, interracial amalgamation takes place mainly through intermarriage. There is no law against such intermarriage. While there may be much opposition within some families there is no general social disapproval. Commonly when a man marries a woman of a different race the friends of both symbolize their good will by attending the wedding and by other social recognition.

This freedom to intermarry not only tends to facilitate the process of amalgamation but also affects the social status of the mixed-bloods in a favorable way. Where interracial marriage is prohibited or where there is a hostile public sentiment, amalgamation may take place, but it takes place more slowly and through irregular unions. These are, in their very nature, secret and there are no official statistics. Because the amalgamation through intermarriage is open and above-board in Hawaii, a statistical record is possible, and because there has been sufficient interest in the matter for a long time very valuable statistical data are available. This is the more valuable to our purpose because it classifies persons according to racial origin, not according to nativity. For example, a child, all of whose great-grandparents came from Portugal, is classified as Portuguese, whereas in other parts of the United States he would be merely "native white of native parentage."

When a pair seek a marriage license each has to supply information as to his or her ancestry. A man might state that his father is a Portuguese-Hawaiian born in Hawaii and his mother, a Japanese-Chinese born in Hawaii, while the

RACE MIXTURE   21

woman might state that her father is German-Hawaiian born in Hawaii and her mother, Spanish born in Spain.

When births are reported for registration there is, similarly, a statement as to the racial origin of the parents and, if there is any doubt as to the accuracy of the information, the Bureau of Vital Statistics can and does check by means of other data on file. Through the use of the marriage and the birth data it is possible to discover the extent and character of the amalgamating process. It is not proposed to present the details of the process at this point, but certain generalizations are offered in order to reveal the process in the large.

In the early days of the fur traders and whalers who brought trade to the ports of Hawaii there was only a small foreign population and foreign women, entirely absent for a long time, were never numerous. There were nearly three times as many white men with native wives as with wives of their own race at as late a date as 1849 and there were more than twice as many persons enumerated as "half caste" as there were Hawaiian born children of foreign parentage. The "half caste" were classified as a part of the foreign population. The number of "half caste" was only a third greater than the number of native women married to foreign men and it is probable that only the children acknowledged by their fathers were counted as "half caste." Such mixed-bloods as may have survived from transient and irregular unions between sailors and Hawaiian women apparently were counted as Hawaiian.

When the plantations were established,—mainly after 1850,—laborers were brought from several foreign countries and thus contacts were established between immigrants and Hawaiians over wider areas. Many plantation laborers, after a few years of service on the plantations, abandoned such service and sought other sorts of economic opportunity in nearly all parts of the Islands so that contacts were established nearly everywhere. Many of these immigrants were without wives and some of them married native women. As the immigrant population increased the rate of out-marriage for Hawaiian women became higher. Conversely, as the number of immigrants became larger and as there came to be more women among them, their rate of out-marriage with Hawaiians decreased, even though the absolute numbers so marrying increased.

In the more recent period, the part-Hawaiians have had an important role in relation to the amalgamation of peoples. Their position is such that they have not been able to develop any strong sentiment of racial preference, certainly not for racial purity. They intermarry pretty freely with both Hawaiians and non-Hawaiians. Their marriages have always tended to correspond to the numerical situation. That is, when there were only a few part-Hawaiians of marriageable age and when there were very few non-Hawaiian women, nearly all of the part-Hawaiian men married Hawaiian women and over half of the women married non-Hawaiian men. As part-Hawaiians became more numerous relatively to the Hawaiians, as non-Hawaiians increased in number and as the sex ratios of the immigrants became more nearly normal, the tendency has been for part-Hawaiian men to marry fewer Hawaiian women, proportionately, and more part-Hawaiian and non-Hawaiian, and corresponding changes have taken place in the marriage practice of the women. Table VIII shows the trend since 1912.

The mixture of Caucasian and Asiatic blood is mainly indirect through the intermarriage of the different kinds of part-Hawaiians. Caucasian-Hawaiians marry Asiatic-Hawaiians or pure Asiatics, and Asiatic-Hawaiians marry pure Caucasians; and the issue is of a three-way mixture. Over five per cent of all marriages in the four years, 1930–34, were of these types.

The relative importance of the various immigrant groups so far as intermarriage with Hawaiians and part-Hawaiians is concerned has been determined, not so much by racial preference or prejudice, as by numbers, length of residence, and sex ratios. The Caucasians of American and North European ancestry have played the most important role in amalgamation by reason not only of their numbers, recently augmented by service men, but also by reason of their long

TABLE VIII

Brides and Grooms of Part-Hawaiians for Two Four-Year Periods

	1912–16	1930–34
Number of part-Hawaiian Grooms	455	1134
Per cent with Hawaiian Brides	39	15
Per cent with part-Hawaiian Brides	48	58
Per cent with non-Hawaiian Brides	13	27
	100	100
Number of part-Hawaiian Brides	645	1461
Per cent with Hawaiian Grooms	24	14
Per cent with part-Hawaiian Grooms	34	42
Per cent with non-Hawaiian Grooms	42	44
	100	100

period of contact. Next come the Chinese, who have been somewhat numerous for a long time. In the case of both the Chinese and the Caucasians of American and North European ancestry there has been a very abnormal sex ratio,—a great excess of men. The Portuguese sex ratio was more nearly normal and hence there has been less inter-marriage with Hawaiians. While the Japanese laborers came, originally, with few women they were able to secure wives from their homeland without much delay or difficulty and so only a few have married non-Japanese. In recent years the Filipinos, who are now numerous and without many women of their own race, are marrying more Hawaiian women than are the Chinese.

Amalgamation among the various immigrant groups is comparatively recent, belonging mainly to this century, and the hybrids are children so largely that the community is not greatly conscious of their existence. Such mixture has been mainly between the Portuguese and "Other Caucasians," a mixture within the Caucasian race. There is a small but increasing amount of marriage between Caucasians and Asiatics and also among the various Asiatic groups. The recent increase of marriages between Chinese and Japanese suggests that marriages of this type may be numerous when the ancient family traditions of the Chinese and the Japanese are further weakened and when old-country nationalistic sentiment has passed away.

Probably the out-marriage of persons of African descent has been facilitated by the fact that, except for a few who came from the mainland of the United States, they are not called Negroes. The first few hundred Africans came mainly from the Cape Verde Islands. They were known as Portuguese and they married Hawaiian women mainly, but also a few Portuguese women. Their descendants are known as Hawaiian or part-Hawaiian or as Portuguese, not as Negroes. Similarly the Porto Ricans with Negro blood are known as Porto Ricans, not as Negroes or part-Negroes and they are classified as Caucasians for census purposes. There is something in a name. If a man with African ancestry known as a Porto Rican goes to a certain barber shop in Honolulu,—one that seeks to attract tourist patronage,— he can get his hair cut. But if a man with African blood is identified as a Negro of mainland origin, he, when he seeks the service of this shop, is told that he has come to the wrong place.

That the number of mixed-bloods will continue to increase and that their proportion of the total population will increase pretty rapidly as soon as immigration ceases to be an important factor is evident from a consideration of the marriages that have taken place in recent years. The marriages of the fourteen years, 1920–34, have been of such a character that the issue of nearly one third will be of mixed racial stock. The marriages of earlier dates count toward a lower rate of mixture, but in the years 1931–1933 about twenty-five per cent of the children born were of mixed blood. Considering the trend of interracial marriage it may be expected that within a generation or two the births of mixed-bloods will be over half of all births if further immigration does not greatly influence the racial composition of the population. By the end of the century it is probable that half of the population will be of mixed racial ancestry.

The Hawaiian, as a pure racial group, is destined to disappear at a comparatively early date in consequence of intermarriage with part-Hawaiians and non-Hawaiians. The Spanish, a very small group, is diminishing at an even more rapid rate. The Portuguese may be expected to show a similar trend before the end of the present decade. The "Other Caucasians," while they contribute materially to the general process of amalgamation, tend to increase on account of new immigration from the American mainland and from Europe. While there is a considerable amount of out-marriage in this group the rate is fairly stable so that the forecast is for a fairly stable white population for a long time unless economic conditions shall reverse the movement of population,—unless the white people of Hawaii shall go to the mainland in significant numbers.

The pure Chinese are still increasing moderately in spite of the fewness of Chinese women, but out-marriage is slowly increasing and birth rates are decreasing. Not improbably there will begin to be a decrease of pure Chinese within ten or fifteen years. Now that the important immigration of Filipinos seems to have reached its end, they may be expected to diminish in numbers and to be succeeded by increasing numbers of part-Filipinos. The Japanese stand out as somewhat exceptional, and still there has been a small increase in out-marriage which, if it continues, will bring them effectually into the amalgamation process.

Some interest attaches to the sectional aspect of race mixture. The main thing to be said is that there are no sectional distinctions of such a character as to indicate a very important sectional difference in the racial and mixed racial character of the future population. The native Hawaiians and the various immigrant groups are widely distributed over the Territory, and in nearly all districts there has been considerable interracial marriage for two or three generations. As between Honolulu and the rest of the Territory, there has been no great difference in the rate of amalgamation excepting as a result of the migration of some part-Hawaiians from the country districts to the city.

Table IX shows the sectional distribution of the various races and of the part-Hawaiians at three dates. Especial attention is called to the ratio of part-Hawaiians to Hawaiians and to non-Hawaiians in Honolulu and the other districts.

TABLE IX

Civilian Population of Honolulu and of All Other Districts at Three Dates
(Census Data)

	1866		1896		1930	
	Honolulu	All Other Districts	Honolulu	All Other Districts	Honolulu	All Other Districts
Hawaiian	10,681	46,444	7,918	23,101	9,675	12,961
Part-Hawaiian	619	1,021	3,468	5,017	14,242	13,982
Chinese	370	836	7,693	13,923	19,334	7,845
Portuguese	230	190	3,833	11,358	12,297	15,291
Other Caucasian	1,457	743	4,208	3,039	16,839	7,519
Japanese			2,381	22,026	47,468	92,163
Filipino					4,776	58,276
All other	164	204	419	636	5,829	9,302
Total	13,521	49,438	29,920	79,100	130,460	217,339
Number of part-Hawaiians to 1,000 Hawaiians . .	57	21	438	217	1,472	1,079
Number of part-Hawaiians to 1,000 non-Hawaiians .	274	528	187	98	125	68

Out of 134 precincts in the Territory there were in 1930 only 29 in which over half of the population was of one racial group, and of this number only four had as many as two-thirds of any one race. The near-equality in the rate

of interracial amalgamation as between Honolulu and the
rest of the Territory does not appear to result from the
existence of similar conditions in the urban and the rural
districts, but rather, from a balance of opposing inequalities.
The rate of amalgamation in both the city and the rural
districts has been affected by relative numbers, by abnormal
sex ratios and by the attitudes of the various racial groups
more or less adverse to out-marriage. Before sugar production became important there was a tendency for the
foreign population to be concentrated in Honolulu and
hence, relatively to the number of natives, there were more
hybrids born in the city. But when the plantations began
to be important, some of the rural districts acquired a
relatively large population of foreigners. For two generations the sectional distribution of the various races has been
favorable to a pretty rapid racial amalgamation in all parts
of the Islands, a few small areas of scanty population excepted.

Usually the social contacts among members of the different racial groups are most numerous and intimate in the
city, and least numerous and intimate in the non-plantation
rural districts. The plantation districts may be rated as
intermediate. Moreover, the non-Hawaiian people of the
city have lived in the Territory for a longer time, on the
average, the more recent immigrants being found mainly on
the plantations. The city has a higher proportion of
citizens and, among the immigrants, there has been greater
progress toward a common culture.

In so far as enlisted men in the army and navy take wives
in Hawaii, they tend to raise the out-marriage rate for the
haole and also for the Portuguese and part-Hawaiians with
whom they intermarry largely. Since the men are stationed
in or near Honolulu their influence counts for a higher rate
of racial amalgamation in the city than in the other districts.

From a consideration of the above mentioned factors one

might suppose that the rate of amalgamation would be much higher in the city than elsewhere. But there are certain factors on the other side. Sex ratios among immigrants have been more highly abnormal in the rural districts at all times. Moreover, some of the non-Hawaiian groups, notably the Chinese and the Caucasian, of American or North European origin,—the *haole*, to use the local name, —have tended to concentrate in Honolulu. In the city their numbers are large enough to permit of the development of a social life more or less segregated according to race and this favors the development of group sentiment adverse to out-marriage. For example there is in Honolulu among the Chinese, especially the more prosperous Chinese, considerable sentiment against marriage with non-Chinese, and young men and women are influenced by this sentiment. But in the rural districts it may happen that the members of a racial group are too few to maintain an organization of their own and the young people may find their social life in racially mixed groups. Under such conditions social control adverse to out-marriage is less effective. This is illustrated by both the Chinese and the civilian *haole*, who marry out of their respective racial groups in higher proportion in the country than in the city.

In 1930, 50.5 per cent of all part-Hawaiians lived in Honolulu, but only 42.7 per cent of the Hawaiians. This tendency of the part-Hawaiians to be concentrated in Honolulu has not been, since the early period, due, directly and mainly, to a higher rate of marriage between Hawaiians and non-Hawaiians, but rather to a tendency on the part of part-Hawaiians born in the country to come to the city. Since 1890 many Chinese have moved into Honolulu and some of them brought part-Hawaiian families. The part-Hawaiians have always been favored for desirable sorts of employment in Honolulu and in response to this there has been a small but steady movement of young men and women from the rural districts. In 1930, 56 per cent of the part-

Hawaiians, 20–44 years of age, lived in Honolulu, but only 50 per cent of those under 20, and 43 per cent of those over 45. The coming of young part-Hawaiians to Honolulu affects marriage rates and birth rates. In the city where part-Hawaiians are relatively numerous, the Hawaiians marry part-Hawaiians in higher proportion than they do in the rural districts where part-Hawaiians are relatively scarce.

If one were able to forecast an extreme stability of population in the sectional sense the outlook would be for a future hybrid population that would not be of a sectionally uniform mixture. In the areas now used for plantation purposes one might expect Japanese and Filipino traits to be more prevalent than in the city, and in a few rural districts Hawaiian traits to be uncommonly prevalent. It is probable, however, that there will be a continued movement among the various peoples so that the hybrid population will tend to approach homogeneity. If, after a hundred years, there are among hybrids sectional differences capable of measurement by anthropologists, it is not probable that they will be recognized popularly in such a way as to interfere seriously with further movement or with social relations.

CHAPTER IV

THE MOVEMENTS OF IMMIGRANTS

IF the members of an immigrant group are occupationally and spacially segregated and if they reside permanently in the area of first settlement, they are able, in only a small way, to enjoy the social contacts essential to their acculturation. Because of their economic situation most new immigrants find it necessary to accept the less desired sorts of employment where they work side by side. Commonly they are able to live together in more or less segregated districts and for obvious reasons they desire to do this. Even with such minimum advantages, many of them are able to improve their economic position and, at the same time, to acquire some knowledge of the larger community life. Especially important is the acquisition of a second language. When immigrant families, after a term of residence in a segregated district, have occasion to move, they may find it feasible to establish homes where they will enjoy wider social contacts and where, consequently, the later stages of acculturation go on more advantageously.

The movements of the peoples of Hawaii are the more easily described because of the relatively simple economic structure of the Territory and because of the controlled character of immigration. During the period of Hawaii's modern economic development there has been one basic employment, agriculture, and most of the time only one important crop, sugar cane. More recently pineapple production has become important and there is a little coffee grown for export. Most immigrant laborers in Hawaii are employed directly by the sugar cane or the pineapple plantations. The cities exist mainly to perform certain services required by the plantations and the plantation population. There is manufacture, merchandising, transportation, finance, research, government. Minor agriculture, dairying, stock raising, and fishing serve to provide part of the foodstuffs required by the plantation population and by the people of the cities. Back of the cities and back of the minor agriculture lie the plantations which create the demand for the products and services of both. As the plantations have increased the magnitude of their operations they have created additional opportunities for urban workers and also for the small farmers and gardeners.

The main occupational and spacial movement of the peoples of Hawaii, 1876–1930, may be visualized as a stream of new immigrants to the plantations and three streams consisting of older immigrants and their sons and daughters moving away from the plantations. The first and largest of these outgoing streams flows beyond the limits of the Territory and subdivides, one branch going toward the Orient and the other to California. The second runs from the plantation to the cities of Honolulu and Hilo, while the third is made up of the families that seek non-plantation agricultural or business opportunities in the rural districts on or near the plantations.

The first of these movements has been going on vigorously for at least a half century. The actual number of persons who immigrated to Hawaii cannot be known accurately because the statistical data are not such that one can always distinguish between the arrival of new immigrants and the return of some who revisited their native land, but the following estimates are sufficiently close to reveal the general character of the movement. Probably 46,000 Chinese immigrants came, mainly before 1898. Nearly half of these returned to China, more than two-thirds of these leaving the Islands before 1900. Very few immigrant Chinese went from Hawaii to California and the great majority of the

Hawaiian born Chinese are still residing in the Territory. About 17,500 Portuguese immigrated to Hawaii, the largest numbers coming in 1878–1886. Including Hawaiian born descendants, about 14,000 have emigrated to the mainland. There are in Hawaii over 27,000 Portuguese, mainly Hawaiian born. The Portuguese men came with families and they are a prolific people.

Only a few of the Spanish, about 8,000 of whom came, mainly 1906–13, are now resident. Out of 4,000 probable survivors of those who immigrated, only 413 were enumerated in Hawaii in 1930 and there were 806 Hawaiian born Spanish. For the most part, those who left went to California, but a few returned to Spain.

About 180,000 Japanese have come to Hawaii and about 126,000, including about 20,000 Hawaiian born children, have emigrated, about 28,000 to California, and the rest to Japan. This return movement to Japan is still going on, twenty-eight years after laborers ceased to come.

About 120,000 Filipinos have been brought to Hawaii and about half of these have left the Territory; about two-thirds returned to the Philippines and the rest went to California.

Other smaller immigrant groups such as the Germans, the Porto Ricans, and the Russians and the Koreans behaved in a somewhat similar way, those who left commonly going to the mainland.

If one considers not only the surviving immigrant laborers but also their descendants in Hawaii and elsewhere it may be said that only a minority of them are to be found in Hawaii today.

In relation to occupational succession in Hawaii the Chinese worked out most of the important patterns of procedure. From 1852 to 1876 Chinese laborers were brought in at an average rate of about a hundred a year. Leaving the plantations after a few years, they were the pioneers in discovering ways through which an immigrant with small savings could make a living in Hawaii aside from plantation labor. The largest number of Chinese came in the ten years 1876–1886, and there was a smaller but important movement in 1890–1897.

The general procedure of those who became independent producers and business men was about as follows. Through saving parts of the wages received from the plantations, individual Chinese men accumulated a few hundred dollars each. Through the organization of large partnerships they secured enough capital to permit of an undertaking in agriculture or business. Sometimes a dozen or more men would be partners in rice growing or gardening. Commonly, for agriculture and gardening, leased land not suitable for the use of plantations was utilized and the improvements were made by the lessees. Probably all the partners would work in connection with their enterprise and, as profits were made, the operations would be extended and other Chinese would be employed at wages. Production was mainly for the Hawaiian market and it was an easy step for one of the partners to set up either a country store to supply goods needed by the workers or a city store to dispose of the farm products. Some became peddlers at first, carrying their packs over the country and purveying to the wants of the native Hawaiians. After they secured enough capital, they set up small stores. Even to this day there are a good many small country stores kept by Chinese who are now old men. In the main they followed old-country methods both in agriculture and in merchandising and a good many of them were successful.

Others came to the city of Honolulu and competed actively for such employment as was open to them. Since there were no large manufacturing establishments they found their opportunity in the many small industries that develop in a growing city and they over-crowded the labor market for both skilled and common labor. As men without families, mainly, they could live at low cost and so they could afford to accept low wages. When this movement to the city was at its height in the eighties there was much antagonism toward the Chinese but after most of them had stabilized their position in the economic life of the community there came to be a more friendly spirit.

The more prosperous Chinese were able to secure wives from their homeland before the Chinese Exclusion Act became effective in Hawaii (1900). Many of their sons, educated in American schools, found employment as clerks, bookkeepers, salesmen, and delivery boys for American firms. In 1930, 80 per cent of the Chinese men, 20–40 years of age, lived in Honolulu and they were engaged in a wide range of occupational activities including common and skilled labor and clerical work. They are carrying on business and financial enterprises of nearly all sorts and they are securing an increasing representation in the professions and also in public employments. Very few run laundries in Honolulu. Young men and young women continue to come from the rural districts in small numbers and when business is normally active they are absorbed into the business life of the community without attracting much attention.

Of those remaining in the country, many are too old to work and only a few of the others are employed at common labor on the plantations. Considerable numbers are in business as owners or employees, others are common laborers or skilled, a few are farmers, gardeners, or poultrymen. The immigrant rice growers, when too old to operate their fields, were unable to secure native Chinese help and so they sold out to Japanese men. For the Chinese the process of occupational stabilization is well advanced and at the present time they are not regarded as creating social problems through the readjustments that are being made.

When the Chinese first came to Honolulu in considerable numbers they lived mainly in a district adjacent to the principal business section of the city and the district is sometimes called Chinatown even today although most of the residents are non-Chinese. Partly because this city district was an area of second settlement, and partly because of the fact that Honolulu people are less race conscious than those on the mainland they did not segregate themselves as fully as was the case among the San Francisco Chinese or among European immigrants found in large American cities. As the city has increased in size and as the second generation Chinese have reached maturity and achieved business success there has been a considerable movement of homes away from the old Chinese district and into newer and more attractive residential areas mainly toward the southeast, their places in the old districts being taken mainly by Japanese.

In these new areas the Chinese, who are mainly native born, either buy or build homes similar to those of neighboring Americans; they furnish their houses with all modern appliances including radio and electric refrigerators, and they plant trees, shrubs, and flowers as do Americans. Commonly visitors who pass through these sections identify the homes as Chinese only by seeing the children playing on the lawns or in the streets.

White people do not consider them objectionable as neighbors and when the Chinese have begun to buy into a neighborhood occupied by white people there has been no consternation nor has there been any neighborhood action to prevent their coming. Commonly their coming has been accompanied by rising prices for real estate and if a white man has preferred to live in some other district he has been able to sell at a good price.

For a long time there have been a few districts in Honolulu in which there is an understanding that property is not sold to non-whites. Real estate men do not show houses in such tracts to non-white prospective buyers or tenants. But a considerable number of white people live outside of such districts and when occasionally a home in such a district is sold, contrary to the understanding, to a man of other ancestry it is likely to pass without any serious manifestation of disapproval.

More briefly the story of occupational and residential succession can be told for other immigrant groups who followed more or less closely the pattern set by the Chinese. The main body of Portuguese immigrants came at almost identical dates with the Chinese, 1878–1886. Because they were married and burdened with the support of families they were not able to leave the plantations and set up their own business enterprises quite as promptly as were the Chinese. As they left the plantations, fewer came to the cities and a larger proportion became farmers. As white people eligible to naturalization, they were favored by the laws relating to the homesteading of land. But a considerable number went into commercial business and others secured city employment at common or skilled labor. Relative to their total number there are fewer Portuguese than Chinese in the cities. But the trend of Portuguese is like that of the Chinese, toward the cities.

In 1930 about 45 per cent of all Portuguese, including nearly 50 per cent of the men 20–44 years of age, were in Honolulu. They too are found in a wide range of occupational activities, common and skilled labor, business and the professions. They are well advanced toward occupational stability and such further developments as there may be are not expected to disturb seriously the equilibrium of employment.

When the Portuguese came to Honolulu many of them established their residence on the slopes of an extinct crater known as the Punchbowl. While it is not far from the central business district its elevation is such that it continues to be a desirable residence area and it is still known as a Portuguese settlement although one sees many non-Portuguese children playing in the streets.

The Portuguese, like the Chinese, are spreading out over

desirable residential areas toward the southeast. In some cases they tend to concentrate in such a way as to create a Portuguese neighborhood, but many are scattered. Some are so situated that their neighbors are mainly of American mainland origin and their society is found mainly in this group. Apparently the Portuguese are beginning to disappear as a separate group so that after a time they will constitute just a part of the white population.

A considerable number of Japanese came to Hawaii in the ten years preceding annexation, 1888–1898. Most of them came without families and in time returned to Japan or went to California. Those who remained in the Territory included most of those who brought wives. The principal body of Japanese men now resident came in the ten years, 1898–1908, after which time the Japanese government did not issue passports to adult male laborers. Among those who came in this latter period were considerable numbers of women and, when the immigration of men ceased in 1908, many of them sent to Japan for their wives or for the so-called picture brides, so that the adult immigration, 1908–1924, was almost entirely of women.

Since the Chinese and Portuguese, who had come at an earlier date, had found most of the available opportunities which immigrants with little capital could make use of, the Japanese were under the necessity of remaining in plantation service for a longer time. For 31 years, 1890–1921, the Japanese were more numerous in plantation employment than the men of any other immigrant group and most of the time they constituted a clear majority of all such employees. But as they were able to find other employment of a more satisfactory character, they left plantation service. In doing this they not only followed the Chinese patterns mainly, but they actually succeeded the Chinese in both the rural districts and the cities.

Pre-eminently the Japanese are the small farmers of Hawaii. Out of 5,955 farms reported in 1930, 4,158 or nearly 70 per cent were operated by Japanese owners or tenants. But these 4,158 farms included only a little over 2 per cent of all farm land in the Territory. Of the 4,158 farms operated by Japanese, 619 were owned by the operators and on 3,539 the operators were tenants. During the twenty-two years after the cessation of Japanese labor immigration, 1908–1930, the population of the Territory was doubled and that of Honolulu nearly tripled. The demand for the products of local farms and gardens increased even more than proportionately. This new demand has been supplied mainly by the Japanese who have been quick to take advantage of new opportunities. While dairying did not belong to the traditional culture of the Japanese, they are now producing a considerable part of the local supply of fresh milk. They have been pioneers in the production of watermelons and strawberries. For a long time, either as laborers or as owners and tenants, the Japanese have produced most of the coffee grown in Hawaii.

The Japanese are also succeeding the Chinese as storekeepers in the country districts. Because of the relatively large Japanese rural population the Japanese merchants have had an advantage over the Chinese, despite the early start of the latter. Immigrants commonly prefer to trade with merchants who speak their language and who are familiar with their needs.

In the cities, the Japanese are in nearly all occupations. There are many common and skilled laborers. Considerable numbers are in the mercantile business. Hundreds of small manufacturing enterprises are owned by Japanese and there are a few of considerable magnitude. Most of the building in the residential sections of the city and some in the central business district is done by Japanese contractors. There are three Japanese banks. The Japanese are represented in the professions by increasing numbers.

Much of the movement of the Japanese from the plantations has occurred since 1915 and, in their effort to establish themselves in other occupations, their competition has modified the labor situation to an important degree. Except for the rapid growth of Honolulu and Hilo, which furnished much opportunity for employment, their competition would have been felt even more. In any case they have been felt to be the disturbing factor in the general employment situation. Since the Japanese are not yet stabilized occupationally, since the group is so large, and since it is not probable that the cities can continue to supply opportunity to rapidly increasing numbers, there is apprehension as to the future while they are further changing their occupational status.

When the Japanese began to come to the cities in large numbers some of them established themselves adjacent to and among the Chinese, but they also established camps or settlements in nearly all parts of the city barring certain areas occupied almost wholly by whites. If they have not actually displaced the Chinese merchants, they have secured a large part of the new trade incident to the growth of the city and, in the district in which Chinese merchants were formerly predominant, the Japanese are becoming more numerous. In the newer residence sections of the city, too, the Japanese have been quick to discover business locations and in most cases they have had the advantage of the presence of a large and growing Japanese population.

In 1930 a third of the people in Honolulu were Japanese and they were widely distributed over its area. In more than two thirds of the precincts at least twenty per cent of the population was Japanese. Commonly they live in small camps or settlements. These are large enough to enable them to have their more intimate social contacts within the group, but too small to prevent outside contacts altogether. The children, in particular, extend their acquaintance to other groups.

Because the majority of the Honolulu Japanese have been in the city for a comparatively short time, less than twenty years, the later stages of their occupational and spacial progress are not so well indicated. Such observations as may be made tend to indicate that in the main they will follow the Chinese pattern, but with a few exceptions. They are quicker to adopt American business methods. They, more than the Chinese, are experimenting with small manufacturing enterprises. Their numbers will increase more rapidly because they are better supplied with wives. As they become prosperous they show a greater tendency to build fine homes and to adopt American standards of consumption. They seem to be making more effort to broaden their social contacts.

Table X is intended to throw light on the sectional distribution of the men of the various racial groups as affected by occupation. It shows that, in general, the immigrant groups that came at the earlier dates are found in the cities more largely while the late-comers such as the Japanese and the Filipinos are mainly in the rural districts. Very small

TABLE X

*Percentage Distribution of Civilian Males 20 Years of Age and over (1930) as Urban and Rural.**

	Urban— Honolulu City and Hilo	The Rural Part of Honolulu County	All Other Rural Districts	Total
Other Caucasian . .	74.2	7.7	18.1	100
Chinese	65.3	13.5	21.2	100
Asiatic-Hawaiian .	60.1	6.8	33.1	100
Caucasian-Hawaiian	59.5	6.8	33.7	100
Portuguese. . . .	55.7	8.0	36.3	100
Hawaiian	47.9	10.3	41.8	100
Spanish	45.7	22.4	31.9	100
Japanese	41.2	15.2	43.6	100
Korean	35.6	23.8	40.6	100
Porto-Rican . . .	34.8	11.8	53.4	100
Filipino	8.2	22.3	69.5	100
All others	60.7	18.7	20.6	100
All races	35.4	16.3	48.3	100

* The order is that of the urban percentage.

groups such as the Spanish and the Korean have been attracted to the cities a little more rapidly than the Portuguese or the Japanese, probably because it is only in the cities that they are numerous enough to maintain a social organization of their own. The Porto Ricans, a small group, contrary to the rule, show little tendency to concentrate in the cities, considering the length of their Hawaiian residence. Apparently they are less able than the members of other immigrant groups to make a satisfactory economic adjustment and more of them, therefore, remain on the plantations.

The rural part of Oahu on which Honolulu stands, is intermediate between the cities and the other rural districts as offering opportunity for small independent enterprises. Because of the proximity of the city there is a larger market for dairy and garden products and for fish. Moreover, there is considerable employment in connection with the military and naval establishments near the city. These opportunities explain the tendency of the Koreans and the Spanish to be concentrated in rural Oahu.

The large movement of population from the rural districts to Honolulu and Hilo has been associated with a large importation of plantation laborers from outside the Territory. It now appears to be probable that the cities can no longer provide employment for any large number of men from the country. Consequently the young men are not coming to the city since 1930 as they did before, but are accepting employment in the country, largely on the plantations. This does away with the need for importing laborers from the Philippines or elsewhere. Possibly one may regard this as a depression phenomenon, but, probably, it marks a permanent shift in the character of the economic situation. Hawaii is approaching a condition of closed resources,—a condition in which the resident population is about large enough to utilize its resources. The outlook is for almost a complete absence of immigration and for a greatly reduced movement within the Territory. If this forecast proves to be correct the further processes of acculturation and amalgamation will be free from such disturbance as might be caused by the intrusion of important new population elements. The probable reduced mobility of population will tend to reduce the rate of interracial amalgamation. While other factors of the situation will work to an opposite result, one may anticipate that as social conditions assume a more stable character there will be, at the least, a reduced rate of increase in the number of interracial marriages.

CHAPTER V

INTERRACIAL MARRIAGE—THE SOCIAL
BACKGROUND

IN Hawaii public sentiment is not opposed to interracial marriage. True, there is much personal and family sentiment adverse thereto and such sentiment may prevail in social sets or groups of considerable size and importance, but it is the part of discretion to confine the expression of such sentiment to the small intimate group. So far as sentiment is expressed in an open and public way it, in general, is not unfavorable to marriage across race lines. For example, when such marriages occur they may be solemnized in any of the churches and, if so, the friends and families of bride and groom symbolize their good will and approval by sitting in the pews, attending the reception, sending presents, and offering felicitations and congratulations. The term, public sentiment, as here used, is defined in such a way as to confine it to such sentiment as is held by people generally or by a group of preponderant influence. An individual whose views are in harmony with public sentiment feels free to give open public expression to them. Not infrequently slogans are coined and used popularly and social ritual may be used to symbolize doctrines in harmony with such sentiment. If antagonistic sentiment prevails in some group of less influence and if its members feel free to give expression to such antagonistic sentiment only within the intimate group of like-minded and under conditions that more or less imply that it is confidential, such sentiment may be important in some ways but it is not *public* sentiment. In Hawaii a man or a woman is free to marry out of his or her race so far as public sentiment is concerned.

The comparatively large number of interracial marriages in Hawaii may be regarded as a consequence of this freedom. This brings us to the consideration of a fundamental question. Why this freedom in Hawaii? Why, in Hawaii, did the people of British and American origin fail to set up the obstacles that are so commonly found where English-speaking people have established contacts with the darker races?

As a first step toward an answer to the above question, it may be said that the laws and the sentiment of a people relating to such marriage are just a part of a social system. Marriage practice must be in conformity with the general pattern of race relations. Where the members of one race deny political, economic and general social equality to the members of another race, and where there are doctrines of racial superiority and inferiority, it is necessary to prohibit interracial marriage. Where the people of different races enjoy political equality, where economic opportunity is not formally limited for any people on grounds of race, and where people meet socially as equals, doctrines of social equality come to be held and there are social rituals to symbolize such equality. Such doctrines and rituals inhibit the public expression of private and family sentiment adverse to interracial marriage and prevent the enactment of prohibitive laws. In short, interracial marriage is free in Hawaii because any attempt to deny freedom would be contrary to the local mores. The question, then, reduces to this: Why in Hawaii are the developing mores [1] of such a

[1] One may question whether the term "mores" can be used in this connection. Do not the Hawaiian customs relating to race relations lack something of the age and sanctity of the mores? Is there sufficient unanimity of sentiment? One must admit of an incompleteness of development, but it is certain that for more than a hundred years there has been a development of sentiment and of a code in response to local conditions. While they are not fully accepted by all sections of the population and while they are subject to challenge in times of crisis, they do, nevertheless, control conduct ordinarily, and they gain in sanctity as a result of the emotions aroused in times of crisis.

character as to imply the social equality of different races and, therefore, to permit of interracial marriage?

When two peoples who differ in religion and other cultural traits and also in physical race traits come to live together in the same land and to maintain economic relations with each other they may or may not intermarry. If marriage across race lines is permitted it will take place, and, through such marriage, there will gradually come into existence a more or less homogeneous mixed-blood population. If such intermarriage is effectively prohibited there will develop a racial caste system, the mixture of blood will take place more slowly, and the people of mixed racial descent will gradually find a place in the caste system.

If there is some inborn tendency on the part of men and women to prefer marriage with those of their own race, if there is some native antipathy toward members of another race, such preference or antipathy is, when unsupported by a social code, not strong enough to prevent a considerable amount of out-marriage. There is the influence of propinquity and there are the purely personal preferences. Not infrequently these personal preferences run counter to such race preferences or antipathies as may exist. Under appropriate circumstances it is easy for a man and a woman who differ racially to fall in love and one may surmise that, in some cases at least, the racial differences are added elements of attractiveness.

If society wishes to prevent the intermarriage of men and women across race lines it must resort to some sort of social control,—public opinion, religious doctrine and ritual, or legal prohibitions or all together. There must be severe penalties for those who do not conform and their mixed blood children must suffer also. So elemental and powerful are the urges that influence choice in marriage that only a strong social control can be effective. Any sort of social control able to prevent interracial marriage for a long time cannot fail to create a caste system.

The decision as to whether interracial marriage is or is not to be permitted appears to be largely a matter of historic accident. The historic situation in Hawaii has been such as to result in freedom of marriage in the sense that interracial marriage is recognized in law and that there is no public sentiment in opposition thereto. The purpose of this chapter is to present the salient features of that historic situation.

In the beginning, the old Hawaiian family system was not very strictly organized. There was an exceptional degree of freedom and, except for the people of superior rank, there was very little in the way of ceremony connected with marriage. Divorce consisted merely in quitting and either party was free to terminate the arrangement at will, but there was some sentiment against changing wives frequently.

Children were, in many cases, given away to friends or relatives and hence they did not necessarily constitute a responsibility of the parents. Infanticide and abortion were practiced without public disapproval and hence a woman who decided to divorce her husband might be as free as he from responsibilities relating to the care of a child.

This freedom had one rather unique feature. When a man or a woman was married this did not deprive him or her of the privilege of marrying again. That is, a man might have two or more wives and, at the same time, each wife might have two or more husbands. This does not appear to have been a true case of group marriage, but merely an exercise of personal choice under conditions of freedom. When a man had two or more wives they were *punalua* to each other and the relationship was recognized. Similarly, two men were *punalua* to each other if they were husbands of the same woman.[2]

---

[2] This punaluan type of marriage arrangement might be regarded as a combination of polygyny and polyandry, but it does not seem to have combined the general social organizations of the two systems. Perhaps the multiple marriage of both men and women prevented the development of either the polygamous or the polyandrous type of family. If polygyny is

The freedom of the Hawaiians in relation to marriage was an important factor in the early interracial marriages. Had there been a strictly organized and regulated family system among the Hawaiians it would have operated to prevent marriage with foreigners because the foreigners who came to Hawaii could not readily conform to the requirement of such regulations. Furthermore, since the Hawaiians had not had any foreign contacts for several centuries they were free from any traditional bias antagonistic to other races. Such biases develop only where there is contact. The Hawaiians were ready for intermarriage if it should seem to be advantageous. They had no preliminary social bias against it.

Some of the few white men who came to Hawaii in the eighteenth or early in the nineteenth century became permanent residents and rendered important services to King Kamehameha as advisers in relation to military and civil affairs. In order to bind these men to Hawaii and to his service, the king gave them Hawaiian women of chiefly rank for wives and, incidentally, recognized them as men of chiefly rank. Doubtless the wives of these men enjoyed certain practical advantages from their marriage to foreign men. The foreigners must have treated their wives with more kindness and consideration than was customary among the Hawaiians, and it is probable that there was for these

regarded as a device for providing husbands for all of the women in a society in which there is a shortage of men, and polyandry as a device for providing wives for all of the men where there is a shortage of women, the punaluan system may be considered as a device for making it possible for all the men and all the women to be married all the time while the sex ratios shift from one side to the other. It is probable that such shifting did take place in Hawaii because of a pretty regular practice of infanticide—female infanticide mainly—and an alternation between warfare and peace. For example, there was a long period of warfare in Hawaii beginning some time before the coming of the first white men and lasting until 1796. These wars were very costly in the lives of men. In at least three important battles, practically the entire force of the defeated army is said to have been put to death. Probably by the end of this war there was a considerable excess of women over men. Then came a long period of peace during which infanticide continued. According to the census of 1890, there were 1379 men over 45 years of age to 1000 women of the same age class.

women a measure of freedom from tabu, which, among the Hawaiians, was especially burdensome upon women.

During the first thirty or forty years of interracial marriage practice there does not appear to have been any occasion for the development of anti-foreign sentiment on the part of Hawaiians. The white men who married Hawaiian women were Hawaiianized. Some of these white husbands of native women enjoyed full rights, receiving land like other chiefs. Their presence did not excite apprehension. Because of their own hereditary rank and also because of the importance of the public service of their husbands, these chiefly wives of white men enjoyed the best social status.

With interracial marriage beginning among the people of high rank, and accorded the king's active approval, and with the advantages of status and also the advantages of a practical character that were enjoyed by the Hawaiian wives of white men, it is not strange that Hawaiian women in early days came to look favorably upon white men as husbands. As the practice of out-marriage was extended to the women of lower rank or no rank, another sort of practical advantage came to be recognized. An Hawaiian woman in response to a question as to the reason for the Hawaiian women's preference for non-Hawaiian husbands said, "The Hawaiian men are not steady workers and good providers. The Chinese men are good to provide, but they are stingy. The white men are good providers and they give their wives more money." It may be said that, as some of the white men gradually acquired wealth, they were able to give their Hawaiian wives not only luxuries, but the status that comes from wealth. If a capable white business man married an Hawaiian woman who owned considerable land his management would increase the income from it and he would be too shrewd to sell it when there was a good prospect for an increase in value. All the larger estates now owned by the descendants of the old Hawaiian chiefs are in the hands of part-Hawaiians whose white paternal ancestors protected their inheritance. Gradually the white people, as they acquired wealth and power, were able to give their mixed-blood descendants better educational advantages than the Hawaiians enjoyed and also to give them superior economic opportunities. All in all, the part-Hawaiians, including some of Chinese ancestry, have come to enjoy an economic and social status superior to that of the Hawaiians. An Hawaiian woman may, therefore, regard marriage to a white or to a Chinese man as favorable to a superior status on the part of her children.

It may be said that when an Hawaiian woman marries a white or a Chinese man of good character she commonly acquires enough of the more advanced culture of her husband relating to the choice and preparation of foods and to household affairs generally—the use of chairs, tables, beds, dishes, cooking utensils, clothing,—so that they are able to live together agreeably. Apparently the women take pride in this cultural progress and sometimes they are very careful to bring their children up to be as much like the father's people as possible.

Before 1900 there were very few cases of marriage of Hawaiian men to non-Hawaiian women. In the earliest period there were no foreign women in Hawaii, and for another generation or two there were very few unmarried women. But even in the more recent years since non-Hawaiian girls and women have become numerous there are only a few who marry Hawaiian men. When such marriages do occur they often turn out to be unsatisfactory to both parties. The Hawaiian man, as provider, does not easily measure up to white or Chinese standards and the non-Hawaiian wife is intolerant of his easy-going ways. Neither is she, as wife, willing to assume the status that belongs to the Hawaiian wife according to tradition. Moreover, Hawaiian men generally consider non-Hawaiian women undesirable as wives.

It will be seen, therefore, that the favorable attitude of

Hawaiians toward out-marriage is a one-way affair, i.e., favorable for the women but not for the men. Partly in consequence of these one-way attitudes and partly because of the abnormal sex ratios of the non-Hawaiians it has come about that among the Hawaiians there are three times as many single men as single women.

But it takes two to make a bargain. If Hawaiian women looked with favor on marriage to non-Hawaiian men, there were white men and men of other races who desired Hawaiian women to be their wives and, so far as law and public opinion were concerned, they were free to follow their inclination. The principal interest relates to this freedom.

When racial contacts are established between the people of two races it usually happens that one of them is more powerful than the other by reason of superior military and economic organization and superior knowledge and technical development and there may or may not be an advantage due to superior numbers. Commonly, the people of superior power undertake to exploit those of inferior power, by means of slavery, peonage, serfdom, trade, or employment at wages. In the beginning the exploitation may be carried on successfully through the superiority of knowledge, technique, and organization, but since some of the exploited race may acquire these advantages they do not serve as a permanent basis for profitable exploitation. If the exploitation is to be permanent with race lines, that is, if all of the exploiters are to be of one race and all the exploited of the other, it is necessary that the exploiting race shall be dominant in a political and military sense so that they may make and administer laws which deprive the members of the other race of equal privilege. For, if the exploited possess equal privileges, some of the more able or fortunate will acquire the superior knowledge and technique of the exploiters and, profiting thereby, will rise to the higher economic status. Likewise some of the less capable or less fortunate members of the exploiting race will fall into the exploited class. After this crossing of the line by members of both races takes place for a considerable period of time economic status will not correspond to race. The only way to perpetuate the exploitation of a racial group, as such, is to deny to it equality of privilege, to deny the abler and more fortunate members the privilege which might permit any considerable number to rise out of their class.

The simplest and most obvious and effective way to do this is through slavery,—slavery extended to all the children of slaves. Under some conditions a system of land ownership with serfdom or peonage may accomplish the same results. Discriminatory rules of employment and discriminatory provision for education may be sufficient to maintain race class lines for a long time. If the people of the exploited race have political rights and if they are so numerous as to be able to bring about political compromises with provisions in their favor, it will not be possible to maintain a racially discriminatory organization of sufficient rigidity to be effective. Hence there must be a denial of political rights where numbers are important.

If a dominant racial group is to be successful in its efforts to maintain a system of discriminatory regulations for the purpose of denying the members of the other race equality of privilege, it is necessary to prevent interracial marriage. If some of the members of the dominant race marry members of the dominated race, i.e., form legally and socially sanctioned unions, they will tend to give to their children the advantages reserved to the more privileged people,— wealth, education, political rights, and social status. Gradually there will come into existence a large number of persons of mixed ancestry and of all shades of mixture, some being indistinguishable in appearance from the people of the dominant race. This tends to increase the rate at which miscegenation goes on and finally the race line becomes so obscure that discriminatory race regulations cannot be enforced. Therefore, if the dominant race is to preserve its status as a dominant race it must prohibit by law and sentiment the marriage of its members to members of the dominated race and such illegitimate children of mixed racial ancestry as may be born must be denied the status of the race of superior privilege.

But if intermarriage is to be effectively prohibited it is necessary to prohibit the sorts of social contact that normally lead to marriage or that imply the possibility of marriage. Out of this need a whole code of social relations arises. People of different races must not eat together, entertain each other socially, or attend the same school. The common forms of address must carry the implication of social inequality. There is, in effect, a ritual of race relations through which race is made to appear to be an impassable barrier to marriage. If any member of the dominant race should have the temerity to marry a member of the dominated race the penalty must be certain and severe,—mobbing, perhaps, or at least social ostracism. So strong are the urges and sentiments that influence personal choice in marriage that a weak form of control is ineffective.

A social system, therefore, in which there are racial discriminations denying political and economic equality of privilege and prohibiting interracial marriage may be seen as one that has been evolved in the interest of perpetuating the advantages enjoyed by a dominant racial group. When such a system is adequately supported by sentiment on both sides, i.e., when it has a religious sanction, it is a caste system.

On the other hand, if the social system is such as to involve the recognition of the peoples of both or all races as having equality of political rights, educational opportunity, and economic and social status, freedom of marriage is implied. Prohibition of interracial marriage is associated with a caste system or with tendencies toward a caste system and freedom in marriage is associated with the mores of equality.

Why did the early British and American residents of Hawaii fail to conform to the mores of the English speaking people? During the first thirty years of mixed marriages there were no white *women* in Hawaii. Public opinion adverse to interracial marriage never develops among men isolated from women of their own race. In a peculiar sense it is the women of America and the British dominions who are the guardians of racial purity. Only where there are families can there develop a sentiment against out-marriage. There were no white families in Hawaii until the missionaries came in 1820 and the resident white men did not communicate with their relatives in England or America. It was just a personal matter so far as they were concerned. They could marry Hawaiian women or remain single. A good many found the Hawaiian women attractive, married them, and reared families, some of the earlier, very large families. Some secured status and landed wealth by such marriage.

When white women began to come to the islands one might expect a gradual development of attitude antagonistic to out-marriage. Within a limited group there has been and is some sentiment of this sort. Very few white women of British or American birth or descent have intermarried with non-white men. Commonly white parents would look with disfavor on the marriage of their children, especially of their daughters, to persons of another race. Similar statements could be made relative to the Chinese and the Japanese. But the important fact is that such sentiment has always remained almost a private or family matter. There may be much family sentiment against out-marriage and such sentiment may extend even to a larger group,—the social set to which one belongs,—but there is no formal public expression of such sentiment. It is something that one talks about in the intimate circle, if at all. Formally and openly, people show approval of mixed marriages. For example, when the son of an influential Chinese man married a woman who was only half Chinese, the Chinese father and mother were sorely grieved. They felt that the family status was reduced and, at first, avoided public functions, where they would have had a sense of humiliation. But the larger social group ignored the matter. The man's parents were not ostracized nor he nor his wife. Sometimes the father and son were entertained at the same social function and treated with the customary respect. The young wife, a woman of good social qualities, received recognition too. Years afterward this father took the initiative; going to a Chinese friend similarly humiliated, he invited him back into the association of his friends saying, "I know how you feel."

It is just this inhibiting of the open expression of sentiment adverse to interracial marriage that is significant. A sentiment that cannot be expressed except in the intimate circle is not able to have much influence on the behavior of persons who have free access to another and larger circle. The inability to express such sentiment openly, to coin slogans and to ostracize those who marry out is evidence of comparative indifference or of a lack of the power necessary to successful dominance, or of both. The question then resolves itself into one relating to this control of expression.

That the early missionaries came from New England where there was no slavery and where there was a developing sentiment against the enslavement of the Negro in any part of the country is a matter of considerable importance. Doubtless their attitude favorable to the freeing of Negroes, whom they had not seen, predisposed them against doctrines and practices that would tend to reduce the Hawaiians, whom they saw, to a status of racial inferiority. Had the missionaries come from the South where racial lines were strictly drawn they would not have been able to accept the situation in Hawaii so readily.

It is significant, too, that the earliest white women in Hawaii were the wives of the missionaries. As missionary people they were bound to see the good in the natives and not to draw race lines more than seemed to be necessary. They had to be friendly in order to accomplish the purpose of their mission. In some cases the friendship of the white men who had married native women was very valuable to the missionaries. According to an old account the Hawaiian chiefs did not consent to the establishment of the mission until they were favorably advised by some of the old white residents who had married native women. If the missionaries were like most Americans their attitudes were adverse to intermarriage between whites and the representatives of the darker races. But if the very existence of the mission depended, for a time, on the good will of these founders of mixed-blood families, they must have seen the wisdom of treating such families with respect.

But the very strategy of the missionary position required that they minimize race as such. To the missionaries some aspects of native life were pretty bad. If they were to attribute the deficiencies in the behavior of Hawaiians to their possession of inferior racial traits they might find it difficult to justify their presence in Hawaii. But if the natives were regarded as possessing good inborn traits and as lacking only those things that might be conferred by the Christian religion and its associated civilization, the call for missionary service was clear.

Doubtless the attitude of the missionaries was influenced, too, by the fact of their close relations with the high chiefs of Hawaii. When the missionaries made their request for the privilege of teaching, the reply of the chiefs was in effect: "Teach us first and we will see if it is good. If it is, you may teach the people." At nearly all times in the most important period of their activity, the missionaries were pretty close to the chiefs of highest authority and it was through the support of the chiefs that the missionaries were able to win so great a following among the common people. The Hawaiian chiefs were accustomed to being treated by their subjects with extreme respect. The missionaries also treated them with respect and in this way a pattern of social relations between whites and Hawaiians was created and this pattern tended to become the standard. Of course the missionary wives had their misgivings as to the effect of such relations on their growing children. They sent some children back to New England to be educated and after a time they set up a private school in which their children could be educated without coming into too close contact with the Hawaiians. But they, personally,—the adult men and women,—continued to meet the Hawaiian men and women in ways that implied social equality.

Considering the experience of many other preliterate peoples, one would say that by 1830 or 1840 the situation in Hawaii had reached the point where the early imposition of the control of some foreign power seemed probable. The Islands had become important to foreign trade. The king was not able to protect his people from wrongs inflicted by foreign traders and transient sailors. He was deeply in debt to the traders and was not able either to pay the debts or to protect himself from the sharp practice of some of the traders. The demands of traders were sometimes enforced by the use of the foreign warships that appeared in the harbor. Things seemed to be approaching the condition which has so often been regarded as furnishing warrant for foreign intervention and, eventually, foreign rule. The years of Hawaiian independence appeared to be nearly at an end.

At this point some of the Americans who had come as missionaries resigned from their relation to the mission and became advisers to the king. Through their leadership there was established a more effective governmental organization, one able to meet its financial and its international obligations and, increasingly, to maintain justice and order within the country. As time went on, white business and professional men were taken into governmental service and so well did the government discharge its functions that for a half century it was able to maintain its independence under kings who were descended from the old Hawaiian chiefs.

Doubtless this continued independence of Hawaii for so long a time was a matter of considerable importance in connection with race relations. Had the white people been dominant in the government, had they been able to rely on even a small foreign military force and on the military support of some colonial power, their behavior toward the Hawaiians had been different. Doubtless they would have created a small white upper class in the political, business and social world with racial lines tending to be sharply drawn. This was done in other places that have been held as colonies or possessions and one cannot see any reason for its not being done in Hawaii if the Hawaiians had lost their independence. At this early date they had made only a little progress toward the acquisition of a superior culture. They were without political experience and they were suffering from the social disorganization incident to the contacts with foreigners. This continuation of a system in which the native king was a personage of authority and dignity, while the Hawaiians were undergoing important cultural changes, was a thing of great importance in that it tended to support the incipient mores of racial equality.

Immigrants from other European countries, the Chinese, the Japanese, and still others have had a part in the development of the race mores of Hawaii, but their part has been less important than that of the Hawaiians and the English-speaking whites. This is, in part, because they came at too late a date. They found a pattern of race relations already in existence and accepted it with only minor modifications on their own account. Furthermore, their position, in the beginning, was not one of great influence. They had neither the influence of preponderant numbers and established position, such as the natives had, nor the education, technical skill, and wealth that enabled the English-speaking residents to acquire leadership. There are, nevertheless, some things to be noted concerning the roles of these peoples.

In the earlier years of Chinese residence after there were numbers sufficient to be of some importance they were willing to play a subordinate part if it was moderately profitable. They came over as plantation laborers and, after completing the terms of their contracts, they would leave the plantation for economic opportunities open to men with initiative and small capital. Some became rice growers or gardeners. Some found more desired employment in the little city of Honolulu. Some engaged in merchandising in a small way. In general, they catered to the wants of their fellow Chinese or to those of the Hawaiians who had but little money to spend. They won such trade as they had by means of low prices and competitive skill. But in any case they were not dominant. Some of them married Hawaiian women and some tried to bring up their children as Chinese. Many, after a time, returned to China and nearly all expected to do so. Hence they were less interested in the long term trends of Hawaiian life.

It was only when the Chinese became numerous and when they aroused the hostility of both whites and Hawaiians that there was some chance that their presence would affect the race mores of the Islands. From about 1882 until 1898 they were leaving the plantations in large numbers. This movement not only deprived the plantations of their humble but useful services, making it necessary to seek new laborers elsewhere, but put the Hawaiians to a disadvantage. They could not compete with the shrewd, resourceful, industrious and thrifty Chinese. They saw the Chinese winning in the struggle for economic status. The Chinese incurred the ill will that commonly comes to an immigrant group that is struggling vigorously and successfully toward a superior economic and social status, the ill will of both whites and Hawaiians in this case.

The literature of the period abounds in expressions of fierce hatred. There were no words in the English language too strong to express the disapprobation of the publicists of the time. Of all undesirable people the Chinese were the worst and the plantation interests were severely condemned for importing them as laborers. A law was passed to restrict, —almost to prohibit,—the bringing of Chinese. But laborers were still needed and a later law provided for a limited importation, but under the condition that they could not remain in Hawaii if they should abandon the employment for which they were brought. The land laws, too, were discriminatory against the Chinese.

The adverse public opinion in relation to the Chinese at this time and their inferior legal status in consequence of the discriminatory laws suggest that the Chinese were being reduced to a position of inferior status which might, in time, be one of inferior caste. But in all this anti-Chinese movement the language of hostility was not in terms of race or color. Public sentiment was directed to their behavior, not to them as representatives of a non-white race. White propagandists did not use their color or other physical race traits to symbolize the things that were held to be mean and contemptible in Chinese character. This was precluded by the very strategy of the situation. If the few thousand white people were to maintain a successful anti-Chinese movement they had to have the co-operation of the much more numerous Hawaiians. To have introduced a race issue would have been antagonistic to such co-operation. Had a white man coined a color slogan to fling at the Chinese, it would have hit the Hawaiians, whose friendly co-operation was necessary, with even greater offense.

But the behavior of the Chinese was, unlike physical race traits, changeable. As they gradually worked out a better economic adjustment, as they acquired the superior status for which they were struggling, as their position was stabilized, and as they acquired greater knowledge of local conditions their behavior was modified and their activities did not so much antagonize the interests of others or excite so great apprehension. Since the anti-Chinese sentiment had been attached to a temporary thing,—a transient type of behavior,—it could not much survive the conditions that gave rise to it. Had the hostile sentiment seized upon race traits as the symbols of Chinese inferiority the attitude of the people toward the Chinese would have had a better chance for permanence.

One might point out that the Japanese at a later date went through an experience of similar character. The smaller groups such as the Korean have not attracted much attention.

In the determination of the character of race relations the part-Hawaiians have had an important role. From an early time there have been men and women of mixed ancestry who have held positions of dignity and power. This status was given them at first by the Hawaiian people. It was a recognition of their rank on the Hawaiian mother's side and also of the rank the white fathers enjoyed through the favor of the Hawaiian king. The white people were in no position to question the rank of these half white men and women. In fact it suited their purpose to give recognition and, because of the education and relationship of these mixed-bloods, they were able to mediate between the natives and the whites.

As time went on the mixed-blood descendants of the old chiefs derived less of their status from their rank under the old order and more of it from the wealth which was created or protected by their white paternal ancestors. So numerous are these part-Hawaiians of varying proportions of Hawaiian blood, so influential are some of them, and so closely related by blood are they to influential white or Chinese families that one cannot in any large group speak against mixed marriage lest he offend people of prominence who have relatives of mixed ancestry. To give offense to such people is not merely a matter of bad taste; it is a blunder in that one thereby jeopardizes his own social status.

The gradual acquisition in Hawaii of a population of considerable racial and cultural diversity has made it difficult if not impossible for any one racial group to maintain rigorous discriminatory and unfriendly attitudes toward other groups. Apparently, race prejudice is most effective where there are just two racial groups. In Hawaii, the introduction of the Japanese after the Chinese, and, then, of the Filipinos and of several smaller groups such as the Koreans and Porto Ricans has tended to prevent the development of sharp race lines with discriminatory regulations. If the white people and the Hawaiians at one time developed a system of friendly interracial co-operation in order better to meet the "Chinese peril," at a later time the Chinese themselves, or their Hawaiian born children were admitted into the friendly co-operation, this time to meet the "Japanese peril." The Japanese, following in large measure the Chinese pattern of economic readjustment, are accepted at a still later date.

With so many peoples, there is no one that is dominant. Sometimes it is said that the white race is dominant in Hawaii but this is not true locally. It is true that most of the wealth is owned by white people, but there is a rising class of non-white property owners and even economic dominance is not purely a matter of ownership of property. Politically, the voters are of so many racial or cultural groups that no politician would dare to raise a race issue. The subscribers to newspapers are racially distributed and no newspaper could afford to affront any of the more important groups of its readers with a race issue. Business men seek the trade of the people of all races and cater to their tastes and preferences. The members of a racial group may be influential if they do not try to dominate, if they adopt the method of bargain, compromise and conciliation, and this truth becomes more evident as the years come and go.

The main point to this chapter is that there is, in Hawaii, an uncommon degree of freedom in relation to interracial marriage and that this freedom is the consequence of the special practices, doctrines and sentiments relating to race that have come out of the historic conditions. The historic situation has favored the development of the mores of racial equality. Because there is no denial of political rights and economic or educational privilege on grounds of race, because racial equality is symbolized, the social code permits of marriage across race lines.

But the private and family sentiment and the sentiment that is held by groups too small or too weak to impose codes or rituals may be important in a way. While a good many people will assume the risk involved in running counter to such sentiment, the majority may be greatly influenced thereby. On the whole, one prefers to meet the expectations of the small intimate group to which he belongs even if it is unable to impose any serious penalty for lack of conformity. While such attitudes may not be given free public expression, while they are not consonant with the doctrines that are symbolized by the general social ritual, they may have pretty adequate recognition within the family circle, the social set, or even within the bounds of one racial group. This is true in particular of the Hawaiians who have not forgotten all of the traditions of their old preliterate culture and who, living in the same physical environment, are constantly reminded of such traditions by mountains and sea and every feature of the landscape. What were and are the attitudes of Hawaiians toward the white people, the Chinese, and the other immigrant peoples? Why have the Hawaiian women been so ready to marry white men and Chinese men? Do they believe them to be superior? If so, superior in what ways? Do they regard their own people as representatives of an inferior race?

In the beginning the attitude of the Hawaiians toward whites appears to have been a natural response to the situation. The Hawaiian people were in the habit of paying high respect to their own chiefs and some of the early white men appeared to them to be of superior rank and accordingly they were treated with the respect due to chiefs. Some of the early white residents appeared to be of inferior status and they were treated as common people. The few men who were chosen, on account of their character and technical skill, to serve the king were accorded the rank of chiefs and they had prestige even above that of the ordinary native chiefs, because of the things they could do and which the Hawaiians could not do, but wanted to be able to do. Their services to the king were of unique value and they could not fail of high prestige. That they should be given women of chiefly rank to be their wives was natural. As Hawaiian chiefs, some of them received valuable grants of land, and some of these lands are in the possession of their descendants even to this day.

All this does not appear to have involved any idea of race superiority. The white men were personally superior in knowledge and skill; that is, they were the possessors of a superior culture. As men who performed important services for the king, they were of high rank. The Hawaiians did not think in terms of biological heredity. They were wholly unaware of the theory or doctrine that the people of some race are born with innate traits superior to those of other races, and so they neither accepted nor rejected it. The superiority of these men as seen by Hawaiians must be defined as something that existed within the social system of the preliterate Hawaiians.

The mixed-blood descendants of these early white men who married Hawaiian women of chiefly rank were accorded the chiefly rank also until, through the decay of the old moral order, the basis of rank was destroyed. Some of the half white daughters are said to have been adopted by queens. The grandson of a white man became co-ruler of the kingdom and a granddaughter married a king. While we have no family records of the mixed-blood families of the humbler sort we have every reason to believe that they suffered no disability on account of race. Such scraps of information as we have suggest that many of the white men who married the women of low status were of an irresponsible sort and that, after a few months or years, they deserted their wives and also their children, if any, to leave the Islands. Doubtless most of the children thus neglected by their fathers were, if they survived, brought up according to the patterns of Hawaiian culture and were regarded as Hawaiians, not as *hapa haole*,—half whites. It was the difference in culture not the difference in color that seemed to be important. Unless a half white child had benefited from the superior culture of his father he was an Hawaiian.

In the course of a half century the situation underwent measurable change. The Hawaiians had made important moves in the direction of adopting the white man's culture. They were using tools of steel. They used cotton goods instead of tapa for clothing. They had learned to read and write. They had gone far in the direction of a commercial economy but, in this economy they had an inferior role. They had formally proclaimed the abolition of tabu, which lay at the base of the old moral order, and had professed the Christian religion. Doubtless they had expected to achieve security and prosperity through the acceptance of these features of the white man's culture, but in this they were disappointed.

The process of acculturation is much more difficult where religion is involved and a people remaining in its own ancient home acquires a new culture more slowly than one that migrates. The Hawaiians made rather slow progress toward the acquisition of the white man's knowledge and skills and especially in the acquisition of the more subtle factors of culture that are so important from the standpoint of its actual utilization. Early hopes for equality of power through the acquisition of the new culture were disappointing. The new tools of steel, the ability to read and write, and even the Christian religion, which they had accepted, formally at least, failed to make them equal to the white man in the things that counted for affluence, power, and security. They were being passed in the race for prestige and their numbers were dwindling. Under such conditions it may be supposed that their notions as to white superiority underwent some change. Even when they learned some of the white man's arts and worshiped his God they could not do what white men did nor did they gain security. Their new mental attitude would be more favorable to the acceptance of the doctrine of superiority of inborn traits in case they became aware of the doctrine through their contact with European and American thought. Probably the attitude of some of them is more or less affected by this doctrine.

But it is not true that the Hawaiians do, in general, believe in this doctrine, or theory, of inborn racial superiority. Commonly they would deny it. They tend to think that the white man's superiority is largely discreditable in a moral sense. An Hawaiian storekeeper cannot, in cold blood, refuse credit to a needy neighbor merely because payment is not probable and so he fails as a merchant. An Hawaiian who has plenty for this week must divide with his friends who are in want and so he does not acquire capital. An Hawaiian tends to think that thrift,—the postponing of enjoyments so that there may be larger enjoyment in the future,—is a mark of selfishness and greed. He would be ashamed to be thrifty like some of the people he knows. Long term planning seems to be a sort of impiety. What is called shrewdness and foresight among business men would, to the Hawaiian, call for names of a less complimentary character. The so-called virtues of the business man are unworthy of a good man. In the moral background from which the Hawaiian passes adverse judgment on business men there is something that comes from the old Hawaiian mores and also something that seems to come from the newer Christian religion. He is too good a man to win the prestige that comes from business success. There is a tendency, too, to look forward to a time when the people who succeed through the use of unworthy means will meet with reverses,—get their just punishment. Some Hawaiians seem to derive a certain satisfaction from reciting stories about successful wrongdoers who finally paid the penalty.

But, on the other hand, there are Hawaiian men more favorably situated and more happily conditioned who appear to be quite unconcerned about the sorts of success they do not win. I visited an old man who derives a modest income from a few acres of land rented to some Chinese. He sat in his humble but comfortable cottage overlooking the sea. Round about were trees and flowering shrubs. Mingled with the gentle lapping of the waves were the voices of his grandchildren at play. On his table lay a Bible in the Hawaiian language and it gave evidence of use. On the walls of the sitting room were pictures,— the Rock of Ages and others of a similar character,— symbolizing his religious faith. His conversation revealed a soul at peace and his kindly countenance testified to his freedom from envy or ill will toward the men of every race. Even when he said that some of his sons had died of *mai haole* (white man's sickness), there was not a trace of bitterness. When about to leave, I asked my interpreter to tell him that I regarded the situation of his old age as one of uncommon happiness and that I congratulated him. His reply, "The goodness of God."

While some of the earlier part-Hawaiians enjoyed high rank as conferred by the Hawaiians and in accordance with the old Hawaiian mores, their superior status in the more recent times comes in a different way. While, among Hawaiians and part-Hawaiians, there is much sentiment that is associated with memories of the old order, the rank derived from that order is not of much practical importance. What counts now is the wealth inherited from some Hawaiian ancestor, but protected by some shrewd white man who married an Hawaiian heiress. Commonly, too, the part-Hawaiians have enjoyed superior educational advantages and more of them are in the preferred occupations, partly through the favor of white business men. Some of the part-Hawaiians are so nearly white that except for their claiming Hawaiian ancestry they would pass as pure white. Naturally these near-whites and others are more or less affected by the ideas current among white people—not merely local white people, but white people elsewhere as represented by their writers. Sometimes the darker part-Hawaiians feel that their lighter complexioned cousins are trying to avoid recognizing them. Commonly part-Hawaiians prefer to marry lighter part-Hawaiians, other things being equal, and a mother is congratulated when her child is especially light colored. With the part-Hawaiians of the last fifty years, the superior social and economic status has seemed to be pretty definitely associated with lightness of complexion. If a dark part-Hawaiian, failing to achieve the higher status of part-Hawaiians, finds his society largely among the Hawaiians, he is pretty sure to call himself an Hawaiian,—to try to pass as a pure Hawaiian. He fears that, if he were to claim his little white blood, the Hawaiians would regard it as snobbery and would make fun of him.

All this points to a changing attitude on the part of Hawaiians. But they have not been slaves nor have they been subjected to a racial code designed to symbolize inferiority. Their attitudes cannot be described in terms that derive their meaning from the experience of slavery and its code. Doubtless they would admit freely that most of the white people they know are superior in education, in business ability, and in economic status, but this is very different from an admission of all-round superiority. Hawaiian

parents may be proud when their daughter marries a good
white or Chinese man because of such superiorities as he
may be believed to possess and they may be glad if their
grandchild is light-complexioned, and still they do not com-
mit themselves to the theory that light-complexioned people
are, in general, superior.

The practical importance of this distinction is not far to
seek. When individual Hawaiians and part-Hawaiians have
superior personal abilities they can put such abilities to
use. They can enjoy the best educational opportunities, and
avenues to distinction are open to them. Although there
is recognition that, for the time being, most of them are inferior to the white men they know, in certain respects, they
are not bound to treat a white man as superior when he is
in fact inferior; they are not under obligation to play the
part of inferiors when they are actually superior. It is just
this distinction that makes the difference between the trend
toward a caste system and the trend toward a social system
characterized by opportunity to pass from one class to another according to ability and character,—a society of open
classes, to use Cooley's term.

CHAPTER VI

THE HAWAIIANS AN AMALGAMATING RACE

In the story of the amalgamation of races in Hawaii the immigrant peoples, especially the white and the Chinese, appear to have played the more active part, while the role of the Hawaiian has been of a more passive character. Through the coming of foreign men, some of whom married native women, the character of the Hawaiian race is being modified, that is, it is becoming part-Hawaiian. The Hawaiians as found by Captain Cook (1778) were already a people of mixed racial origin but they had been isolated for so long a time that they may be regarded as a people of stabilized race mixture and they had a stable social organization. This new intrusion of foreign blood in the last century and a half is further complicating the mixture and the time has been too short to permit of its stabilization or of the development of a stable social organization. During the first half century of contacts, while the patterns of race relations were being worked out, the Hawaiians constituted so large a part of the population that their practices and attitudes were of prime importance. It was, on the one side, the Hawaiians, and, on the other, all of the immigrant peoples. For a period at the beginning, 1790–1819, the initiative belonged to the Hawaiians, and, in later times, when the initiative passed to the foreigners, the traditions and attitudes of the Hawaiian people set the limits within which such initiative could be exercised.

Before 1820 there were only a few score of white men in Hawaii. According to the status given them by the Hawaiian people, about twenty were of chiefly rank. They were the men of greater ability or more stability of character who were chosen by Kamehameha to serve him in the more important capacities and he, in order to bind these men to his service, gave them women of chiefly rank,—sometimes of high rank,—to be their wives, and in some cases at least he allotted to them extensive tracts of land such as chiefs might receive. But the majority of the white residents before 1820 were mere deserters from the sailing ships that touched at the ports of Hawaii and, by the Hawaiians, they were recognized as men of inferior status. Some married women of ordinary status and received little allotments of land[1] such as common Hawaiian farmers received. But whether of high or of low status these men, if they received wives and land, were regarded as Hawaiians and in fact they were Hawaiianized if they remained long enough.

There is much information about the families of the white men who married Hawaiian women of superior rank. The upper class Hawaiians had always been greatly interested in genealogy because a man's hereditary rank was his most valuable possession. The white men were able to write and some of them left written records which are treasured by their descendants, who have an added sense of their own importance because of the facts of their family history. These marriages of more than a hundred years ago acquire a more romantic character as they recede into the distance. Family sentiment increases. One might even say that myths relating to the ancestors are gradually developing. Sometimes it is difficult to winnow the solid historic fact from the stories affected by myth.

Most of the white men who, in the early days, married Hawaiian women of chiefly rank had reasonably large families. While the old Hawaiian moral order was not too greatly weakened, the girls of chiefly rank were carefully protected so that there would be no question concerning the paternity of their children. It was a matter of maintain-

[1] Jarves, *History of the Hawaiian Islands* (to the year 1846), p. 91.

AN HAWAIIAN GIRL OF THE NATIVE RACE

ing the status of chiefs. This protection would, in the nature of things, tend to protect from the venereal diseases, which were prevalent soon after the coming of white explorers. These women, who presumably enjoyed such protection and who married white men of stable character and superior status, were commonly the mothers of good sized families ranging from four to twelve children each. There were a few that were even larger. Moreover, there were few if any stillbirths and the infant mortality was much lower than that of the people generally. Clearly these women were normally fertile and their children were born with the physical vigor necessary to survival. Even in later times, when the old Hawaiian moral order had so far fallen into decay that even daughters who were descended from chiefly families did not commonly enjoy the protection to which reference has been made, there were certain girls who because of some special circumstance in their upbringing may be supposed to have been exceptions. Two were brought up by queens and one had a missionary guardian in whose home she lived. These women, too, had large families. It is a matter of some interest that several white men who were no longer young, and also some Chinese men of a later date, seem to have had a preference for marrying very young girls,—girls of only fourteen or fifteen years, in some cases. One may surmise that they knew of the ravages of the venereal diseases and that they were taking precautions. There is a record of one man who divorced his wife because of her unfaithfulness. There is testimony that the white men who married upper class Hawaiian women protected them and, for the most part, their wives appear to have been faithful.

On the average, the Hawaiian and part-Hawaiian women of our family histories [2] who had white or Chinese husbands

[2] In the files of the Department of Sociology at the University of Hawaii are the data of the family histories of the descendants of white and Chinese men who married native Hawaiian women at so early a date that there have been four to six generations of their hybrid descendants. The data were collected and organized by Miss Margaret Lam.

raised more children to maturity than did those who were married to Hawaiian men. For example, one such woman was the mother of eight children all of whom lived to maturity and married. Another was the mother of six all of whom lived to maturity and married. Another was the mother of six, five of whom lived to maturity and married, the other having died as a youth from smallpox. Another woman was the mother of sixteen, nine of whom lived to maturity while another was the mother of five, four of whom lived to maturity. Other similar cases could be cited. During the time when these women were bearing large families the population was undergoing great losses by excess of deaths over births. Probably, on the average, Hawaiian married women of that time did not much exceed one surviving child each. In the family histories the majority of the married women whose youth or early married life belonged to the period of maximum social disorganization had either no children or only one or two who survived infancy. The growth of the hybrid families depended mainly on the superior fertility of a comparatively small number. For example, in a family of eight children all of whom married there was one daughter who was the mother of six children who survived infancy while the seven wives of her five brothers were the mothers of only five surviving children in all, and her two sisters left but one living child. Because of the superior effective fertility of the women who married white or Chinese men, their contribution to the later population was much more than proportionate to their numbers.

Table XI shows the average number of children who survived infancy for four generations of women. The first generation consists of two Hawaiian women who married white men, one bearing six children and the other eight, fourteen in all. In the second generation are the married daughters and the daughters-in-law of these two women, and in the third and fourth generations, similarly the married granddaughters and great-granddaughters and the wives of grandsons and great-grandsons.

TABLE XI

Hybrid Children Who Survived Infancy Four Generations

	NUMBER OF MARRIED WOMEN	NUMBER OF CHILDREN WHO SURVIVED INFANCY	AVERAGE NUMBERS WHO SURVIVED INFANCY
First Generation . . .	2	14	7
Second Generation . .	17	23	1.35
Third Generation . . .	21	81	3.85
Fourth Generation* . .	77	238	3.09

* Some of the 77 women are of an age such that their families cannot be considered to be complete.

The low ratio of children to married women for the second generation corresponds with the general experience of the Hawaiian people of that period. The youth and middle life of the members of this second generation included the years of great social disorganization which followed the abolition of tabu, 1819–1836. During one four-year period,—from the census of 1832 to that of 1836,—the population decreased by about 15 per cent and there was a marked decrease during the whole century.

Because of the character of the marriages of the sons and daughters of these early white founders of mixed-blood families, the tendency was for the mixed-blood descendants in the next generation to become dark mixed-bloods preponderantly. Nearly all the sons and about half of the daughters married pure Hawaiians and so the majority of the children were one quarter white and three quarters of the native stock. Except for the lower average effective fertility of the mothers of the darker hybrids, nearly three quarters of this generation would have been of the dark and nearly one quarter of the light mixture. In fact, about 61 per cent were of the dark mixture, 3.5 per cent of half-and-half mixture, and 35.5 per cent of the light mixture.

The marriage ratios of the second generation of mixture were much like those of the first except that more of the part-Hawaiians married each other and, in respect to this, the same trend continued in the third and later generations. Since the lighter colored part-Hawaiian women married white men more commonly than did the dark, the part-Hawaiian women who married part-Hawaiian men were on the average of a little darker mixture than were the men they married. In general, the trend all through the nineteenth century was for part-Hawaiians to be absorbed back into the Hawaiian group, mainly, to become dark part-Hawaiians.

Table XII shows the tendency of dark part-Hawaiians to outnumber the light for three generations of race mixture. The figures show the number of mixed-blood descendants of three white men classified according to their fractional share of Hawaiian blood.

TABLE XII

Three Generations of Race Mixture

PART-HAWAIIANS OF THREE GENERATIONS CLASSIFIED ACCORDING TO FRACTIONAL SHARE OF HAWAIIAN BLOOD	HAWAIIAN							TOTAL
	7/8	3/4	5/8	1/2	3/8	1/4	1/8	
First generation of mixture . . .				17				17
Second generation of mixture . . .		17		1		10		28
Third generation of mixture . . .	20		13	12	6		8	59

The first generation was, of course, 50 per cent of Hawaiian blood; the second averaged 53.8 per cent, and the third 59 per cent. It is still too early to have the complete data for the fourth generation, but it is known that there is beginning to be a trend in the opposite direction on account of the increasing proportion of part-Hawaiians who are marrying non-Hawaiians. This tendency of the marriages of part-Hawaiians to be mainly with Hawaiians was, in the beginning, a natural consequence of the numerical situation,—the fact that the great body of population was made up of Hawaiians,—and it continued until the numerical situation had been modified by the immigration of large numbers of foreigners and until there had been sufficient acculturation to facilitate marriage between the immigrants and the part-Hawaiians.

In addition to the score or so of white men who were recognized as of superior status and who made their permanent residence in Hawaii there were others who were of inferior status and who, for the most part, were only temporary residents. Perhaps there were as many as 80 of these at the end of Kamehameha's reign (1819), but others had come and gone. Some of these white men married native women of the lower social status,—married them in the sense that they lived with them as husbands permanently or for a time, but the number who so married is not known. Nor is it known how many children survived from such unions or from unions of a more transient and irregular sort. Some of these men are said to have been of an irresponsible character and it is probable that after a few years they left the Islands, deserting their wives and also their children if there were any. In view of the high infant mortality of this period, especially high in the areas most frequented by white men, in view of the prevalence of abortion and infanticide with the highest incidence in the same areas, and in view of the very high general death rates, we may suppose that the number of surviving descendants of these early white men of inferior rank was relatively small. Moreover, it is probable that many of them were brought up in Hawaiian families with little or no benefit of foreign culture so that they would be, culturally, Hawaiians as distinguished from the half-white children who were cared for by their fathers. Doubtless the descendants of these pretty fully Hawaiianized half-white children were in the first and the second generations almost wholly of the dark mixture and, having no ground for pride of ancestry, many permitted the memory of their white ancestry to perish. There is, therefore, today a probable population of several thousand who have a little unknown or unclaimed white blood, excepting as the situation has been modified by later mixture. This tendency of dark part-Hawaiians who lack any especial cultural evidence of their white ancestry and who have no special pride of ancestry to claim to be pure Hawaiians continues even to the present time.

TABLE XIII

Population of Hawaii, 1853
Census Data and Computations

I. Native population including mixed-bloods

	Honolulu District	All Other Districts	The Kingdom
Male	5,572	31,507	37,079
Female	4,703	29,237	33,940
	10,275	60,744	71,019
Married men	2,823	17,525	20,348
Married women			
To native men	2,822	17,525	20,347
To foreign men	118	301	419
	2,940	17,826	20,766

II. Foreign population, including 291 who were born in Hawaii

	Honolulu District	All Other Districts	The Kingdom
Male	906	825	1,731
Female	274	114	388
	1,180	939	2,119
Age—both sexes			
Under 20 years	333	50	383
20 years and over	780	642	1,422
Not reported	67	247	314
Married males			
To native women	118	301	419
To foreign women	107	51	158
Married females			
To native man	1		1
To foreign men	107	51	158

The rather abundant data of the census of 1853 make it possible to get a measure of the frequency of out-marriage on the part of Hawaiian women and foreign men and also to determine the difference between the city and rural practices. From Table XIII it may be seen that while the foreign population of 1853, especially the foreign women, tended to be concentrated in Honolulu, the native Hawaiians still resided mainly in the outside districts. To each 1,000 Hawaiians there were in Honolulu 115 foreigners whereas, in all other districts there were only 15. Of the 419 native women married to foreigners, 51 were classified as half caste and 20 of these lived in Honolulu. Of the 419 foreign men, 12 were Chinese, a few, not over 20, may have been Negro and the rest were white. Naturally the out-marriage rate for Hawaiian women was higher in Honolulu where 4 per cent of their husbands were foreign born. In the other districts only 1.7 per cent of the married women had foreign husbands. Apparently there was just one Hawaiian or part-Hawaiian man whose wife was a foreigner. Probably she was a Tahitian.

There are for the years between 1853 to 1896 no direct data as to the marital status of Hawaiian women with a racial classification of their husbands, but from the slowly growing number of part-Hawaiians, one may infer that the number of Hawaiians married to foreigners increased at only a moderate rate. While there were nearly thirty-five times as many foreign men resident in the Islands in 1896 as in 1853, the number with native wives had multiplied by less than three. As the white population increased through immigration, the number of women increased more than proportionately so that the men had a better opportunity to marry women of their own race. There was also an increase in the social control of the white community adverse to out-marriage. What was true of the white people was in large measure true of the Chinese also.

When the census of 1896 was taken a special effort was

made to discover the paternity of the part-Hawaiians.
While there are no direct data as to maternity, the data relating to paternity and other data enable one to make a
sufficiently close estimate as to the number with Hawaiian
and the number with part-Hawaiian mothers.

From these figures one may then make a not too inaccurate estimate as to the number of Hawaiian women who
had foreign husbands and the number who were married to
part-Hawaiian men.

TABLE XIV

Paternity of Part-Hawaiians (Census of 1896)

Race of Fathers	Male	Female	Total
Hawaiian	429	462	891
Part-Hawaiian	1147	1179	2326
All non-Hawaiian	2673	2595	5268
American	665	647	1312
British	590	531	1121
German	168	159	327
French	39	30	69
Norwegian	25	28	53
Portuguese	296	246	542
Japanese	32	45	77
Chinese	656	731	1387
South Sea Islander	52	39	91
All other	150	139	289
Total	4249	4236	8485

According to the census of 1896 there were 5535 Hawaiian
and 817 part-Hawaiian married men, 6352 in all. There were
6455 Hawaiian and 970 part-Hawaiian married women, 7425
in all. There will be but scant error if one assumes that all
the Hawaiian and part-Hawaiian married men had wives who
were either Hawaiian or part-Hawaiian. On the basis of this
assumption the difference between 7425 and 6352, or 1053,
is the number of Hawaiian and part-Hawaiian women married to non-Hawaiians.

The racial character of the 970 husbands of part-Hawaiian

TABLE XV

Maternity of Part-Hawaiians (1896)

Paternity Mainly According to the Census		Maternity As Estimated	
Hawaiian	891	Part-Hawaiian	891
Part-Hawaiian	2326	Hawaiian	1693
		Part-Hawaiian	633
			2326
Non-Hawaiian			
White			
American	1312		
British	1121		
German	327		
French	69		
Norwegian	53		
Portuguese*	300	Hawaiian	2182
Other white	250	Part-Hawaiian	1250
Total white	3432		3432
Non-white			
Chinese	1387		
Japanese	77		
Negro*	281	Hawaiian	1586
South Sea Islander	91	Part-Hawaiian	250
Total non-white	1836		1836
Total	8485	Hawaiian	5461
		Part-Hawaiian	3024
			8485

* The Portuguese, who came in large numbers, 1878–1886, as plantation laborers were, for the most part, accompanied by their families and for twenty years there was only a little marriage with Hawaiian women. The paternity of the Portuguese-Hawaiians of 1896 is to be credited mainly to the earlier Portuguese immigrants,—deserters from whaling ships,—some of whom were Negroes.

women may be estimated partly from the data of the family histories and from the more recent statistical data as to brides and grooms with racial classifications. There are also the data of the 1896 census relating to the average number of surviving children, racially classified.

TABLE XVI

Marital Relations of Hawaiians in 1896
(An Estimate)

RACES OF MARRIED MEN	RACES OF MARRIED WOMEN			
	Hawaiian	Part-Hawaiian	Non-Hawaiian*	Total
Hawaiian	5,215	320		5,535
Part-Hawaiian . .	607	210		817
Non-Hawaiian . .	633	440	12,135	13,208
Total	6,455	970	12,135	19,560

* There were 3746 of the wives of non-Hawaiians mainly Chinese and Japanese who were not residents of Hawaii.

For nearly all of the years since 1912, there are very satisfactory data as to the marriages of the men and women of all the racial and mixed racial groups recognized for census purposes. The groups are (1) the Hawaiian, (2) Caucasian-Hawaiian, (3) Asiatic-Hawaiian, (4) Portuguese, (5) Porto Rican, (6) Spanish, (7) Other Caucasian, (8) Chinese, (9) Japanese, (10) Korean, and (11) Filipino. When candidates apply for a license to marry they are required to furnish data as to name, birthplace, and race or race mixture of themselves and also of their parents. From these data are made statistical tables showing how many brides of each racial group are married by the grooms of each group.

The following table for 1932–33 is a sample. In order to read it one regards the last column at the right as showing the total number of grooms of each specified racial group named at the left side of the page and the last line at the bottom, in similar manner, shows the number of brides of each specified group named at the top. If there were from each and every group some men who were married to women of each and every group the numbers so marrying would occupy all the other small rectangular spaces and the numbers,

TABLE XVII

Brides and Grooms in Hawaii for the Year 1932–1933

RACES OF GROOMS	RACES OF BRIDES												
	Hawaiian	Caucasian-Hawaiian	Asiatic-Hawaiian	Portuguese	Porto Rican	Spanish	Other Caucasian	Chinese	Japanese	Korean	Filipino	All Others	Total
Hawaiian	56	20	24	6			2	3	1			1	113
Caucasian-Hawaiian	18	65	36	21		1	11	8	4	1	1	1	167
Asiatic-Hawaiian	13	32	28	11	2		3	18	3	1	1		112
Portuguese	6	24	12	181	2	3	22	9	6	1	1	3	270
Porto Rican	2	3		4	47	1	3						60
Spanish				4		4		1			2		11
Other Caucasian	6	37	18	83	3	5	311	2	6			5	476
Chinese	6	7	20	5	1		1	119	6			1	166
Japanese	4	6	12	4		1	1	9	806	1			844
Korean	1		3	1				1	1	30			37
Filipino	22	7	22	21	10	2	8	2	12	3	259		368
All others	1	3	3	1	1		1	1				2	13
Total	135	204	178	342	66	17	363	173	845	37	264	13	2637

where found, show the precise number of marriages of each racial type. Neglecting the "all others" column and line, we may note that of the 121 possible ways of pairing, 91 were used this year. For the four-year period 1930–34, 108 ways were used. The column at the extreme left is read as follows: There were 56 Hawaiian brides in the Territory who were united in marriage with Hawaiian grooms, 18 with Caucasian-Hawaiian, 13 with Asiatic-Hawaiian, 6 with Portuguese grooms, and so on, 135 in all.

Because of the smallness of the numbers married in any one year, the figures may not be representative and this is especially true of the smaller racial groups. I have, therefore, combined four such tables into one, making four tables for sixteen years, one for the four years, 1912–16, one for 1920–24, one for 1924–28, and one for 1930–34. (The period, 1916–20, is omitted because some of the data are wanting, and for 1928–30 in order to get the most recent data into the last table.)

It will be observed that the various specified racial groups are not according to any strict anthropological classification. It is necessary to follow the census classifications. Doubtless the Portuguese and the Spanish are about alike in racial traits as well as in old-country culture traits. Possibly one might classify the Chinese, the Japanese, and the Koreans as belonging to one race. Nevertheless each of the various peoples specified has in Hawaii a separate identity. They are culture groups and social groups as well as statistical groups although the group solidarity is not highly developed in the case of the Caucasian-Hawaiians or the Asiatic-Hawaiians and although it is decreasing pretty rapidly for some of the others. The tables thus made indicate the trends in a pretty satisfactory way excepting for certain groups where there was an occasional temporary disturbing factor. The four tables are to be found in the appendix, the present interest relating solely to marriage trends among the Hawaiians.

The following table shows the recent racial trend in marriage for the Hawaiian men and women separately.

TABLE XVIII

*Hawaiian Grooms with a Racial Classification
of Their Brides for Four Four-Year Periods*

Absolute Numbers

Races of Brides	1912–16	1920–24	1924–28	1930–34
Hawaiian	821	584	528	258
Part-Hawaiian	154	173	243	225
Non-Hawaiian	43	38	59	63
Total	1018	795	830	546

Number to each 1000 Grooms

Races of Brides				
Hawaiian	807	735	636	472
Part-Hawaiian	151	218	293	412
Non-Hawaiian	42	47	71	116
Total	1000	1000	1000	1000

*Hawaiian Brides with a Racial Classification
of Their Grooms for Four Four-Year Periods*

Absolute Numbers

Races of Grooms	1912–16	1920–24	1924–28	1930–34
Hawaiian	821	584	528	258
Part-Hawaiian	179	202	212	166
Non-Hawaiian	366	354	415	240
Total	1366	1140	1155	664

Number to each 1000 Brides

Races of Grooms				
Hawaiian	601	512	457	389
Part-Hawaiian	131	177	184	250
Non-Hawaiian	268	311	359	361
Total	1000	1000	1000	1000

Steadily the Hawaiian population decreases in proportion to the part-Hawaiian. According to the census classifications there were, in 1910, 208 Hawaiians to 100 part-Hawaiians; but in 1920 there were only 131; and, in 1930, only 80. Formerly the situation was one in which a few part-Hawaiians lived among the Hawaiians but in the near future there will be only a few Hawaiians living among the part-Hawaiians. Considering merely the relative numbers and the influence of propinquity, one would expect to see a steady decrease in the rate of in-marriage among the Hawaiians and a steady increase in the rate of their out-marriage with part-Hawaiians. For similar reasons and also on account of the further acculturation of immigrants as well as Hawaiians the Hawaiian rate of out-marriage with non-Hawaiians steadily rises. No longer are the Hawaiians suffering from an excess of deaths over births, but the majority of the children born to Hawaiian women, 58 per cent in recent years, are only part-Hawaiian. The Hawaiians are an amalgamating people.

CHAPTER VII

THE ROLE OF THE MIXED–BLOODS

In the discussion of interracial marriage among the Hawaiians it was necessary to make frequent reference to the part-Hawaiians with whom they intermarry more freely than with others. But such references fail to indicate adequately the role of the mixed-bloods in the general process of racial amalgamation. We come now to a consideration of this role.

The role of the mixed-blood depends largely on the character of the social organization, whether it be a caste society in which interracial marriage is prohibited or whether it be a society of open classes permitting such marriage. A caste system is organized in such a way as to prevent the free functioning of the mixed-bloods as a liaison group and hence it retards the mutually conditioned processes of amalgamation and assimilation. If a society is free in the sense that interracial marriage is permitted by law and public opinion, the hybrid population resulting from mixed marriages serves freely as a liaison group between the parent races. It is able to do this because it is intermediate. It is intermediate in color and the other physical traits that serve for identification and, perhaps also, the less easily measured traits of biological inheritance such as temperament. It also tends to occupy an intermediate social position and it is intermediate in culture.

A society in which law and public opinion permit of interracial marriage is not necessarily one in which the people are indifferent to such matters. Along with such freedom of marriage there may be much adverse family sentiment and there may even be racial groups or social sets of considerable size and importance in which sentiment opposed to out-marriage is expressed. The distinction is between public opinion and the opinion of some group too small or too weak to be regarded as the public.

The mixed-bloods in a free society have the function of a liaison group just because there is this sentiment adverse to out-marriage. The liaison group by reason of its being intermediate tends to reduce the strength of such sentiment. If a man's family or social set disapproves of his marriage with a member of another race the disapproval is not so strong if the wife is half of his own racial stock and when she is seven-eighths, disapproval may approach the vanishing point. This will not seem to be true to people who belong to a society characterized by a caste system. In such a society, or even in one with strong caste tendencies, there is a ritualistic code and the social penalties for the violation of the code may be equally severe, no matter whether one marries a woman wholly of another race or one who has only enough of the blood of the other race to permit of identification.

In a society with strong caste tendencies such as that of American states with a large Negro population, the lighter the color of the mulatto, the greater the presumption of illegitimacy somewhere in the family line and this seems to give added warrant for adverse discrimination. In many cases the inferiority of social status contributes to the development of personal traits that tend to justify the exclusion of hybrids from the society of the race of superior status. But in a free society it is otherwise. There are no publicly proclaimed doctrines or socially enforced codes adverse to such marriage. The presumption that the mixed blood population had its origin in socially sanctioned unions tends to give them a good social status. Because of the relative freedom of opportunity there are some who possess

ANCESTRY, KOREAN–HAWAIIAN

wealth, education, and refinement such as to qualify them for admission to the best society. In a society in which marriage is free there comes into existence, gradually, a population of so many shades of color, so many sorts of mixture, and so many gradations of culture and refinement, that there is no sharp line of cleavage. There may be people whose personal attitudes are such that they would be willing to fight on the issue of racial purity, but there is no clear indication as to where the line of battle should be drawn and, besides, the possible fighters are not organized and disciplined. They have no slogans and so the issue is lost by default. The outcome is determined by the accidents affecting contacts and by personal preference. In a highly mobile population there tends to be a general weakening of social control so that the individual is relatively free to follow his own inclinations. And where people are free, their personal preferences frequently lead to marriage across race lines.

A real social group, as distinguished from a statistical aggregation, is one with memories common to its members and with common traditions. There is social solidarity because the members share in the same sentiment and regard themselves as having common interests. This is true, no matter whether the distinctions that unite the members and set them apart from others are based on race, on nationalistic sentiment, on religion, or on some other cultural difference. Within such a group, loyalty is required and there is a sense of obligation. There are penalties of a more or less severe and subtle character for individuals who fail to conform to group standards. The sentiment of such a social group is always and necessarily adverse to the marriage of its members to outsiders, for such marriage tends to lessen its solidarity. No matter whether the persons so marrying shall bring into the group mates who do not share in its traditions or whether they shall withdraw or be expelled from the group, there is a weakening of morale and of ability to maintain standards and status. This is true even in a community in which there is no law or public opinion adverse to interracial marriage.

The freedom, therefore, of mixed-bloods to intermarry with members of the pure racial groups depends on the absence of traditions capable of creating a strong sense of group solidarity. As long as the group is little more than a statistical aggregation its members are in fact marginal members of the two parent groups, with leanings toward one or the other. They are not "members one of another." They tend to live like the parent groups and to conform to their standards, not having standards of their own. There is, therefore, no sentiment adverse to intermarriage with the parent groups and such marriage will be without hindrance excepting as there may be adverse sentiment in the parent groups. Since the adverse sentiment of such parent groups is not, in the beginning, strong enough to prevent the out-marriage that gives rise to the hybrid population, it may be presumed that it will be even less effective in relation to marriage with the hybrids who are nearer to them in blood and in culture.

But when a mixed-blood group, through the passing of generations, comes to be remote from the ancestors of pure racial stock and when it comes to have traditions of its own, it too will have a degree of group solidarity and this necessarily involves sentiment adverse to out-marriage. Such a group might, in time, acquire all the traits of a pure racial group so far as these matters are concerned and, in such case, its members would regard themselves as members of a racially pure, not of a hybrid group. In fact, this is just what has happened to the various peoples of the world who think that they are of pure racial descent and develop sentiment for racial purity.

In Hawaii the mixed-bloods have discharged their function as members of a liaison group with a comparatively high degree of freedom, in the sense that adverse sentiment in the parent groups has not been very strong and it has been nearly absent among the mixed-bloods until recent years. But there are two groups of mixed-bloods that are now large enough and old enough to show a little trend in the direction of group solidarity. The younger and smaller of these groups, the Chinese-Hawaiian, is just beginning to develop group consciousness. The larger and older, the Caucasian-Hawaiian, represents a more advanced stage of development toward social solidarity.

While there were a few Chinese in Hawaii before 1850, and while a comparatively large proportion of them left descendants of mixed Hawaiian ancestry, the absolute numbers are pretty small. Of the 1387 Chinese-Hawaiians returned for census purposes in 1896, about 300 were of mature years and these were widely scattered so that they did not constitute a social group. Not until the number of adults increased considerably and not until there came to be a degree of concentration in Honolulu were the conditions favorable to the development of group consciousness. The movement of Chinese-Hawaiians from the rural districts to Honolulu, in the beginning, does not appear to have been an independent movement, but was associated with the coming of the Chinese to the city. In 1910, 472 adult Asiatic-Hawaiians or 48.2 per cent of all such adults resided in Honolulu. In 1920 the number in the city was 1061, or 56.4 per cent; and by 1930 it had increased to 1604, or 57.3 per cent.[1]

Evidence of the existence of almost no Chinese-Hawaiian group consciousness can be found for the time before 1910. Middle-aged Chinese-Hawaiians are mainly representative of the earlier status. They are a first generation of half-and-

[1] For the census year 1896 there are data for the Chinese-Hawaiians but since the censuses have been taken under the authority of the U. S. Congress the Chinese-Hawaiians, the Japanese-Hawaiians, the Korean-Hawaiians and the Filipino-Hawaiians are all combined into one statistical group known as Asiatic-Hawaiians. Up to 1920 one makes only a negligible error if he assumes that all of the adult Asiatic-Hawaiians are of Chinese ancestry and the error is not very great even up to 1930.

half mixture, their fathers being Chinese and their mothers, mainly, pure Hawaiian. In their youth they constituted a group only in the statistical sense. The traditions of their early homes were, on the one hand, Chinese, and on the other, Hawaiian. There were no Chinese-Hawaiian traditions. There was an accommodation, but it was of too recent an origin to be regarded as traditional. These children were exposed to the influence of two sorts of cultural tradition. They ate rice with the Chinese father and poi with the Hawaiian mother. In some homes the Hawaiian language was used and in others the Chinese, mainly, but commonly both were used imperfectly. In some cases the ritual associated with the birth of children was observed in the Chinese way, and in others, according to the Hawaiian custom and, often enough, there was something of both. The children practiced ancestor worship with the father, and they were taught to observe other Chinese rites. They also attended the Christian churches with their mothers and, from their mothers, they also learned to observe some of the customs that had come down from the old Hawaiian religion.

So far as it was possible in Hawaii, some of the more resolute and ambitious Chinese men of the earlier period trained their mixed-blood sons according to the Chinese pattern until they were ten or twelve years of age and then sent them to China where they completed their education. Commonly these sons returned to Hawaii with Chinese wives or Chinese wives were secured later and they and their children were accepted by the Chinese community in Honolulu.

Out of this situation came typical problems of adjustment. The Chinese, at first unorganized and of a low social status, gradually developed organization and acquired an economic status superior to that of the Hawaiians. In general, the Chinese fathers of the more ambitious sort desired to bring their children within the circle of Chinese

ANCESTRY, CHINESE–HAWAIIAN

influence and prestige. At first such a father could be pretty sure of success if he had his children educated as Chinese and if they were of good personal character as seen by the Chinese. But as the Chinese community came to be more fully organized, as standards became stricter and more definite, the tendency was to exclude the mixed-bloods unless they were above average in ability and influence. Some of the Chinese fathers failed to have their children accepted as Chinese. The failure might be due to the refusal of the Chinese to accept them or it might be due to the preponderant influence of the Hawaiian community in determining the tastes and tendencies of the children.

Running through hundreds of personal stories of the Chinese-Hawaiians is the constant recognition of the business superiority of the Chinese. Chinese men are "industrious," "thrifty," "shrewd," the Hawaiians are not. The Chinese fathers tried to make good business men out of their sons. After educating them they introduced them to business. Here, too, the mixed-bloods turned out to be intermediate. They are not satisfied to fall to the economic level of the Hawaiians and most of them are unable to reach the Chinese level of competency. Some would prefer to be regarded as members of the Chinese community and if they are pretty successful in business, in a profession, or in politics, the Chinese accept them. Others, not able to win recognition, are resentful toward the Chinese and still unwilling to be identified as Hawaiians.

If one were to write a drama relating to the life of the more ambitious Chinese-Hawaiians who are over thirty years of age, he would utilize the tragedy inherent in the situation of people who do not quite belong either to one parental group or to the other and who, because their numbers are too small and because they are not bound together by common traditions, do not have a group of their own able to confer satisfactory status.

But the majority of the Chinese-Hawaiians were brought up more like Hawaiians. The fathers, some of whom were much older than the mothers, might die while the children were young and in that case the mother might give the children to her relatives or she might marry an Hawaiian man; and, either way, the children would be brought up much like Hawaiians. Some of the less ambitious of the Chinese men lived in the families of their wives, spoke the Hawaiian language and were content to see their children brought up mainly according to the Hawaiian pattern. This was commonly true in communities in which there were only a few Chinese. Some of the Chinese men deserted their Hawaiian wives, sometimes with a money allowance, and returned to China, taking, possibly, one son to be educated in the Chinese way while the other children would become Hawaiian in culture. Sometimes a Chinese man dismissed his Hawaiian wife [2] and brought a wife from China, in which case the father might take some of the children and bring them up as Chinese while the others were raised as Hawaiians by the mother.

In general, the Hawaiians were willing to accept the mixed-blood children on terms of equality. If the children were not, through the father's influence, conditioned unfavorably toward the Hawaiians they were not greatly adverse to the acceptance of such status as they could win as Hawaiians. The middle-aged Chinese-Hawaiians who have been interviewed for our case studies speak of their "leaning," some, toward the Chinese side, but, many more, toward the Hawaiian side. This tendency to "lean" one way

[2] Not always did these Chinese take the trouble to have a marriage ceremony according to law and this facilitated the separation, if it came. It is not necessary to charge the Chinese men with this neglect as if it were with the intention of deserting their Hawaiian wives. It was mainly a consequence of their lack of familiarity with the laws of Hawaii. Not only was there a failure to observe the procedure essential to valid marriage under Hawaiian law in the case of marriage to Hawaiian women, but also when Chinese men married women of their own race there was, in hundreds of cases, a similar neglect.

or the other is highly significant of the fact that these earlier Chinese-Hawaiians had their social relations with the Chinese, with the Hawaiians or with both, not among themselves. But because of the full acceptance given them by the Hawaiians, the personality traits of most have not been so much affected by their marginal position as one familiar with hybrid groups elsewhere might expect.

But this first generation situation is, in the nature of things, transient. When Chinese-Hawaiians marry they sometimes marry Hawaiians, sometimes Caucasian-Hawaiians; sometimes they marry each other and sometimes Chinese or other non-Hawaiians. In any case the situation for the Chinese-Hawaiians of the second generation of mixture is not like that of their parents. If a Chinese-Hawaiian man marries an Hawaiian woman there is not much doubt as to the racial status,—"leaning,"—of their children. As three-quarter-blood Hawaiians without any contact with or influence from a Chinese father they would be established in their social contacts definitely with the Hawaiians or, more recently, they might tend to associate mainly with the Chinese-Hawaiians who are now coming to be a social group. In case a Chinese-Hawaiian woman marries a Chinese man, there is greater uncertainty as to the racial status of their children. Even the three-quarter-blood Chinese will not be welcomed into the Chinese community of Honolulu unless his personal character or his family connections recommend him. Should such a young man fail to make Chinese social status, he may continue to live in a racial no-man's-land for a long time unless he is willing to identify himself with the becoming-self-conscious Chinese-Hawaiian group. If two Chinese-Hawaiians of the first generation of mixture marry each other, their children will be of a half-and-half mixture like the first generation, but they are in a different position in relation to culture and social status. The early home environment of such children is different, in that there is no direct contact with either Chinese or Hawaiian parents. The parents are of the same culture status. The home does not present the sharp cultural contrasts that are found where pure Chinese marry pure Hawaiians. The children are beginning to be brought up as Chinese-Hawaiians, that is they are coming to share in the developing traditions of the Chinese-Hawaiian social group.

This beginning of the development of a true Chinese-Hawaiian social group is, in part, a consequence of increasing numbers and, in part, of increasing remoteness from the racially pure progenitors. As long as the founders of families of mixed ancestry are living, their experiences and personal traits do not serve well the needs of the myth-maker. But when they have passed away it is as natural for legends and myths to come into existence as for flowers to blossom in the springtime. The creation of legends and myths is in response to a demand. Excepting as one is able, imaginatively, to enter into the past of his people he is not a real member of society. The demand of children for the "once-upon-a-time" or the "when-I-was-young" stories is a demand for full membership in their social group and the story is not satisfactory unless it helps the hearer to conceive of himself as a worthy member of a worthy society.[3] To the extent that the stories, as originally told, fail to meet the demands, they are subject to revision in the re-telling so that, in time, they become the treasured spiritual possessions of a people. Their truth is the truth of art.

When people possess common memories and when they share in the possession of a history, of legends and of myths they feel that they have common interests and obligations. Myths and legends are especially valuable in that they help to define ideals, to set up standards and to create bonds of unity. They have this value largely because they have

[3] "A tradition of historic greatness is an invaluable aid, if not an absolute prerequisite, to nationality." E. B. Reuter, *The American Race Problem*, p. 406.

been freed from inconsequential and prosaic facts of history and have been enriched by the imagination in such a way that they serve to arouse sentiment.

Old people enjoy a certain advantage as mythmakers. Since, presumably, the memory of an old man runs back further than do the memories of his hearers, he may place his story in time so that he need not fear contradiction. This means that in dealing with the past he is not bound down too closely to the facts but is free to be creative.

In a little friendly group of women one of them, an elderly Chinese-Hawaiian woman, responding to a few questions about the older Chinese-Hawaiian families, spoke about as follows (this woman was the widow of a white man and, when she made the effort, could use English of an almost standard character, but as she became more interested she tended to introduce Hawaiian words and the special structure that belongs to the language of many bilingual people in Hawaii):

"The Hawaiians always did like Chinese people very much. They are the only nationality they go with. You see they go with no other people like they do with the Chinese. That's why today there are so many Chinese-Hawaiians, you see. Oh, they like to marry Chinese because they are good workers. They are good workers. . . .

"Chinese men pick the most beautiful women of the country. Sure, the most beautiful women, the prettiest women. Maybe not always the good looking, but the best behavior. These Chinese knew who were the best families and they picked out the prettiest girl, too. The *pake* [Chinese] knew the best families. They come to the house and ask plenty questions and that's how they find out. Oh, they smart people. They no want the low class people; they look for the best class. My mother was one of the prettiest women. Of course, we belong to the *alii* [chiefly] class. My father was the first Chinese doctor in Hawaii. He was a runaway from China. Went to Australia and then to California and by and by, of course, he came here,—about 1871. I lived with my grandmother and she brought me up in Hawaiian style. . . .

"Hawaiian ladies like to marry Chinese better than *haole* [white]. The Chinese man take care of wife good. They no hit wife, they treat her good and they give them the best. Hawaiian lady marry Chinese man and she just like queen at home. Chinese men treat good. Especially, Chinese New Year, they give their wives one week vacation to have good time. They give them one hundred dollars to spend for anything—to have a good time. . . .

"Yes, Hawaiians like to have their daughters marry Chinese. Sometime you hear so-and-so have *pake* son-in-law. They say "good" mind you, they handle girl so good. They so smart to win girl. If no smart how can they win pretty women? They bring little thing every time they come to the house. . . .

"Hawaiian women say they don't like to marry *haole* men because they have to cook. If they marry Chinese they sit down like a queen—don't have to cook. The Chinese men cook. They used to say that if you marry *haole* your hair smell of smoke, because you have to do the cooking, but if you marry Chinese your hair smell of sandalwood. . . .

"You can't say that all the *hapa-pake* [half-Chinese] associate only with each other. We associate only with people of our class. We can't associate with people down Kakaako way. The first class Hawaiian not allow to associate with second class. May be poor, but blood good. I associate with pure Hawaiian, *hapa-pake* and, maybe, *hapa-haole* if they are of my class. I don't care for any people not in my class. Not because I am Chinese-Hawaiian must I associate with them. Maybe in school we say, 'hello,' but not familiar friend."[4]

In the course of the conversation another woman made confirmatory remarks from time to time and a few questions were asked. In other interviews similar beliefs were avowed.

Here is a basis for the developing myth relating to the superiority of the Chinese-Hawaiians. They are descendants of the superior Chinese and the superior Hawaiians. This myth is pretty sure to win general acceptance because it is attractive not only to the Chinese-Hawaiians, but also to the Chinese and to many white people. As the Chinese see it, the superiority of Chinese-Hawaiians over the Caucasian-Hawaiians points to the superiority of the Chinese

[4] From a case study, University of Hawaii collection, made by Margaret Lam.

over Caucasians. To the Caucasian racial purist the myth has value in that it constitutes a further argument against the out-marriage of whites who are supposed not to mix well with the darker races because of their own great superiority.

The importance to our purpose of this beginning of the making of myths by the Chinese-Hawaiians comes from the fact that it is so near to the beginning and hence so little effective in the way of creating social solidarity. While it is important to note that among the mixed-blood families of the earlier origin there is some development of family sentiment, it must be remembered that more than four-fifths of the adult Chinese-Hawaiians are of the first generation half-and-half mixture, that they are too young and too near the origin of their families to permit of the development of traditions. The group, as a whole, has discharged its function as a liaison group with an almost maximum degree of freedom. That is, they intermarry freely with both the parent groups and also with the other group of mixed-bloods, the Caucasian-Hawaiians. For example, in the four years, 1912–16, there were 321 Asiatic-Hawaiian brides and grooms, all or nearly all being Chinese-Hawaiians. Only 34 married each other, 17 pairs; 127 had Hawaiian brides or grooms; 52, Chinese; 68, Caucasian-Hawaiian; and 40 married into still other racial groups.

Not only does the absence of group solidarity make it possible for the members to marry out in large proportion, but also the out-marriage tends to prevent the development of group solidarity. Commonly if eight or ten Chinese-Hawaiian women meet socially it will be found that some of their husbands are Hawaiian, some Chinese, some Caucasian-Hawaiian and some Asiatic-Hawaiian. Since, in any intimate group, the conversation must be of such a character as to imply that the persons present are genuinely entitled to the society of each other, it would not be possible in any such Chinese-Hawaiian group to carry on the sort of conversation that would be necessary to the creation of Chinese-Hawaiian group sentiment. Any remark which might imply that they, as members of the group, were under obligations of loyalty to the group would be in effect, a criticism of some of the persons present and this would be resented. Even among Chinese-Hawaiians who have married within the group, freedom to cultivate group sentiment may be qualified by the fact that some of the brothers and sisters have married otherwise.

The Caucasian-Hawaiian group is older, larger, and more conscious of itself as a group than is the Asiatic-Hawaiian. To a considerable extent it is made up of the descendants of American, British, and other North European men who married Hawaiian women in the late eighteenth or first half of the nineteenth century. But there are many who are of the first generation of mixture and among the Caucasian parents are Portuguese and Spanish, as well as other Europeans. It remains true, however, that the great majority are of American or North European ancestry.

While there are many who are of the first or the second generation of mixture, the descendants of the old families are so numerous and so much more prominent that one tends to think of them as the typical representatives of this group. As early as 1853 there were 368 foreign men reported as married to native, and 51 to "half-caste" women. At this time there may have been about a thousand persons of mixed racial ancestry and some of them were of the third generation of mixture. Probably more than ninety-five per cent of the mixed-bloods were part white. At the present time some of the older families have as many as four or five hundred living members and some are in the sixth generation of mixture. In the creation of Caucasian-Hawaiian group tradition these old families are playing the leading part.

The Caucasian-Hawaiians, like the Chinese-Hawaiians, at first occupied a purely marginal position between the two

PARENTAGE
Father, Irish-Hawaiian
Mother, American (white)-Hawaiian

racial groups, but they have had more time to develop sentiment relating to the historic past of their families and to create legends and myths. The founders of these families, being more remote in time, serve better the needs of myth-makers. It is easier, in the story telling, to draw the remote ancestors in heroic proportions, and to color their experiences with romance. The Hawaiians and especially the part-Hawaiians of the earlier origin look back with great interest to the time just before and the time soon after the coming of white men, a time when their chiefs still ruled and when their dignity rested secure on the basis of the old moral order. This tends to be the golden age of Hawaiian tradition. There were great chiefs in those days, tabu chiefs, who were considered to be divine and before whom the people prostrated themselves. The stories of their prowess are well known and they are told with greater art to more deeply interested listeners as the heroic age recedes further into the past. What makes these stories the more interesting is that several thousand of the Caucasian-Hawaiians are able to trace their ancestry back to these old chiefs.

Perhaps as many as twenty of the early white residents married Hawaiian women of chiefly rank. Mainly these men were common or not much above common sailors before they came to Hawaii, but, because of their services, they were elevated to chiefly rank. Their association with the chiefs, their marriage to women of chiefly rank, their receiving grants of land which later became landed estates, all tend to exalt them in the minds of their descendants. In the olden days the chiefs preserved their genealogy with great care since their status as chiefs depended on it, but today it is the part-Hawaiian rather than the Hawaiian who keeps the record of family history.

The fact that these white men came from far-away countries quite unknown to the Hawaiians tends to involve their doings with a certain glamour. Sometimes the family has stories relating to the pre-Hawaiian part of their lives.

Some part-Hawaiians even claim descent from a cousin of Lady Jane Grey and others trace their lines back to the Duke of Wellington whose grandson is said to have come to Hawaii. Even the common sailors had come from strange and far-away lands and they were able to do many wonderful things. It is easy to see how the later descendants of these men and their chiefly wives are able to elaborate such bits of information as these men left into the most interesting of legends.

If one is not over-stolid he likes to think of his life as coming from a past that was characterized by noble sentiment. One seems to validate his claim to a high status in this way. We tend to invest the personal relations of our parents and more remote ancestors with a wealth of romance if there is any basis for it in fact or in legend. This is especially true of people whose ancestry is in some way out of the ordinary. What could be more favorable to myth and legend than the marriage of these Hawaiian women of ancient chiefly lineage to the wonderful white men who came from far-away strange lands?

Of course there were Hawaiian women who were not of chiefly rank and some of the white men led such colorless lives as to furnish little or no material for romance. Perhaps these were in a great majority. But it must be remembered that, while a person has only two parents and four grandparents he may have thirty-two ancestors in the more remote fifth generation, and he is in poor luck, indeed, if there is not at least one of them of whom he may be proud. The old Hawaiians and their modern descendants are like other peoples in that they tend to trace their ancestry back to the progenitor of most glorious memory.

It is easy to see how the continuing intermixture of families favors the development of common traditions. Just as chivalry in Europe or *Bushido* in Japan, once a tradition of an upper class of privilege and power, is now becoming a possession of the masses, so, in Hawaii, the legend and the romance originally centering around the names of a few of the more distinguished ancestors now tend to become a common possession of all Caucasian-Hawaiians. Not only will all Caucasian-Hawaiians be sharers in the traditions of the more distinguished ancestors, but, through intermarriage, it will not be many generations until practically all will be in fact descendants of the few progenitors of chiefly rank. Probably there are three or four thousand such descendants even at the present time.

One might mention two other things favorable to the growth of local traditions in Hawaii. Places in Hawaii are not anonymous. They are not designated merely in mathematical terms,—so far north of a base line, so far west of a principal meridian. Every little area of a few acres had a name and many of these names survive. Each spot is unique in respect to its character as a part of the landscape. Every mountain and hill, almost every prominent rock, every valley and every coastal plain, every inlet from the sea and every headland, has its name and its associations and they are to the Hawaiians, and also to Caucasian-Hawaiians, perpetual reminders of the things of history and legend that have value for sentiment. It is easy to love a land like Hawaii. Not only is it beautiful, but it is identifiable in all its parts.

And, finally, Hawaii enjoys a considerable degree of isolation, and there was more isolation formerly than there is now. While there has been stimulus from the outside world, the distance has tended to protect from the confusion that comes from the undue multiplication of inconsequential and short lived interests. There has been repose as well as stimulus. Local people have not been so much in the whirl of the transient interests of the big outside world as to prevent the development of local interests and traditions.

Because of the greater degree of social solidarity among the Caucasian-Hawaiians, their marriages are more largely within the group than are those of the Chinese-Hawaiians.

To this extent they are discharging their liaison function less effectively. During the years, 1912–16, for example, 352 to the thousand of Caucasian-Hawaiian brides and grooms were married to each other while among the Asiatic-Hawaiians the ratio was only 107 to the thousand. But with such favorable conditions as there have been, the Caucasian-Hawaiians have not been able to develop a strong group solidarity in a little more than a century.

When a social group has a rich heritage of ancient tradition, its members tend to have their social relations controlled by group sentiment and this is, in general, adverse to out-marriage. Under the conditions that prevail in Hawaii the index of in-marriage preference for any racial or mixed racial group tends to be also an index of its social solidarity. Preference, as here used, refers to individual attitudes as determined largely by the sentiment of the family and other intimate groups. One tends to do what is expected of him,—expected by those who are nearest to him,—if he feels that his status as a member of the group is a matter of vital importance. Preference is socially conditioned. Moreover, preference and its opposite involves not only the attitude of any particular group that may be under consideration, but also that of other groups with which it is more or less in contact. It takes two to make a bargain. Preference and its opposite work from both sides.

I have, in a more or less arbitrary way, computed indexes of in-marriage preference for four periods and for various racial and mixed racial groups in Hawaii. The indexes are based primarily on the actual marriage practice of the peoples, but allowances are made for certain numerical factors such as the relative size of the groups and the abnormal sex ratios,—factors that affect marriage practice irrespective of preference.[5]

The variability of such indexes of in-marriage preference according to the degree of social solidarity may be seen

[5] For the method of these computations see Appendix, page 327.

from a comparison of the indexes of several racial groups
for the period, 1912–16. Of all the peoples of Hawaii, the
Japanese had the highest index of in-marriage preference,
996. They came to Hawaii with ancient, highly organized,
and very sacred traditions; that is, they possessed group
solidarity in high degree. The individuals are controlled by
group sentiment and tradition and they have not lived in
Hawaii long enough to permit of any serious weakening of
such control. The large size of the group, too, is favorable
to the persistence of solidarity.

The Hawaiian index, much lower than that of the Japanese, was 722. Once the possessors of distinctive and
effective traditions of a primitive sort, they have experienced
such changes in the last century and a half that their old
traditions are largely lost or, if retained, they are in a
weakened condition. The decay of the Hawaiian mores
went on the more rapidly because of the unfitness of the
traditions of a primitive moral order in a world of modern
industry. Their low degree of group solidarity is reflected
by a low index of in-marriage preference.

But the Caucasian-Hawaiian index was still lower, 404.
At the best, their traditions lack the age necessary to great
effectiveness and not all of the Caucasian-Hawaians share in
the possession of such traditions as there are. But still
lower was the index of the Asiatic-Hawaiian group, 159.
If the traditions of the Caucasian-Hawaiians lack age, this
lack is even more notable in the case of the Asiatic-Hawaiians and even higher proportions of the people fail to
share in the possession of these incipient traditions.

In one respect the indexes of the Caucasian-Hawaiians
and Asiatic-Hawaiians differ from those of all the so-called
pure racial groups. In the case of each and every pure
group the trend of the index of in-marriage preference is
downward. As the influence of the old racial cultures
diminishes, there is a decrease of social solidarity and a trend
toward more out-marriage. The Hawaiian index fell from

722, 1912–16, to 517, 1930–34. Although the Japanese are most persistent in their traditions, their index fell from 996 to 955. But while all of the indexes of the pure racial groups were falling those of the two mixed blood groups were rising: that of the Caucasian-Hawaiians rose from 404, 1912–16, to 464, 1930–34, and at the same time the Asiatic-Hawaiian index rose from 159 to 361.

This lack of effective group solidarity among the Caucasian-Hawaiians and still more among the Asiatic-Hawaiians is confirmed by the testimony found in hundreds of case studies. Individuals have their associations determined largely by the accidents of location and the members of neither group are much concentrated or segregated according to race. Their intimate friends are often outside of their own group. So true is this that one would be guilty of but little exaggeration if he were to say that the Chinese-Hawaiians and other Asiatic-Hawaiians constitute merely a statistical, not a social, group.

There is a little, but not much, social distance between the Caucasian-Hawaiians and the Asiatic-Hawaiians. As an older group of mixed ancestry the Caucasian-Hawaiians have more members who are prominent in some way. The leaders of the whole Hawaiian and part-Hawaiian group are found mainly among the Caucasian-Hawaiians. The Chinese-Hawaiians, in seeking positions of higher dignity, find the Caucasian-Hawaiians more or less entrenched and with a tendency to resist the claims of members of the newer group. It is a case of the people of superior power and prestige trying to maintain their position as against new competitors, but since there is a racial difference there is a tendency on the part of Chinese-Hawaiians to charge racial pride. Often they say that they don't care to associate with Caucasian-Hawaiians because they are so *haole-fied* (like whites and with the pride of white ancestry).

It is hard to mention these things without exaggeration. Never is there any deep resentment and, commonly, behavior is affected in only a moderate degree. While Caucasian-Hawaiians, as members of a group of greater age and prestige, may regard themselves as superior to the Chinese-Hawaiian, the members of both groups are associated in nearly all sorts of social activity and it is not difficult for Chinese-Hawaiians of sufficient age and ability to win recognition and positions of leadership.

Because of the weakness of group sentiment there is an increasing rate of intermarriage between the two groups of part-Hawaiians. In the four years, 1912–16, 9 per cent of the Caucasian-Hawaiian brides and grooms wedded Asiatic-Hawaiians, but 17 per cent so wedded, 1930–34. On account of such marriages and also on account of marriages between Caucasians and Asiatic-Hawaiians and Asiatics and Caucasian-Hawaiians there is coming into existence a considerable statistical group of a three-way mixture, that is, of people who have Caucasian, Asiatic and Hawaiian ancestry. This is evident from recent marriage and birth data. In the year 1931–32, there were born of known paternity 1088 children who were classified as Asiatic-Hawaiian, but 412 or nearly 38 per cent of these had Caucasian ancestry also. In the four years, 1930–34, there were 1045 marriages of such racial character that the children will be classified as Asiatic-Hawaiian, but of this number, there were 570, or 54 per cent, whose issue will have Caucasian blood also.

It is known that there were a few children of this three-way type of mixture born more than seventy years ago, but the great majority are still under 25 years of age. Probably, in 1930, they numbered, all in all, about 4500, a number equal to a third of all the Asiatic-Hawaiians. But because of the youth of most of them they have not as yet done much in the way of conditioning social attitudes. But the character of their future influence is easily seen. It will be their role to destroy the low wall of separation between the two part-Hawaiian groups so that the amalgamation will hasten to its completion.

During the next twenty or thirty years the Asiatic-Hawaiians as a statistical group will increase in numbers more rapidly than the Caucasian-Hawaiians, if the present arbitrary method of classifying the people of the three-way mixture continues to be used. A little later the Caucasian-Hawaiians will begin to diminish in numbers and, eventually, there will be one part-Hawaiian group of complex mixture known statistically as Asiatic-Hawaiians, but having Caucasian as well as Asiatic ancestry. But while in the case of the people of the three-way mixture, the Caucasian ancestry is ignored for statistical purposes it is the Caucasian-Hawaiian tradition that will be chiefly influential in the amalgamated group of part-Hawaiians, the traditions having their origin largely in the families of the early white men who married Hawaiian women of chiefly rank.

When part-Hawaiians marry in their own group they, in general, prefer those who are lighter complexioned than themselves, that is, persons with less Hawaiian blood. Of course, there are other grounds of preference. If a dark part-Hawaiian has a good position and income and if he is a man of good personal traits, he will be able to secure a lighter colored wife. Hawaiian and part-Hawaiian women are keenly aware of the advantages that come from having husbands who are good providers and they talk about such matters freely. Every girl knows that to make a good marriage she must marry a man who has a good and steady income.

The lighter complexioned Caucasian-Hawaiians are, in many cases, the sons and daughters of white men of character and ability and such men not only give their children superior educational opportunities, but also, they help them to secure superior positions. White employers and executives, who tend to favor the lighter complexioned part-Hawaiians for the positions of greater dignity and income, would say that they are more capable. Irrespective of native ability, it may be said that their educational and general social background is better, commonly. If a boy knows that there is opportunity for him dependent only on his education and character, he has the incentive to make the appropriate effort. It is true, also, that superiority of social status is an important factor toward the maintenance of those moral standards which are important in relation to positions of responsibility. One has more to lose through dereliction. One's whole scheme of life is affected by the sort of success that seems to be attainable. Differences in opportunity are reflected in personality traits and personality traits condition opportunity. The effects are cumulative. In the long run, differences in character and training due to differential opportunity may be so important and persistent as to seem to be due to differences in biological heredity.

On the other hand, if a part-Hawaiian boy is three quarters or seven eighths of Hawaiian blood, he has no white or Chinese father to train him or to emphasize the importance of education. Probably the home will not be able to do much in the way of finding a superior position for him and he tends to take the status of Hawaiians. Not always, but commonly, superiority of status among part-Hawaiians is associated with lightness of complexion. Not improbably the preference for the light complexioned in marriage was, in the beginning, just a preference for persons of superior status. At first the light complexion was associated with the superiority of the status, then it became a sign of superiority, and now tends to be regarded as superior in itself.

When the statistical groups now known as Caucasian-Hawaiian and Asiatic-Hawaiian shall be amalgamated into one in the sense that all or nearly all will be of a three-way mixture,—Caucasian-Asiatic-Hawaiian,—the amalgamation will still be incomplete in a biological sense. At one extreme there will be some who are almost pure Hawaiian and at the other, those who will be almost pure Caucasian or, maybe, almost pure Chinese or Japanese, while the majority will occupy intermediate positions. Not until the mixture becomes more nearly homogeneous may it be regarded as a stable race mixture. Not until the people cease to notice and consider the differences in color, or in the other physical traits that serve for identification, will there be a complete disappearance of the social problems incident to race contacts. The speed that will characterize the later stages of amalgamation, i.e., the creation of a more homogeneous mixture, will depend largely on whether people do or do not observe and think about the differences in fractional mixture.

Whether people do observe and give consideration to such differences depends not so much on mere visibility as on the motivation as affected by the social situation. Where there are important vested interests to be maintained by a race of superior as against a race of inferior privilege, people become very expert in the detection of race traits so that almost invisible differences serve to place one in his proper caste group. But in a society in which there are so many races and so many ancestral and fractional types of race mixture as are in prospect for Hawaii and where the caste principle does not prevail there can be no dominance by any one type, certainly not by any one fractional type of part-Hawaiian. Under these conditions the part-Hawaiian man, no matter what his complexion, will see that his only chance for important influence or leadership will depend on making friends among and co-operating with all part-Hawaiians, including those who are not of his own fractional mixture. The situation will compel him to ignore differences in color even when they are plainly visible. So far as the more open and public expression of sentiment is concerned, this is practically true even now and the further multiplication of the gradations of mixture will serve only to establish this part of the code more firmly.

At the beginning of this chapter attention was called to the fact that in a society of free interracial marriage it is the function of the mixed-bloods to serve as a liaison group facilitating the amalgamation of the parent races. It now remains to be pointed out that the various gradations of mixture within a mixed-blood group serve as a series of liaison groups between the extremes and that they perform this function so much the more efficiently because there are so many gradations and such small intervals of difference. In such a situation any tendency toward the creation of codes and doctrines adverse to free marriage or toward the open expression of adverse sentiment is tabu. It may be expected therefore that the later stages of amalgamation among the part-Hawaiians will go on with little retardation excepting such as may result from secondary factors such as place of residence and economic status.

So far, the interest has been mainly in the intermarriage of the two groups of part-Hawaiians with the Hawaiians and with each other. But their intermarriage with Caucasians, Chinese, Japanese and others is no less significant. Caucasians and also Chinese are more disposed to marry part-Hawaiians than those who pass as pure Hawaiians. In the four years, 1930–34, Caucasian men married 30 per cent of the Caucasian-Hawaiian brides and only 13 per cent of the Hawaiian. Similarly Chinese men married 10 per cent of the Asiatic-Hawaiian brides but only 3 per cent of the Hawaiian. But the Filipinos have resided in the Territory for so short a time that there are very few Filipino-Hawaiians to serve as a liaison group and they marry a higher proportion of the Hawaiian than of the Asiatic-Hawaiian women, 15 per cent of the Hawaiian and 11 per cent of the Asiatic-Hawaiian, 1930–34. The comparatively high rate of out-marriage among the Caucasians and the Chinese is explainable largely by reference to the presence in the community of relatively large liaison groups. Similarly the comparatively low rates of out-marriage among the Japanese and the Filipinos is in part explainable by reference to the almost complete lack of hybrid liaison groups, a lack due largely to the recency of their immigration.

Reference has been made to economic advantage as a factor affecting the attitude of part-Hawaiian girls toward marriage with white men. But there is something more and probably more important. Always there is the side of romance. Romantic love does not flourish most between persons who have always known each other. Such persons know each other so well that they are not mutually interesting. Knowledge may be so complete as to leave nothing to the imagination. One can dream about some person whose life is largely a closed book. The village belle is won by the stranger. White men in Hawaii are comparatively few. They belong to a race of high prestige and, commonly, they live outside of the world of the part-Hawaiian girls. If by chance or design a young white man of good personal traits comes into this world for a time the stage is set for a romance.

Table XIX shows the racial character of the brides and grooms of part-Hawaiians for the four years, 1930–34. It may be noted that the Asiatic-Hawaiians intermarry in higher proportion with the Hawaiians than do the Caucasian-Hawaiians. The Asiatic-Hawaiians intermarry more largely with Asiatics than with Caucasians, while the Caucasian-Hawaiians appear to prefer Caucasians. It may be seen, too, that the Caucasian-Hawaiian men, in larger proportion than the women, marry Hawaiians, while the opposite is true in the case of the Asiatic-Hawaiians. One may note the low rate of in-marriage for both groups and the comparatively high rate of out-marriage with both Caucasians and Asiatics. Through intermarriage with all of the so-called pure racial groups the part-Hawaiians are multiplying in numbers and to this extent the rate of increase for the pure racial groups is checked.

Under the condition of a high rate of out-marriage on the part of both Hawaiians and part-Hawaiians, the tendency is for the mixed-blood population to increase at an extraordinarily rapid rate. Since the rate of out-marriage has been

TABLE XIX

Marriages of Caucasian-Hawaiians and Asiatic-Hawaiians
for the Four Years 1930–1934

RACE OF PERSONS MARRIED	ABSOLUTE NUMBERS			
	Brides of Caucasian-Hawaiian Men	Grooms of Caucasian-Hawaiian Women	Brides of Asiatic-Hawaiian Men	Grooms of Asiatic-Hawaiian Women
Hawaiian	98	95	68	130
Caucasian-Hawaiian	268	268	135	134
Asiatic-Hawaiian .	134	135	119	119
Portuguese, Spanish and other Caucasian	137	260	45	102
Chinese	20	31	55	69
Japanese	20	28	14	36
Korean	3	3	1	6
Filipino	1	41		74
Porto Rican and all others	9	19	7	11
Total	690	880	444	681
	NUMBERS TO 1000			
Hawaiian	142	108	153	192
Caucasian-Hawaiian	389	305	304	196
Asiatic-Hawaiian .	194	154	268	175
Portuguese, Spanish and other Caucasian	198	296	102	149
Chinese	29	35	124	101
Japanese	29	32	31	53
Korean	4	3	2	9
Filipino	1	46		109
Porto Rican and all others	14	21	16	16
Total	1000	1000	1000	1000

increasing in the last thirty years, the part-Hawaiian population is increasing at an accelerated rate. For example,
from 1896 to 1910, 13½ years, the average annual rate of
increase of part-Hawaiians was 2.8 per cent. For the 9¾
years, 1910 to 1920, the average annual rate was 3.7 per

cent and, from 1920 to 1930, 10¼ years, the average annual rate was 4.7 per cent. The following table is intended to show something of the complexity of the amalgamating process and, at the same time, to reveal the cause of the

TABLE XX

Maternity and Paternity of Part-Hawaiian Children of Known Paternity Born in the Year 1931–1932

	RACE OF CHILDREN		
	Caucasian-Hawaiian	Asiatic-Hawaiian	Total Part-Hawaiian
Born to Hawaiian mothers			
The fathers, Caucasian-Hawaiian	101		101
The fathers, Asiatic-Hawaiian .		84	84
The fathers, Caucasian . . .	121		121
The fathers, Asiatic		173	173
Total to Hawaiian mothers .	222	257	479
Born to Caucasian-Hawaiian mothers			
The fathers, Hawaiian	107		107
The fathers, Caucasian-Hawaiian	229		229
The fathers, Asiatic-Hawaiian .		119	119
The fathers, Caucasian . . .	146		146
The fathers, Asiatic		89	89
Total to Caucasian-Hawaiian mothers	482	208	690
Born to Asiatic-Hawaiian mothers			
The fathers, Hawaiian		118	118
The fathers, Caucasian-Hawaiian		97	97
The fathers, Asiatic-Hawaiian .		106	106
The fathers, Caucasian . . .		54	54
The fathers, Asiatic		125	125
Total to Asiatic-Hawaiian mothers		500	500
Born to non-Hawaiian mothers			
The fathers, Hawaiian	34	25	59
The fathers, Caucasian-Hawaiian	89	27	116
The fathers, Asiatic-Hawaiian .		71	71
Total to non-Hawaiian mothers	123	123	246
Total births of part-Hawaiian children	827	1088	1915

high rate of increase. The reader will note that only 1190 out of 1915 part-Hawaiian children of known paternity were born to part-Hawaiian mothers in that year, that is, only 62 per cent.

To the 1915 children of known paternity must be added 30, for those of unknown paternity. Since there were 417 deaths of part-Hawaiians the net increase was 1528, or 4.9 per cent, the part-Hawaiian population being 30,759. This may be compared with 1.3 per cent, the approximate rate of natural increase for the rest of the population in recent years. It is easy to see that the numerical importance of the part-Hawaiians is increasing now as never before. Their percentage of the total population of the Territory was, in 1910, 6.5; in 1920, 7.0; in 1930, 7.6; and these gains were made despite the very large immigration. Now that the period of large immigration appears to be ended, the part-Hawaiian percentage will rise more rapidly. Probably they will constitute nearly eleven per cent of the population by 1940 and, if the situation is not seriously affected by further immigration, the majority of all of the people of Hawaii may be part-Hawaiians by the end of the present century. This gain will, of course, take place at the expense of all of the so-called pure racial groups. Looking forward two or three hundred years one may envisage the population of Hawaii as made up almost wholly of people who will be descendants of the old Hawaiians. But they will also be descendants of the peoples of Europe and of those of Asia. They will be approaching a condition of a stable race mixture and they will call themselves Hawaiians. They will be culturally homogeneous. The practical social problems incident to the contact of races will not have been solved, but they will have disappeared, thanks to the multiplication of hybrids and to their acculturation.

Chapter VIII

THE HAOLE, THE PAKE AND THE PORTEGEE

PRELIMINARY to a consideration of intermarriage between white people in Hawaii and the people of other races it seems best to define certain terms which have a local significance. It is not possible accurately to describe the Hawaiian racial situation in terms whose meanings do not correspond to the distinctions actually made in Hawaii. During the greater part of the century and a half of race contacts in Hawaii the Hawaiian people constituted the great body of population and this was especially true in the early period in which the patterns of thought were being worked out. If, therefore, we are to use the racial classifications intelligently we must get at their meaning through a consideration of Hawaiian experience and thought.

The first thing to be said about the white people of Hawaii is that, by the local people, they are not commonly called white. One speaks of Americans, British and Portuguese, not of whites. One does not speak of the Hawaiians as colored. The people of Asiatic birth or ancestry are called Chinese, Japanese or Korean; that is, they are classified according to national origin, not according to race.

In continental United States the people of the white race take themselves for granted and they classify the others and assign them their place in the social order. They are able to ignore any point of view different from their own. In Hawaii the white people were, for a long time, so few that the Hawaiians, who took themselves for granted, named and placed the other peoples. Of course they had to place the British and the Americans near the top, but the name, hä'o le, was Hawaiian and it is best understood from the standpoint of Hawaiian experience. It has been necessary, therefore, in Hawaii for white people to see themselves somewhat as Hawaiians see them. They have accepted the Hawaiian designation, *haole*, and, of course, it has affected their conception of their role and their behavior.

The word, *haole*, in the beginning meant stranger or outsider. It did not, at first, refer to color, but since nearly all of the early strangers were white men it came to be applied in its unmodified form only to white people. When a few Negroes came they were at first called *haole eleele* (black outsider). Since there were only a few Negroes, this use was unimportant and the word came to be applied only to whites.

Almost from the beginning, there were some white men who occupied positions of power and prestige. When white men, mainly British and American, came to be somewhat numerous they occupied most of the important professional positions and they were the executives and administrators, the owners of property and the initiators of policy. Of course there were many who occupied positions of minor importance, but even they were better paid than others and the way was more open to them for promotion. Thus the word came gradually to stand for a class of superior economic and social status. At first it was made up of Americans and British, but Norwegians and Germans, even though they came as plantation laborers, made *haole* status pretty freely as they won superior positions. Since the Hawaiians had long been familiar with a system of social distinctions based on rank or class and since they were not, in the beginning, race conscious, it is reasonable to assume that the term, *haole*, was, for a long time, more significant of rank than of race. But as Hawaiians and part-Hawaiians in the more recent times have been learning to speak the English language and, with it, taking over other elements of American and European culture, they are more or less coming to think in terms of race.

It must be emphasized that the term, *haole,* acquired its meaning from Hawaiian experience and attitudes and that its use has become current among all the other peoples because it stands for something they feel to be unique in the position of this group. As a local classificatory term its meaning is maintained not so much by the *haole* as by the others. When some of the German plantation laborers won a better economic status the decision whether they were to be regarded as *haole* lay in part with the *haole* who might or might not give them social recognition, but more largely with the Hawaiians and others who might or might not be willing to treat them as *haole.*

Not always is the word significant of good will. There are the so-called *haole*-haters and, maybe, the envious. In some cases there seems to be a rankling sense of injustice. Sometimes there is respect for the *power* of *haole,* but not for their *goodness* and, sometimes, not for either. When one part-Hawaiian speaks of another as *haolefied* he is calling attention to some of his less gracious traits.

When the Chinese came in sufficient numbers to attract attention it was obvious that, while they were strangers, they were different, and they were not called *haole.* A Chinese man was, *pa ké.* In China the word, *pak ye* (uncle), was used not only when addressing an uncle, but also as a term of respect when a child addressed an elder. It appears that the early Chinese men who married Hawaiian women were trying to train the children in their own and other families to show respect to age according to Chinese usage. They told the young people to say *pakye* and as this was mispronounced it became *pa ké.* But naturally enough, it was not used as a term of respect. It was equivalent merely to Chinese. In the period, 1884–1900, when there was so much ill will toward the Chinese on account of their leaving the plantations and competing for the jobs that the Hawaiians wanted, the word, *pake,* acquired a meaning quite the opposite of what was intended. The hated and despised *pake.* Just as *haole* came to stand for an upper class so *pake* for a time came to stand for an inferior class.

The Hawaiian names of the other immigrant peoples were formed by modifying the English names in such a way as to make them pronounceable on the basis of Hawaiian phonetic achievement. For example, the sounds of *t* and *k* were not clearly discriminated and likewise *l* and *r,* and since the Hawaiians did not have the sounds represented by *g, s,* or *z* they changed the word Portuguese to *Pokiki.* Later, when they had made some progress toward the acquisition of English, a compromise pronunciation, *Portegee,* came to be used by Hawaiians and, from them it was learned by the other immigrant peoples.

But the linguistic influence of the Hawaiians has been decreasing so that in the case of the later immigrants, the English-speaking people did not, in general, accept similar compromises but maintained the correct pronunciation, which gradually tends to be accepted by all others. The Japanese, at first *Kepani* to the Hawaiians, are becoming Japanese. The *Poko Liko* are becoming Porto Ricans, the *Pilipino,* the Filipinos.

If one makes a study of the classificatory terms used for census and other official uses in Hawaii in the nineteenth century, he finds evidence of a reticence to use terms significant of race distinctions. The white men who were prominent in the administrative and statistical work of the kingdom were mainly Americans and they were familiar with the terms of racial distinction used in the United States. But at no time did they classify people as white and colored. The Chinese were never classified as Mongolian or yellow. The few Negroes who had come from the Cape Verde Islands were called Portuguese. Twice the word "Negro" was used in footnotes, once, to give the information that there were 20 such persons in Honolulu in 1853 and, once, to state that the mixed-blood Portuguese-Hawaiians of 1896 were, mainly, not the children of the Portuguese plantation laborers who had come after 1877, but of the earlier Portuguese, who had come on whaling ships, and that many of these were Negroes.

It is not that the idea of race was lacking in the American community. Popularly, the so-called Portuguese from the Cape Verde Islands were known among the English-speaking people as black Portuguese and the others as white Portuguese. The official reticence toward the use of racial terms appears to have grown out of a recognition that, under Hawaiian conditions, such use would tend toward the acceptance of ideas adverse to the system of race relations that was in course of development. It would be difficult to utilize American racial terminology in Hawaii without incurring the risk of introducing American race doctrine.

When the first census under the authority of the United States Congress was taken (1900), the usual mainland racial classifications were used, but the local peoples were not always classified as might have been expected. The population as a whole was classified as "white" and "colored." The Negroes, Chinese, and Japanese were the colored. The Hawaiians and their mixed-blood descendants and also the South Sea Islanders were classified with the people of European descent as white. Apparently the foreign-born Portuguese of Negro blood and also the mixed-blood members of their families were classified as Negroes.

In 1910 and in later census years the people have been classified according to a compromise system somewhat like the one used locally in the previous century. From the standpoint of our present interest the important thing is the way the whites are classified. Instead of the word, "white," used for the classification of mainland people the word, "Caucasian," is used and Caucasians are subdivided into four classes, "Portuguese," "Porto Rican," "Spanish," and "other Caucasian." [1] In 1910 the "other Caucasians" were mainly the people who were known locally as *haole*, but since all Caucasians but the pure Portuguese, pure Porto Rican, and pure Spanish were included, the term was destined to stand for a group of decreasing homogeneity as new immigrants might come or as there should be inter-Caucasian mixture. At the present time only about 60 per cent of the civilian "other Caucasians" are of *haole* status or, if adults only are considered, about 80 per cent. Among the others there are about 5000 persons of European birth or ancestry who have not yet attained to *haole* status and about 5000 part-Portuguese, part-Porto-Rican and part-Spanish who are minors mainly and who, for the most part, are not recognized as *haole*.

Among the European immigrants of the nineteenth century the Portuguese were unique in relation to the status achieved. Coming mainly as plantation laborers they did not as promptly improve their status as did the Germans and Norwegians. The Portuguese were much more numerous. Mainly they were illiterate and for a generation they were indifferent to schooling. In general culture they differed more from the *haole* than did most of the other European immigrants. Because they were numerous and because their status was a humble one for a long time, there came to be a pretty definite mental set in relation to them. That is, they were regarded as a separate people, the "Portegee."

If one considers the attitude of white people only, the racial status of the Portuguese in Hawaii does not differ greatly from that of many of the European immigrant groups on the mainland. There has always been a tendency on the part of the people of the old American stock to regard the newer immigrants as if they were of a different race and this is especially true in relation to those immigrants who have differed most in culture from Americans. In many sections

---

[1] Where this term is not defined by its position in a series, quotation marks are used to suggest its special meaning.

with large foreign populations the word, "white," has been used colloquially in such a way as to exclude certain classes of Europeans, and such usage tends to persist as long as the foreign language is used for communication within the family. In so far as the status of the Portuguese in Hawaii may differ from that of such mainland immigrant peoples, the difference seems to be a consequence of their being involved in a general system of race relations in which the ideas and attitudes of Hawaiians, part-Hawaiians and Orientals are important.

But as the Hawaiians are gradually abandoning their native language and using the English language in its place they are coming under the influence of American doctrines. Distinctions which originally were based wholly or mainly on rank are acquiring racial significance or a more distinct racial significance. A similar statement could be made relative to the other immigrant groups. Just as the Japanese, originally thought of as the people from Japan and a people who had their own language and a special economic position in the community, tend to be regarded as a race, so also the Portuguese.

As the Hawaiian language gradually passes out of use and as the old Hawaiian way of thinking becomes less important, the term, *haole,* may be forgotten and, with it, the system of social relations that gave the term its meaning. The slowness of the Portuguese progress toward the achievement of *haole* status may mean that the majority will never achieve it—it may cease to exist too soon. But when the people of Hawaii are popularly classified after two or three generations it is probable that there will be no Portuguese. There will be just native white people of native parentage for census purposes and the descendants of the present *haole* and of the present Portuguese if otherwise unmixed will be classified together as white. But for a time the tendency to regard the Portuguese as a race will be a factor in their social relations.

CHAPTER IX

THE BRIDES OF THE HAOLE MEN

THE intermarriage of white people in Hawaii with the people of the other racial groups presents certain features of unique interest. Many men and few women have so married. The great majority of the men were of American or of British origin and this was especially true in the nineteenth century. The Americans and the British are known, the world over, as being more race conscious than other peoples. American contacts with Indians on the frontier and with Negro slaves, freedmen, and their descendants have resulted in a very definite system of race mores highly adverse to marriage with non-whites. Indeed, interracial marriage is prohibited by law in about two thirds of the American states and where such prohibitions do not exist it is a testimonial not so much to the absence of adverse public sentiment as to the absence of non-white people. If there are very few non-whites, it may be that legislative bodies give no attention to the matter. British experience in governing and exploiting the native peoples of the "far flung empire" has had a similar effect on the attitude of British people. This is most evident among those who live outside of the British Isles but, in considerable measure, even those who remain in the homeland are race conscious. The sentiment of the English-speaking community in South Africa is much like that of South Carolinians. Canada has been as alert to restrict Oriental immigration as the United States. The "White Australian" policy is well known.

Why, of all the white peoples of the world, have the race conscious Americans and British played the leading role in amalgamation with the Hawaiians? It is not merely that the Americans and the British, as seafaring peoples, were the first to be represented by considerable numbers in Hawaii. Most of the time for fifty years there have been more white Portuguese resident in Hawaii than British and American civilians combined. But while the Portuguese in Brazil do not appear to be greatly adverse to intermarriage with non-whites, those in Hawaii have, even in the more recent years, intermarried with Hawaiians less than the Americans and British have. The civilian *haole* men have been much less numerous since 1878 than the Chinese and they have been better provided with women of their own race, but they have, nevertheless, intermarried with Hawaiian and part-Hawaiian women more than the Chinese have.

The explanation of the rather free out-marriage practice of Americans and British in Hawaii is found mainly in the special character of their social situation. True it is that most of the early American residents came from the North, where race sentiment was not so strong as in the slave states, but this does not seem to have been decisive. When a Southerner comes to Hawaii and lives under certain social conditions he is just about as likely to marry a dark complexioned woman as a Northerner is. It is more a matter of his social situation in Hawaii than it is of the influence of his old home community. The most important thing is just the being away from home—away from his parents, relatives, and neighbors. So long as a man is a member of a community he tends to conform to its standards. There are, of course, a few people of the emancipated sort who may be comparatively indifferent to the opinion of their people and there are some who are of the rebel type. But most people find it almost impossible, when they are real members of a community, to run counter to what "everybody" expects of them. A man escapes from the control of his community by leaving it and, the farther away from home and the less the communication with the old home people, the greater the freedom.

Men of resourcefulness and resolute character are often able, when they leave their old homes, to find a place in society in the new community quite similar to what they occupied in the old. The member of the Masonic Order finds a lodge in the new town. Church members find a church of their own sect. Professional men find their professional associations. But there are many men who are unable to carry their social environment with them. Their course in a new community is determined advantageously or otherwise by the accidents of the situation. Following the line of least resistance they tend to make such adjustments of behavior and attitude as are necessary in order to get on in the sort of society they happen to be in. A man is so fundamentally a social being that it is much more important for him to enjoy something approaching normal human relationships than it is that he shall have his first choice as to the character of the people with whom he associates.

The early Americans and British who became residents of Hawaii did not commonly come direct from their old home towns. They were men accustomed to a seafaring life and, if one could know the stories about their going to sea, it would be found that many had experienced some sort of break with their families. For example, there was a high-born Scottish lad who, according to the family account, did not like his stepmother. He considered himself mistreated, ran away from home, changed his name, taking that of his mother's father, and went to sea. He fought under Admiral Nelson at Trafalgar, and in time he reached Hawaii, where he married an Hawaiian woman. In the story there is no reference to any communication with his father or with the people of his old boyhood community. He appears to have cut himself off completely.

It was the emancipation of the early American and British

men from the moral control of their native lands that made
them free to marry in Hawaii. Something like this is true
even in the more recent times. Some twenty-five years ago
a family of German origin lived on one of the islands where
there were several hundred Germans—enough to maintain
a church and a school in which the German language was
used. The church was the center of a community life.
From it the dead were buried and in it the weddings were
solemnized. In it Christmas and the other church festivals
were celebrated. The family had a son who, in the course
of time, came to Honolulu for better employment opportunities. In connection with his work, he was sent to still another
island where he soon married a beautiful part-Hawaiian
girl. His parents were grievously disappointed for they
wanted him to have a German wife. But he was two hundred
miles from home, was lonesome, was entertained in the
home of a good part-Hawaiian family and just naturally fell
in love with one of the girls.

It is this being away from home that results in so many
marriages between the men in military and naval service and
the brunettes of Hawaii. The men are mainly young and un-
sophisticated. They come over with ordinary American
attitudes on the race question. For many, their enlistment
marks their first extended experience away from home.
Ordinarily they do not enjoy any sort of social contacts
with the *haole* residents of Honolulu because there is too
much difference in economic and social status. Besides,
they are transient newcomers in a community that has
settled traditions, and in such a community the newcomer
is never as readily accepted as in communities too young to
have traditions. The boys are homesick, bored with the
routine of army and navy life, and, in seeking social
diversion, they get acquainted with girls of darker complexion. These girls find the romance the more thrilling
because the boys are *haole* and, perhaps, because they wear
the uniform. Often enough, too, the girl's mother actively

encourages the affair by giving the youth what he most feels the need of—a home place to which he can go and be mothered a little.

Commonly it is said that the marriages that result from such associations are transient affairs, lasting only till the term of service expires or until the regiment is transferred. But one could make out a fairly long list of names of the men who have asked for their discharge in Hawaii and who have remained to discharge their responsibilities as husbands and fathers. One young man from a Southern state is said to have sung with others the song, one line of which runs, "You may call 'em Hawaiians, but they look like niggers to me." But, a year or two later, he married a girl who appears to be a pure Hawaiian and, for years, he has been working to support her and their children. Of course he could not take his family back to Georgia. Some of the men who marry light colored part-Hawaiians do take them to the mainland, and, in a few cases at least, back to the old home, but I know of none who have returned to a home in the "Old South."

Marriage choice is influenced in considerable measure by economic and social status. Commonly there would be objection to marriage with a person of markedly inferior status even if there were no question of race. There is also the question of education and refinement. Because of the large proportion of resident *haole* who have greater wealth or superior positions and because of the superior educational and social advantages enjoyed by many, it is a group that would be segregated to a certain extent even if there were no question of race. The effect of this may, however, be exaggerated. There are some *haole* who clearly belong to the common people. Some of the part-Hawaiians and of the other non-whites have achieved a superior economic status and, from the standpoint of education and refinement, are qualified for participation in the society of cultivated people.

It will be seen that the type of social organization that permits of interracial marriage, is one that makes the conditions of competition so nearly equal that such obstacles to intermarriage as arise from difference in income, education and refinement tend to become independent of race. If one could make a precise and accurate statement as to the degree to which such obstacles do tend to prevent the out-marriage of "other Caucasians" it would be true only temporarily. The lines based on economic and social status tend, more and more, to cut across race lines.

In 1853, 67 per cent of the foreign men outside of Honolulu, mainly *haole,* were married to Hawaiian and part-Hawaiian women, while in the city, only 17 per cent were so married. At all times intermarriage between *haole* men and the women of other races has gone on more freely in the rural districts than among civilians in the city, but the rates are not so far apart now as they were in 1853.

The way people marry is affected by the location of their residence. If the members of a racial group are spatially segregated there will be less out-marriage. The civilian "other Caucasians" tend to be concentrated in Honolulu where 69 per cent of them were found in 1930. Here it is possible for them to maintain a degree of segregation. There are residence areas in which, according to a "gentlemen's agreement" among realtors, houses and building lots are not sold to others. There are schools in which most of the pupils are *haole.* There are churches mainly attended by *haole.* There is a considerable degree of segregation in relation to the more intimate sorts of social contacts and this is especially true in relation to the young people of marriageable age. True to Hawaiian traditions, there are no rigid rules concerning such matters and exceptions may be noted. Nevertheless, the families that have lived in Honolulu long enough to find a definite place in *haole* society are able to go in the direction of friendly interracial social affairs as far as may be necessary to

PARENTAGE
Father, English-Hawaiian
Mother, Japanese-Hawaiian

symbolize the Hawaiian spirit of interracial good will without much jeopardy to the future racial purity of their families.

So far as the city is concerned the intermarriage of "other Caucasians" to the men and women of other racial groups is mainly on account of the residence of many newcomers, or *malihinis*, to use the Hawaiian word. Many of these are in military and naval service, but there are many civilians who have resided in Honolulu not more than a few years and who have not found any real position in *haole* society. Among the *malihinis* there are considerable numbers who are of the emancipated type, and they marry out of their racial group much more freely than do the old residents of established social position. For example, during a certain recent year, 1926–7, 42 per cent of all "other Caucasian" grooms in the Territory were "service men" and all of these were in or near Honolulu. Of such "service men" 62 per cent were married to women who were not of their own racial group. In Honolulu 38 per cent of the civilian "other Caucasian" grooms married out and, while there are no statistical data relative to this point, it may be said that the majority of them were of the emancipated *malihini* type, not members of the old families.

But in the rural parts of the Territory it is otherwise. The number of *haole* in a rural district may be too small to permit of much social segregation and residence is more stable. Social contacts between *haole* and other peoples tend to be more continuous and intimate than in the city. A good many of the older rural *haole* can converse in the Hawaiian language and the younger Hawaiians commonly speak English. The village churchyard where the ancestors of *haole* families lie buried near Hawaiians may symbolize a tradition of friendly family relations that extends over the greater part of a century. Every social group tends to create sentiment adverse to out-marriage, but a group so small and scattered as that of the rural *haole* is not able to do this very effectively and there are things in the family tradition of some of the more influential families that tend to reduce the adverse sentiment to uncommonly small proportions. In the year, 1926–7, 45 per cent of the "other Caucasian" grooms (civilian) of the rural districts were married to brides of racial groups other than their own.

When "other Caucasian" men marry out the general tendency of choice is about as might be expected. Mainly they marry Portuguese and part-Hawaiians. Comparatively few marry Orientals. The Portuguese as representatives of a white race are preferred over non-whites, especially by service men.[1] Since these men have little or no part in local tradition it may be supposed that to them the Portuguese are just another white immigrant people.

Brides of Civilians and of Service Men Who Were Married in the Year 1926–1927

RACE OF BRIDES	ABSOLUTE NUMBERS		NUMBER TO 1000	
	Civilians	Service Men	Civilians	Service Men
Hawaiian	16	13	54	60
Caucasian-Hawaiian	33	21	112	98
Asiatic-Hawaiian .	9	5	31	23
Portuguese . . .	37	74	125	343
Porto Rican . . .	2	4	7	19
Spanish	2	7	7	33
Other Caucasian . .	178	83	603	384
Chinese	3	1	10	4
Japanese	8	5	27	23
Korean		1		4
Filipino				
All other	7	2	24	9
Total	295	216	1000	1000

[1] The out-marriage rates of "other Caucasian" men are affected considerably by the inclusion of men stationed in and near Honolulu for military or naval service. The extent and character of this influence may be seen from the data of the above table. In the year, 1926–27, 42 per cent of the "other Caucasian" grooms were service men while 58 per cent were civilians. Of the civilians, 40 per cent married women not of their own racial group while for the service men the rate of out-marriage was 62 per cent and the rate for both combined was 48.9 per cent.

In the preceding sections there has been little or no reference to interracial marriage between "other Caucasian"
women and men of other races. There were very few such
marriages in the nineteenth century and there are not many
even in recent years. This may be explained in part by reference to the abnormal sex ratio. There have always been
fewer women than men and this would be expected to favor
the out-marriage of men rather than women. But there are
two other factors of greater probable importance. The marriage between a white man and an Hawaiian woman results
commonly in a better working arrangement than one between
a white woman and an Hawaiian man. In the former case the
man, if a fairly good representative of his people, expects
to provide an adequate income for the support of his wife
and children and commonly this is better than an Hawaiian
woman would expect from a husband of her own race. Feeling that she has made a good match she is willing to modify
her way of life reasonably so as to suit her white husband.
Moreover, such cultural changes are in line with her ambition for an improved social status. The family status seems
to depend more on the husband and so the wife gains a
better status and is happy. But a white wife of an Hawaiian man is likely to expect better support and treatment
than she gets and while unwilling to accept her husband's
status she is not able to modify his much.

And then there is the subtle influence of social sentiment
adverse to interracial marriage. Where this sentiment
exists even in a moderate degree among white people, it
seems so much worse for a woman to marry out of the
race than it does for a man. In spite of the fact that it is
the son who perpetuates the family name, an American
father is much more shocked at the thought of his daughter's
marrying a representative of another race than he would
be if it were his son. A son is expected to have more freedom and to be responsible for his own action. The daughter
is especially to be protected by her father and if she flouts

the paternal control it has more effect on the status of the family as a whole. A family may hold its head up pretty well in spite of the errant behavior of a wayward son, but it is mortally humiliated if the daughter goes wrong. The daughter must conform her conduct more precisely to family or neighborhood sentiment. Moreover, in the nineteenth century there were very few if any *haole* women detached from their families and of the emancipated sort. Even at the present time when there are some such women in Hawaii they are less numerous than men of the same type. Consequently there have been only a few "other Caucasian" women who have married outside of their own race in Hawaii and they, mainly, in the more recent times.

There are in Honolulu a few *haole* women who are wives of Chinese, Japanese, Korean, Filipino and Indian men. Most of these women were, before their marriage, residents of the mainland. In most cases a young man of Asiatic birth or ancestry attended college on the mainland and the social relations and the romance that preceded marriage center around some campus. Some of the men were citizens of Hawaii before they went to college. Probably some were attracted to Hawaii after their marriage by its reputation for interracial good will. It would be going too far to say that Hawaii has become a haven for husbands and wives who, on account of race, experience social embarrassments elsewhere, but there seems to be a little tendency in this direction.

On account of the prominence of these college men and their *haole* wives their role is more important than their small numbers may indicate. The men, commonly, are brilliant professional men or they are in business positions of some importance. Their wives are women of refinement. These women receive social recognition as *haole* and still there is some curtailment of social opportunity on account of their husbands, not a curtailment due to malice or to a social code, but just in consequence of the fact that, to most white people, the Oriental husband does not seem quite to "belong." To a certain extent these women have been able to find social diversion among themselves, but they do not restrict themselves to the society of one another. It is still too early to speak of the social situation as it will develop for their children except that they enjoy good educational advantages, they make a good appearance and appear to be well endowed intellectually.

Table XXI shows the in-marriage and the out-marriage rates for the "other Caucasian" men and women for the four four-year periods. While the out-marriage rates for

TABLE XXI

Brides and Grooms of "Other Caucasians"
Including Enlisted Men

Brides of "Other Caucasian" Men   Number to 1000

	1912–16	1920–24	1924–28	1930–34
Hawaiian	85	56	66	22
Caucasian-Hawaiian	119	122	103	83
Asiatic-Hawaiian	14	19	27	29
Portuguese	157	172	183	179
Porto Rican	14	13	17	13
Spanish	14	11	13	10
Other Caucasian	574	561	530	618
Chinese	5	8	10	12
Japanese	2	8	19	14
Korean		1	2	5
Filipino	5	2	2	1
All other	11	27	28	14
Total	1000	1000	1000	1000

Grooms of "Other Caucasian" Women   Number to 1000

Hawaiian	11	1	4	6
Caucasian-Hawaiian	29	14	37	41
Asiatic-Hawaiian		4	4	7
Portuguese	19	12	19	40
Porto Rican	1		1	6
Spanish		1	2	2
Other Caucasian	925	911	897	866
Chinese		3	1	4
Japanese		5	2	7
Korean	1	1	1	
Filipino	7	3	3	16
All other	7	45	29	5
Total	1000	1000	1000	1000

the women are low, there is a moderate increase for each period. But while the rates for men were comparatively high, the trend, which was upward until 1928, turned pretty sharply downward after that date. Probably this reversal of trend was due in part to a legal obstacle and in part to a temporary modification of attitude affecting the choice of brides.[2]

[2] Formerly some of the men in army or navy service secured in Hawaii divorces from the wives they had left on the mainland, and then they could marry local women. But, since 1928, such men have, for the most part, been unable to secure the jurisdiction of the local court, it being held that the stationing of men in Hawaii does not give them domicile for divorce purposes. Following this there was a decrease in divorces to "other Caucasian" men, a decrease in the number married yearly and a decrease in their rate of out-marriage.

The further reduction in the out-marriage rate of "other Caucasian" men after 1931 is accounted for in a different way, i.e., by reference to a crisis situation in which race feeling was accentuated. In the autumn of 1931 the wife of a young naval officer claimed that she had been raped by several young men. Later, she identified five men, mainly of Hawaiian or part-Hawaiian ancestry, as her assailants. These men were indicted and tried before a jury. The case resulted in mistrial, the members of the jury being unable to agree on a verdict. While further investigations were being made one of the alleged assailants was assaulted, supposedly by men or officers of the navy, and another, one with an Hawaiian name, was shot and killed. The police captured the slayers almost immediately while they were driving a car and, apparently, seeking a safe place for the disposal of the dead body. The husband and the mother of the woman alleged to have been assaulted were tried, convicted and sentenced to terms in prison. Their sentences were, however, commuted to one hour and that hour was served at the Governor's office.

During the trial of the alleged rapists, many local people, largely non-whites, followed the proceedings more or less closely. Some of the people, mainly whites, accepted the testimony of the chief witness for the prosecution as true, but others including nearly all of the non-whites saw inconsistencies in the testimony and were unconvinced as to the guilt of the men,—indeed, many were convinced of their innocence,—and there was a tendency to invent theories as to what actually happened on the night of the alleged raping.

The noted criminal lawyer of Chicago who defended the husband and the mother a few months later staged the case dramatically in such a way that mainland race prejudice was brought to bear on the local community very effectively and there was, of course, a response by the community. All in all these two cases and the related events and allegations had the effect of creating race feeling of a more intense character than the Territory had known for a long time. This feeling was strongest among the Hawaiians including part-Hawaiians and the white people of brief residence including the military population. Naturally the hatreds thus engendered would reduce not only the number of marriages of service men, but more especially, the number of intermarriages with the women of other racial groups.

The tables that show the marriage practice of the "other Caucasians" do not always indicate attitudes of preference fairly. For example, "other Caucasian" men marry more than ten times as many Portuguese as Spanish women, but this seems to result from the fewness of Spanish relative to Portuguese in the Territory and not from any important difference in attitude. So far as attitude of civilian "other Caucasians" is concerned the order of preference in out-marriage is about as follows: (1) Portuguese and Spanish; (2) Caucasian-Hawaiian; (3) Hawaiian, Asiatic-Hawaiian and Porto Rican; (4) the people of Oriental birth or ancestry.

It has been estimated that in 1930 there were, in Hawaii, 46,311 racial hybrids of Hawaiian origin and that, of this number, 30,360, or 65 per cent, could claim "other Caucasian" ancestry.[3] In spite of the adverse attitude of British

The Marriage of "Other Caucasian" Men

Race of Brides	Number to 1000		
	1924–28	1928–31	1931–34
Other Caucasian	530	561	637
Portuguese and Spanish	196	213	175
Hawaiian and part-Hawaiian	196	167	128
All others, including Chinese, Japanese, Korean and Porto Rican	78	59	60

and of white Americans toward intermarriage with non-white peoples the *haole* are participating in the general process of interracial amalgamation through the marriage relationship to a greater extent than are most of the other peoples and, among the men who live in Honolulu, those who have come from the mainland somewhat recently are more given to the practice of out-marriage than those who belong to the old families of Hawaii.

[3] See pages 15–18.

CHAPTER X

THE MARRIAGE OF PORTUGUESE

In a study devoted to interracial marriage in Hawaii and to the interracial social relations that condition such marriages, it is uncommonly difficult to deal adequately with the Portuguese. This is because they are, according to American popular classifications, of the same race as the "other Caucasians"—the white race. One might seize upon the distinction made by physical anthropologists between the Mediterranean race and the Nordic race, excepting that such distinction does not seem to have anything to do with the actual situation. A brown-eyed Englishman of the Mediterranean type is still an Englishman socially. A blue-eyed Portuguese,—really of Norwegian ancestry, but reared by Portuguese foster parents in Portugal,—is Portuguese in the social sense. While most Americans and British are race-conscious, they do not commonly take much account merely of brown eyes and a complexion no darker than that of the Portuguese, these being regarded popularly as minor differences within a race, not as marks of race difference.

And still one cannot fail to recognize the existence of a tendency on the part of the peoples of Hawaii to regard the Portuguese as belonging to a different race. Perhaps the tendency is not destined to be permanent, but, in the past at least, it has been a factor affecting the social relations of the two peoples. The problem is to recognize and describe it without exaggerating it.

The earlier Portuguese residents consisted of three or four hundred sailors who had been in the service of whaling ships. They accumulated gradually from about 1830 to

1878. Probably over half were real Portuguese while the others were Negroes from the Cape Verde Islands. It is said that most of the Negroes and some of the whites married Hawaiian women, while some of the whites secured wives from their native land.

The main body of Portuguese immigrants came in the period, 1878–1886, to serve as plantation laborers. They were brought mainly on the initiative of the Hawaiian government, an agent of which did the recruiting in the Azores and the Madeira Islands. The planters themselves tended to prefer Chinese laborers because the cost of importation was very much lower and because it was necessary to pay higher wages to the Portuguese on account of their having families to support. But white men of influence in governmental affairs were considering the future population and they wanted more white people, fewer Chinese. From the standpoint of this interest it was desirable to bring families, not men merely. But this involved paying the passage of so many women and children that it was burdensome to the plantations. There appears to have been worked out a compromise plan. The agent was to send some women and children, but not in more than a certain proportion, and the government was to pay part of the expense. But the military laws of Portugal prevented the free emigration of able-bodied young men if they were subject to military service as reservists, and so it was necessary to accept a good many middle-aged men with families too large to suit the planters.

During this period of immigration there was a tendency on the part of public officials in Hawaii to defend their policy by extolling the character of the Portuguese immigrants. The growing white population was a matter for congratulation, but the idea was expressed without the use of the word "white" or of other terms with a clear racial meaning. The Portuguese were even lauded for their "good citizenship" although they were aliens in fact.

But while the governmental propaganda was thus favorable, it is not clear that it did much to improve the actual status of the immigrants and their families. Possibly it did help toward certain legislative enactments which gave to the Portuguese rights and privileges that were withheld from the Chinese, and these were of real value. But all the time there was, among the English-speaking residents, a current of sentiment toward the Portuguese not unlike the sentiment of mainland communities toward new immigrants from southern Europe, and for a long time there was not much relationship between Portuguese and "other Caucasians" except such as was necessarily connected with employment and business.

But the Portuguese have been making substantial progress in an economic way. The few who remain in plantation service are often found in superior positions. Some are independent small farmers, some are skilled laborers, many are in business. A few have won distinction in the professions. As they have, through the acquisition of the English language, come into closer communication with the *haole* and, as increasing numbers have won recognition in the business and professional world, there is an increasing demand for general social recognition and an increasing sensitiveness to anything that seems to imply social inferiority. Some would like to see the word, Portuguese, drop out of use and more especially, the word, "Portegee." They are Americans. Some are, by their achievements, giving the term Portuguese a position of greater dignity. Some of those who have enjoyed the better educational advantages are becoming familiar with the historic achievement of the Portuguese as navigators, artists, and literary men and they are acquiring thereby a pride of Portuguese ancestry.

Such sentiment as there is among the non-white peoples antagonistic to the recognition of Portuguese as *haole* seems to be a consequence of the general competitive situation. All of the non-*haole* groups have in their social status suffered more or less from poverty and lack of education.

ANCESTRY, PORTUGUESE

Now there is a general tendency,—a competitive struggle, —on the part of the more ambitious men of all these groups to rise to the *haole* level of comfort and influence. To the non-white peoples it is pretty clear that they mu.t win, if at all, as representatives of their respective racial groups. A Chinese man can rise only so far as this is possible within the Chinese group. In order to rise he must help the group as a whole to rise. Now if the more capable Portuguese are able to win recognition as *haole* and thus to escape the limitations experienced by their competitors, it seems to be an unfair advantage.

For nearly a quarter-century after the beginning of the immigration of Portuguese plantation laborers, there was very little intermarriage between them or their sons and daughters and any of the other peoples of Hawaii. Their sex ratio was not far from normal. Since they lived in families, mainly, and since they were fairly numerous they were able to maintain old-country social standards and hence to maintain attitudes adverse to out-marriage. Their inferior economic status tended to prevent the development of intimate social relations with the *haole*. Like nearly all other immigrants, they were isolated because of their language. Cultural differences including religion were obstacles to the kind of social contacts that are favorable to out-marriage.

Considering the nature of the obstacles, one would expect to see a rising rate of out-marriage as the Portuguese improved their economic position and as they underwent acculturation to the American pattern. There has been a notable increase in the number of marriages between Portuguese and other Caucasians since the beginning of the present century. While the marriages are commonly between men and women of humble status, there have been some marriages involving families of superior status and the number of such may be expected to increase.

Intermarriage between Portuguese and Spanish appears

to be very free. In language, in religion, and in old country culture they are much alike. The Spanish are too few in number to maintain institutions of their own and they, especially those born and educated in Hawaii, tend to be drawn into the circle of Portuguese social life. Because of the greater numbers of Portuguese this is for them only a minor matter, but it means the early disappearance of the Spanish by amalgamation with the Portuguese.

The Porto Ricans are nominally, at least, of the same religion as the Portuguese and Spanish; they are partly of Spanish ancestry and they have been under Spanish cultural influences for several hundred years. But there seems to be among the Portuguese, especially in recent years, an attitude less favorable to intermarriage with Porto Ricans than with Spanish. The Porto Ricans have resided in Hawaii for a longer time than have the main body of the Spanish and this would lead one to expect a higher rate of outmarriage. The Porto Rican group, while larger than the Spanish, is too small to maintain Porto Rican institutions. If the Porto Ricans are not so much drawn into the circle of Portuguese influence as the Spanish are, it must be on account of something in the Portuguese attitude. The Porto Ricans are, for the most part, of Spanish-Negro-Indian mixture,—sometimes a light mixture, sometimes a dark,— and it seems that the Portuguese who are not greatly race conscious in Portugal or Brazil, are, in Hawaii, developing sentiment adverse to marriage with persons of Negro ancestry. Perhaps this is evidence of their Americanization. While thirty per cent of all Spanish brides and grooms, 1930–34, were married to Portuguese, less than 9 per cent of the Porto-Ricans were so married.

So far as the Portuguese intermarry with Orientals, it is with the Filipinos, mainly. The Filipinos are mainly of the same religion, the sex ratio of the Filipinos is highly abnormal and there is no strong local Filipino sentiment adverse to out-marriage.

The Portuguese are fairly well distributed as between the city of Honolulu and the rural districts. In the country as well as in the city, they are sufficiently numerous to maintain a social life of their own. In all Portuguese communities there are Catholic churches and in some there are parochial schools attended largely by Portuguese children. Consequently the influence of Portuguese sentiment is about equally effective in the city and in the country. The per cent of out-marriage is somewhat higher in the city, but this seems to be a consequence of the fact that the racial groups with which they intermarry most freely are found mainly in Honolulu. The out-marriage rate for Portuguese men for 1926–7 was, in Honolulu, 34 per cent, and elsewhere, 29 per cent. Because of the presence of large numbers of service men in and near Honolulu the out-marriage rate for Portuguese women in the city was higher, 42 per cent, while in the rest of the Territory, their rate, 30 per cent, was nearly the same as that of the men.

From Table XXII it will be seen that the percentage of out-marriage has been increasing considerably since 1912. In the period, 1930–34, 46 per cent of the Portuguese brides had non-Portuguese grooms, while among the men 28 per cent married out of the group. Of both sexes, 62 per cent married in and 38 per cent out. If one seeks an explanation of the recent important rise in the out-marriage rate of the Portuguese, he must consider not only the changes in culture and economic status that have been taking place, but also the presence of a moderately large and increasing number of part-Portuguese most of whom are classified as Caucasian-Hawaiian or "other Caucasian." For the Portuguese, liaison groups have begun to function effectively.

As in the case of other groups, the actual marriage practice sometimes fails to indicate preference, this mainly on account of the difference in the size of the various racial groups. Allowing for certain other factors, the factor of attitude or preference seems to be favorable to marriage

TABLE XXII

Brides and Grooms Wedded to Portuguese

Brides of Portuguese Men	Number to 1000			
	1912–16	1920–24	1924–28	1930–34
Hawaiian	38	60	62	34
Caucasian-Hawaiian	28	69	96	86
Asiatic-Hawaiian	12	7	27	41
Portuguese	877	801	726	716
Porto Rican	2	20	30	23
Spanish	14	11	21	10
Other Caucasian	15	14	22	55
Chinese		5	4	10
Japanese		3	7	13
Korean				1
Filipino	1			3
All other	13	10	5	8
Total	1000	1000	1000	1000

Grooms of Portuguese Women				
Hawaiian	20	13	23	16
Caucasian-Hawaiian	14	33	38	53
Asiatic-Hawaiian	6	10	11	24
Portuguese	690	590	541	539
Porto Rican	28	18	31	15
Spanish	13	9	11	9
Other Caucasian	154	231	269	257
Chinese	9	6	8	8
Japanese	5	4	8	11
Korean	6	4		2
Filipino	42	57	42	59
All other	13	25	18	7
Total	1000	1000	1000	1000

of Portuguese in about the following order: (1) Portuguese; (2) Spanish; (3) Other Caucasian; (4) Caucasian-Hawaiian; (5) Porto Rican; (6) Asiatic-Hawaiian; (7) Hawaiian; (8) Filipinos; (9) Chinese; (10) Korean; (11) Japanese.

For census and other statistical purposes the part-Portuguese children are not classified as Portuguese, but, in their social relations, many belong to the Portuguese group. In the four years, 1930–34, there were 760 weddings of Portuguese to Portuguese and 949 of Portuguese to non-Portuguese. Doubtless after another generation there will be in

Hawaii more part-Portuguese than pure Portuguese and it is probable that they will intermarry pretty freely with the pure Portuguese. It may be seen that the Portuguese as a statistical group will soon begin to decrease in number. Indeed, any statistical group that is so defined as to exclude hybrids is destined to extinction when the rate of out-marriage is high. But while the Portuguese as a statistical group will soon begin to dwindle, the social group will increase for a considerable time. The lines of social cleavage will, however, become less and less distinct. The census and other data may be used to measure the double process of social assimilation and biological amalgamation.

CHAPTER XI

CHINESE FAMILIALISM AND INTERRACIAL MARRIAGE

THE actual behavior of the members of an immigrant group is the result of at least two sets of factors. There is the body of custom and tradition that they bring from their native land and there is the practical situation in which they find themselves in the new environment. The Chinese mores are very unfavorable to marriage with non-Chinese. Their situation in Hawaii was, for the early immigrants, unusually favorable to such marriage. Their actual marriage practice, extending over a period of more than eighty years, has varied to correspond with their changing situation in Hawaii.

In the case of certain immigrant peoples who came from European countries to America two or more generations ago there has been a fairly definite pattern of marriage behavior. At first, influenced apparently by considerations related to language, religion and other things that belong to culture, the members of each group married almost exclusively among themselves. But as generation followed generation and as they came to use the English language and to act and think more like the other people of their respective communities, intermarriage with the others gradually increased. For example, in the writer's native state, Wisconsin, intermarriage between second and third generation Irish and Germans and between both and the people of the old American stock has occurred with gradually increasing frequency in the last fifty years.

In American colonial times the Germans,—"Pennsylvania

Dutch,"—the English, and the Irish of Pennsylvania maintained themselves as separate peoples, their traditions and their attitudes toward one another being highly adverse to intermarriage. But among their descendants, who, in the early part of the nineteenth century, migrated to southeastern Ohio there was considerable intermarriage. When the descendants of these Ohioans came to Wisconsin, mainly 1850–1870, there were some mixed German-Irish, English-German, English-Irish, and some of more complex mixture. Nevertheless, there were some of pure English, pure German or pure Irish ancestry. In Wisconsin the three sorts of names continue to the present time,—the German being Americanized as to spelling in many cases. Those of German ancestry do not speak with a German accent. And the names are popularly recognized merely as American names and do not serve for a classification of the people. The further amalgamation of these three peoples in Wisconsin seems to be taking place without any apparent influence from the side of the culture of their European ancestors. The experience of these peoples may be regarded as conforming to a general pattern, a pattern involving a minimum amount of intermarriage at first but a gradually and steadily increasing amount as the peoples became more alike culturally.

But the Chinese marriage behavior in Hawaii has not been according to this pattern. A large proportion of the few Chinese immigrants, who came before 1852, married Hawaiian women. Of those who came in 1852–1875, a smaller proportion were so married. Still smaller was the proportion of those who came in 1876–1898. Moreover, in the last ten years during which time nearly all of the Chinese grooms have been Hawaiian born and American educated there has been a lower proportion of out-marriage than there was during the first decade of the century when most of the grooms were foreign born. The Chinese men of Hawaii up to 1924 married within their own group more and more as the term of their residence lengthened and as they became more like Americans in culture. This is a statement relating to the past and is not to be taken as involving a forecast.

This failure to conform to the pattern is explicable in part by reference to the changing situation of people who are the inheritors of an ancient and very sacred tradition. But there is also the fact that their Hawaiian-born children, in acquiring the English language and other elements of American culture, have become familiar with those ideas about race that have developed among English-speaking peoples in the last century or two.

Among the religions that influence marriage choice and family life, ancestor worship stands pre-eminent. It matters not whether a Chinese man be a Confucianist, a Buddhist or a Taoist, an important part of his religion is ancestor worship. Since marriage is entered upon, not primarily in the interest of the groom and his bride, but in that of the family, it follows that the choice of husband or wife is determined, not by the young people, but by the heads of the families who are older and supposedly wiser. Since the avowed purpose of marriage is to provide for the continued worship of the family ancestors, no father would choose for his son a wife who did not share the tradition of ancestor worship or who, presumably, would fail in loyalty to his family. Moreover, the son's wife, according to Chinese custom, lives in the home of her husband's parents and serves the mother. Under the conditions of Hawaiian life a Chinese mother would not ordinarily find a non-Chinese woman acceptable as a daughter-in-law nor would the daughter-in-law find her position tolerable.

From a consideration of Chinese custom and sentiment it may be seen that there would have been, in the earlier period of Chinese residence in Hawaii, little or no out-marriage if there had been a normal Chinese community, that is, if the immigrant men had been accompanied by their families as were the Portuguese who came after 1878.

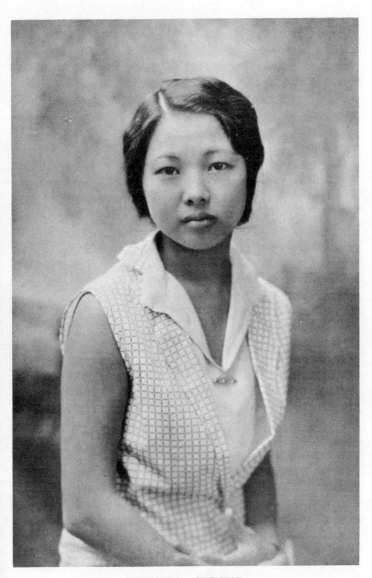

ANCESTRY, CHINESE

Had men and women been about equal in number it is certain that Chinese parents would have arranged for the marriage of their sons and daughters within the group and that there would have been a strong sentiment against any other sort of marriage.

In all, about forty thousand Chinese men came to Hawaii in the nineteenth century but many, after a stay of some years, returned to their native land so that there were only about twenty thousand resident in 1900. Commonly the men were young and unmarried and the majority of those who were married left their wives at the homes of their fathers. They intended to return to the old home after a few years, and leaving the wives behind was in line with custom. But there were many who did, in fact, prolong their residence in Hawaii. Some did not save enough to enable them to return with a sufficiently improved economic status. Others were making so much money they could not afford to leave. Even when their residence was prolonged it appears that most of the men were very slow to bring their wives or to secure wives from the old country, —very slow compared with the Japanese.

One of the causes of this slowness is found in the practice of foot-binding among the women of the districts from which most of the Chinese came. A woman with bound feet could not do much under Hawaiian conditions to help her husband earn a living for their family and so it was necessary for a man to save some money or to establish himself in some business that would yield a better than average income before he could afford to bring a wife. In the case of one dialect group, the Hak-ka, foot-binding was not practiced and they had wives in higher proportion than the others. But, for the main body of Chinese, this handicap resulted in a sort of economic selection. Before 1900, when the American Exclusion Act became effective in Hawaii, most of the small number of prosperous Chinese men secured wives from China while most of the others remained unmarried. After 1900, when the Chinese Exclusion Act became effective in Hawaii, only the few men who were in the "excepted classes"—professional men, the more important merchants and government officials—could bring Chinese wives.

There were few if any Chinese women in Hawaii until 1865 when 52 came on one ship. For a long time the number of women was not more than two or three per cent of the adult population and even in 1900 there were only about seven women to a hundred men or, if the Hak-ka-speaking be excepted, about five to a hundred. After that date the increase of Chinese women came about mainly through the maturing of Hawaiian-born girls. Since there were only a few Chinese women the increase was slow despite the large size of their families.

But the comparatively high rate of out-marriage among the early Chinese immigrants is not to be regarded wholly as a matter of opportunity,—the lack of opportunity to secure Chinese wives. The social obstacles to out-marriage such as would exist normally in a real Chinese community were not effective. There was no local Chinese community sentiment to control their conduct and so far as the old Chinese family traditions still had a hold on them they were able to work out a sort of compromise scheme that did not seem at first to involve a real break with their families or with the old traditions.

Probably there were about four hundred legal marriages of Chinese men to Hawaiian women in the period, 1840–1870. The information for the years, 1871–1899, is less satisfactory but it is probable that in this period there were four or five hundred marriages.[1] In addition to the legal marriages

[1] From 1838 to 1871 there was a law requiring a foreigner to be naturalized as a subject of the king of Hawaii and to establish his character and give evidence of an intention to reside permanently in the Islands before he could marry an Hawaiian woman. During this period there were about four hundred Chinese who were naturalized and in nearly all cases it was for the purpose of marriage. After 1871, when this law was repealed, naturalizations of Chinese were very rare till, in the three years, 1890–92, they became numerous, but for another purpose.

there may have been several hundred cases in which Chinese men lived with Hawaiian women as wives without a legal ceremony of marriage and in some cases the informal marriages were of a permanent character, the husbands discharging their obligations as husbands and fathers as well as did those who were legally married. Not improbably there were, in all, as many as twelve or fifteen hundred Chinese men who had, before 1900, entered into marital relations with native women. But most of such marriages had been terminated by death or separation.[2] It is probable that in 1871 about 200, or 11 per cent, of the Chinese men in Hawaii, were living with Hawaiian and part-Hawaiian wives. Similarly there were nearly 360 or only about 2 per cent of the resident Chinese men so married in 1900.

From 1900 to 1916 marriages between Chinese immigrants and Hawaiian or part-Hawaiian women were in absolute numbers more numerous than at any other time, so that the number so married at the end of the period was about 550. In this period there were a good many of the immigrants who were achieving economic competency and the Chinese Exclusion Law prevented their securing wives from their old homes. Since 1916 there has been a marked decrease in marriages to Hawaiian women and this has been made up only in part by an increase of marriage with part-Hawaiian women.

In the period before 1900 it appears that a considerable proportion of the Chinese men who married Hawaiian women did not remain with them permanently, but after a time they returned to China where their improved economic status enabled them to marry well and to raise families

---

[2] It is the belief of old residents that the Chinese men who married Hawaiian women were more dependable than were the white men and that more of the Chinese marriages lasted for life. But there were a good many separations. On the one hand, separations were very common among the Hawaiians and an Hawaiian woman would often take the initiative. On the other hand, there was the desire of the husband to go back to China or to bring a wife from China. There was no strong public opinion among either the Hawaiians or the Chinese to restrain them from acting according to their inclinations.

according to the custom of their people. Here is a suggestion to the effect that many such men, in marrying non-
Chinese women were not intending to abandon Chinese custom. The marriage was merely a temporary adjustment to
the situation in a foreign country. Eventually they would
conform to Chinese custom and raise Chinese sons to perpetuate the family name and the worship of the ancestors.
It was this way of regarding it that made it possible for
them to marry non-Chinese women so freely. Had it been
necessary for a man to feel that he was staking the whole
future of his family on such an alliance or that he was making a definite break with his family there would not have
been so many marriages to Hawaiian women.

But they were running a greater risk than they knew.
Social relations have a way of undergoing unobserved transformation. If a Chinese man started out thinking of his
Hawaiian wife as a temporary convenience it would often
happen that there would come to be real sentiment. The
day by day life would reveal each to the other as human
and there would would be a growth of insight and understanding. The co-operation of family life and especially
the joint responsibility for the care of children would finally
create bonds of sentiment too strong to be broken.

The way sentiment unexpectedly comes to dominate a
situation can be seen only as one considers actual cases.
According to Hawaiian custom it was very common for
mothers to give their babes to relatives or friends. About
fifteen years ago the Chinese husband of an Hawaiian
woman had consented to the giving away of an expected
child in which he did not appear to be much interested.
All the arrangements had been made. But when the child was
born, behold, it was a *boy* and the Chinese attitudes of the
father asserted themselves. Give away his *boy?* Of course
not. Such a thing was not to be thought of.

One of the consequences of this growth of sentiment was
the tendency on the part of the more resourceful Chinese

men to bring up their mixed-blood children as Chinese. Such children were taught to behave as Chinese children are expected to behave. They participated in the rites of ancestor worship with their fathers and the Chinese festivals were observed. When Chinese language schools were established these part-Chinese children were sent to them to be educated as Chinese. Some of the more prosperous men even sent their hybrid sons to China when they were about twelve years old to be educated and when they returned they brought Chinese wives. No matter what these men may have intended at first they were coming to realize the real character of their commitments. Sentiment of a more personal character had come in and the old traditions had to make terms with it. After all, one must depend on his sons to carry on, even if their mother is not Chinese.

Of course there was not always a development of such sentiment. The Chinese are not all alike. There are the men of the more stolid and unresponsive sort as well as those capable of quick response. Much, too, would depend on the character of the Hawaiian woman a man married. There is no definite information as to the proportion of these early marriages that were terminated by desertion and the proportion that lasted for life, but on the basis of indirect data I have estimated that the majority, possibly two-thirds, turned out to be of a permanent character.

Because of the fewness of Chinese women who immigrated before 1900 and because of the operation of the American Chinese exclusion law after that date, the Chinese men have for a generation been confined to four choices in relation to marriage: (1) A few of them, commonly the more prosperous, were able to secure the Hawaiian-born Chinese girls as they reached marriageable age and it appears that about as many as possible did this. (2) They could go back to China to marry. Before 1910 this was the most common procedure for those who married at all. Some remained in China permanently, but others returned to

Hawaii to earn the support of the wives they could not bring. (3) They could marry Hawaiian or part-Hawaiian women or, rarely, the women of other races. Several hundred did this. (4) They could remain unmarried. This is what a large majority did and so today Hawaii has several thousand old Chinese men who have no families. They are so old and they have been absent from their old home villages so long and with so little communication, being illiterate mainly, that their old country family relationship is little more than a memory. For Chinese this is a tragedy.

Table XXIII shows data relating to the highly abnormal sex ratio of the Chinese in Hawaii and to its trend toward the normal, 1900–1930; also the marital condition of both men and women and estimates as to the location of the

TABLE XXIII

Marital Status of the Chinese at Four Census Dates

Males 15 Years of Age and over	1900	1910	1920	1930
		(Census Data)		
Total number	20,297	14,434	12,414	11,453
Married	5,146	5,674	5,460	5,037
Single, Widowed, and Divorced	15,151	8,760	6,954	6,416
		(Estimated)		
China	3,362	3,539	2,334	1,270
Hawaii	1,784	2,135	3,126	3,767
Race of wives in Hawaii				
Chinese	1,409	1,550	2,376	2,990
Hawaiian	310	400	410	225
Part-Hawaiian	50	150	270	422
All other	15	35	70	130
Females 15 Years of Age and over		(Census Data)		
Total Number	1,803	2,104	3,718	5,677
Married	1,409	1,555	2,416	3,212
Single, Widowed, and Divorced	394	549	1,302	2,465
		(Estimated)		
Chinese	1,410	1,550	2,376	2,990
Hawaiian		1	7	25
Part-Hawaiian		1	20	95
All other		3	13	102

wives of the men and as to the race of both wives and
husbands.

As long as the Chinese were widely scattered over the
Islands and as long as the number of Chinese women was
almost negligibly small it was not possible for an effective
social control to develop. But before 1900 there was the
beginning of a movement to Honolulu which has continued
down to the present so that in 1930, 71 per cent of all the
Chinese lived in Honolulu, and, of the females over 15 years
of age, 78 per cent. Gradually there has come to be a real
Chinese community, a community of families. Among these
families are a good many that are wealthy or at least moderately prosperous. There are hundreds of Chinese societies.
Some of them are organized for business purposes, some for
social and others for the purpose of charitable assistance
to the old immigrant men who have no families of their own.
Still others are for local civic purposes. As the Chinese of
Hawaii have come to know more about China,—the greatness of its area and population and the antiquity of its civilization,—they have developed a new appreciation of its
traditions and a new sense of their own dignity as representatives of a great people. Naturally there are organizations
for the perpetuation of Chinese culture in Hawaii and others
that make contributions of money for the support of educational and political activities in China. All of these organizations are definitely Chinese in the sense that none but
Chinese are members. Not the least important thing about
them is their ability to confer status on their members.

One of the consequences of the increasing respect of the
Chinese for things Chinese is a rising status in the community
generally. As they tend to be more fully satisfied with the
status they can confer upon each other they win higher
respect from the other peoples. Commonly in the case of
the new immigrants, the influential white people tend to
select out of the immigrant group the men whom they treat
as leaders. Possibly the immigrants will for a time accept

such men as leaders or spokesmen. But they never get out of such leadership a sense of their own dignity. It represents a form of submission. But when such a group reaches a point where it can select its own leaders and have them accepted by the community at large there is the beginning of an era of improving status.

All this means that after a period of social disorganization in a foreign land the Chinese are developing a new organization and that the conduct of the people is coming to be controlled more by group sentiment. If one would stand well in Chinese society he must conform his conduct to its standards. This new control is not a mere reinstating of old country standards. Pretty largely it is a control in the interest of successful adjustment in Hawaii and in the case of the younger people the standards tend to be American. Nevertheless, there is something that comes from the old Chinese culture and it is significant.

This development of Chinese community life is confined almost entirely to Honolulu, their numbers being too small in most other places. To the extent that social control has been reinstated in Honolulu on the basis of the Chinese mores, the parents have been able to select mates for their sons and daughters. Such selection always counts on the side of marriage within the group.

In the competition of the Chinese men for brides of their own race it often happens that the advantage lies with the older man who has accumulated property as against the Hawaiian born young man who has not demonstrated his ability. The parents tend to prefer a man of means as son-in-law. One young man, referring to this, said, "A Chinese young man cannot find a Chinese bride until he has made himself." One result of this is the deferring of marriage by Chinese young men and another is the out-marriage of a considerable number of young men who are unable to secure brides of their own race.

If one seeks a statistical basis for an opinion as to the

attitude of the Chinese toward out-marriage, it is not sufficient to consider merely the relative number of men who have married non-Chinese. Even more significant are the number who did not marry at all because Chinese women were not available and the number who are postponing marriage and struggling for an improved economic status so that they may secure Chinese brides. While it is true that some of the more emancipated Chinese young men have married non-Chinese or part-Chinese women, primarily because of personal attraction, it remains true that the shortage of Chinese women has been the more important factor. Parents find it hard to continue to insist on their son's marrying a Chinese girl if they cannot find him the girl. The parents of the higher economic and social status are commonly able to do this, and hence among the prosperous there is less out-marriage. Among those Chinese who have achieved a good status in this developing Chinese community there is a definite attitude adverse to out-marriage. When a son or a daughter in such a family is married to a non-Chinese there is the most severe parental disapproval. A son may be disinherited and a daughter may be denied the privilege of social relations with her brothers and sisters. In some cases the family feels so deeply humiliated by the out-marriage of one of its members that it withdraws from society.

Reference has been made to the fact that in the country districts the Chinese are too few to maintain organization. The few Chinese boys and girls attend schools in which their association is mainly with non-Chinese children and the young people, if they are not to exclude themselves almost wholly from social life, must find their society in racially mixed groups. While only a minority of the Chinese who marry are in the rural districts, a larger proportion of those who do marry are married to non-Chinese. Perhaps this is the principal reason for the steady movement of youth to the city. An old Chinese man cannot afford to give up his business in a rural community but he sends his children to the city so that, coming under the influence of a Chinese community, they will marry Chinese.

For the year, 1926–27, Honolulu was given as the residence of 82 per cent of all Chinese grooms and of 83 per cent of all Chinese brides despite the fact that it had only about 67 per cent of the Chinese population at that time. During the same year, only 20 per cent of the Chinese grooms in Honolulu were married to non-Chinese while in the rest of the Territory 44 per cent were so married. The corresponding percentages of out-marriage for Chinese women were, for the city, 9 per cent and, in all other districts, 28 per cent.

Of the Chinese men who married out of their own racial group, the great majority have married Hawaiian or part-Hawaiian women,—Hawaiian women, mainly, up to about 1916 and, thereafter, mainly, part-Hawaiian. Among part-Hawaiians the preference,—both sides considered,—has favored marriage with Chinese-Hawaiian women; but in certain years there have been more Caucasian-Hawaiian than Asiatic-Hawaiian brides.

There have been only a few marriages between Chinese men and white women and these mainly with Portuguese. Since 1912, the trend toward marriage with Japanese women is such as to suggest that it may become important when the influence of their respective family systems has decreased considerably. But even now Chinese parents seem to be not as strongly opposed to their son's marriage to a Japanese girl as to marriage with a girl of some other racial group.

Not much need be said as to the marriage of Chinese women. Before 1920 there were so few Chinese women in proportion to the number of men that there was very little, if any, out-marriage among them. Since that date there has been a moderate trend in the direction of increased out-marriage and this is more true in the country districts than in the city. In some cases a girl may live in a community in which there is no marriageable Chinese man. In other cases the family does not in fact belong to the Chinese community even if it is in the city. Under some circumstances a girl of pure Chinese blood may become, in her attitudes and mannerisms, so "American" that she does not like Chinese society, and that she would be a misfit in a typical Chinese home. And then there are the personal preferences of a romantic sort that are pretty sure to affect conduct where racial lines are no more strictly drawn than they are in Hawaii.

The trend of marriage practice among the Chinese men and women since 1912 may be seen from Table XXIV.

TABLE XXIV

Marriage of Chinese Men and Women

Brides of Chinese Men	Number to 1000			
	1912–16	1920–24	1924–28	1930–34
Hawaiian	240	79	69	34
Caucasian-Hawaiian	35	49	63	67
Asiatic-Hawaiian	96	58	54	101
Portuguese and Spanish	25	17	18	13
Other Caucasian		5	2	6
Chinese	583	765	763	728
Japanese	4	11	24	34
Korean		2	2	6
All other	17	14	5	11
Total	1000	1000	1000	1000
Grooms of Chinese Women				
Hawaiian	10	19	10	22
Caucasian-Hawaiian		16	33	34
Asiatic-Hawaiian	20	36	35	48
Portuguese and Spanish		10	7	13
Other Caucasian	20	27	34	48
Chinese	944	878	833	791
Japanese	3	4	25	31
Korean	3		3	5
All other		10	20	8
Total	1000	1000	1000	1000

Among Americans who have given a little attention to Hawaiian statistics there is a belief that the attitude of the

Chinese in Hawaii has been uncommonly favorable to marriage with Hawaiian women. They are contrasted with the Japanese who are supposed to have a very different disposition. To make the contrast more striking the Chinese are sometimes represented as uncommonly free from the influence of sentiment adverse to interracial marriage and amalgamation. This tends to become a myth. Possibly the myth had its origin in the undoubted fact that a relatively large number of the few Chinese immigrants of the earliest period did marry Hawaiian women. But more recently it has received support from misunderstood official statistics relating to the Asiatic-Hawaiian population. The 12,592 Asiatic-Hawaiians enumerated in 1930 are supposed to be, for the most part, Chinese-Hawaiians and the birth of about a thousand Asiatic-Hawaiian children a year seems to point to the existence of several thousand Chinese who are married to Hawaiians. But in recent years, fewer than 12 percent of such children have had Chinese fathers and only 5 per cent Chinese mothers. Much more numerous are those who have Chinese grandfathers or great-grandfathers. Table XXV shows the racial paternity and maternity of the Asiatic-Hawaiian children born in the two years, 1931–33. The birth of 247 Asiatic-Hawaiian children of Chinese paternity in two years indicates that there are about 650 Chinese men with Hawaiian or part-Hawaiian wives.

If one is interested in the probable future trend of marriage practice among the Chinese he must exercise considerable care in the use of past experience. The early social situation of the Chinese in Hawaii was highly abnormal due to lack of women. The changes in their marriage behavior have resulted mainly from the tendency of the group to become normal in its age and sex ratios. Within ten or fifteen years the age and sex ratios will become nearly normal if the situation is not modified further by migration. Further progress toward American modes of thought and conduct will take place. With the passing of the first generation a

TABLE XXV

Paternity and Maternity of the Asiatic-Hawaiian Children Born in the Two Years, 1931–1933

RACE OF FATHERS	Hawaiian	Caucasian-Hawaiian	Asiatic-Hawaiian	Chinese	Japanese	Filipino	All Others	Total
							RACE OF MOTHERS	
Hawaiian			243	25	16	1	2	287
Caucasian-Hawaiian			204	25	24	4	2	259
Asiatic-Hawaiian	175	217	212	54	20		62	740
Chinese	59	61	127					247
Japanese	49	46	58					153
Filipino	200	58	76					334
All other	15	9	31					55
Total	498	391	951	104	60	5	66	2075

considerable weakening of Chinese family tradition may be expected. The younger people are being individualized, their improved economic position being favorable to this. Through literature, through the movies and through social contact with white people they are becoming familiar with a different conception of family life. Probably there is nothing that works more to the undermining of the old family system than the growing interest among the young people in a romantic conception of marriage. It is romance against tradition. In the not distant future it will be the custom for young people to make their own marriage arrangements. Some do this now and in other cases a son may really make his own choice while the parents go through the usual formalities of betrothal,—a sort of compromise arrangement. Future trends in Chinese marriage behavior will not be determined mainly by the factors that have been most important in the past, that is, by the approach of the Chinese to normal age and sex ratios, but by factors of a more complex character relating to cultural assimilation and to the attitudes as they shall develop in Hawaii of the Chinese and others toward interracial marriage.

Looking forward one may expect either that most of the rural Chinese will come to Honolulu or to a few centers or that, through the improved means of travel and communication, they will in some other way come under the social influence of an organized Chinese society. This will count toward a diminished rate of out-marriage.

In so far as the social solidarity of the group is based on old Chinese traditions there will be a tendency toward disorganization when the influential foreign born shall have passed away. But their organization is not based solely, perhaps not very largely, on the old tradition. They are organized to facilitate a realization of their interests in Hawaii. The Chinese Chamber of Commerce, the Kau Tom post of the American Legion, the Chinese University Club, and the Chinese Civic Association have not been organized to maintain ancient tradition. When there was only one local post of the American Legion the Chinese who had seen service were eligible to membership, but only four or five joined. But when the Kau Tom post was organized especially for the Chinese there were sixty members.

When the native-born and educated Chinese men shall have become almost if not quite indistinguishable from white Americans in language and the rest of the things that belong to culture will they abandon such Chinese organizations and participate in the activities of similar organizations of an interracial character or will they perpetuate organizations of separate Chinese sort? Will there be perpetuated a Chinese society with its own standards, with its own need for solidarity and with its own loyalties or will the Chinese lose their identity as Chinese and become just an indistinguishable and unnoted part of the general population? That is, will they be completely assimilated and amalgamated or will they remain Chinese?

The answer to this question does not depend solely on the Chinese. What will be the attitude of the other peoples and particularly of the white people? This raises the whole question of the future of race relations in Hawaii and, since other groups are involved, the consideration of this question will be postponed to a special chapter. One thing, however, may be said in passing. The Chinese will not give up their separate organizations unless they are freely welcomed into the interracial organizations of greatest prestige and on a footing of absolute equality. Unless they may have both security and equality of status in the larger society they will maintain their own organizations.

Chapter XII

THE JAPANESE AN ORGANIZED GROUP

THE number of Japanese in Hawaii, including their Hawaiian-born descendants, is greater than that of any other of the peoples of Hawaii. In 1930 nearly 38 per cent of the population was of Japanese birth or ancestry. Their sex ratio was more nearly normal than average, there being 861 females to 1000 males, as compared with 549 females to 1000 males for the rest of the population. The Japanese had 44 per cent of the female population and in the year 1934–5, 37.5 per cent of the children born were of pure Japanese ancestry. While the number of births and their share of the total births is decreasing and while there is some loss of Japanese population by excess of departures over arrivals, there is every reason to believe that they will continue to be sufficiently numerous to have an important role in Hawaii for a long time. For this reason anything that pertains to their behavior is a matter of uncommon importance.

But the Japanese have not resided in Hawaii for so long a time as the British, the Americans, the Portuguese, or the Chinese and hence there have not been so many interesting and significant developments. In relation to the cycle of change which immigrant peoples undergo in the new environment they occupy a less advanced position. Such trends of behavior as may be observed have not continued for so long a time and hence their meaning is less certain.

The outstanding fact about the marriage of Japanese in Hawaii is that they have married within their own group in higher proportion than any other of the peoples of Hawaii.

ANCESTRY, JAPANESE

Popularly, this is taken as evidence of something exceptional in the attitude of Japanese and there is a measure of truth in this view. The Japanese ethical system, like the Chinese, is based on ancestor worship. Filial piety ranks high in the list of virtues. Marriage is undertaken in the interest of the family and so according to old custom the parents select wives for their sons and husbands for their daughters. When the selection is made in this way marriage with persons of another race or people never takes place.

While Japanese feudalism, as a military organization, was abolished two generations ago, the sentiment of the people in relation to distinctions of rank and class changes slowly and hence the importance of not marrying below the level of the family. The formal procedure of betrothal is designed to protect a family from any such humiliation. The go-betweens,—the intermediaries who serve the two families in arranging a betrothal,—are supposed to know enough of the families so that they will not undertake to arrange an inappropriate match. But this is not enough. Each family may submit a list of ancestors and relatives to the other and there may be an investigation relating to the general family status, the personal character of each person on the list being considered. If a Japanese son has an ancestor or an uncle, cousin or other relative who has suffered from any one of certain diseases or who has been convicted of an infamous crime, he suffers in his status and the chance for a good marriage is lessened. So important is the function of the go-between and so important the investigation, that if a marriage were consummated without this ceremony of betrothal it would not be respectable. In so far as Japanese attitudes have been adverse to out-marriage it appears to be mainly not a matter of race or nationality but of religion and family status.

If one were to go a step further in the comparison of Japanese and Chinese attitudes, it would be necessary to admit that, to the Japanese, the family system is not quite as sacred as it is to the Chinese. For two generations the people of Japan have been undergoing political, economic and educational developments of profound importance. Not only is there a new technology in industry, but there is the beginning of fundamental changes in the general direction of secularization. Having in mind the common people, one may say that the Japanese, if not emancipated from the old mores, are at least more disposed to approach certain problems in a reflective way than the Chinese are. It is easier for them to work out compromise arrangements which may involve some disloyalty to ancient tradition but which are accepted because they are advantageous. When young men in Hawaii, educated in American schools and indoctrinated with the ideas of chivalry and romance, want to choose their own brides, a problem is created for the parents. In the solution of this problem the Japanese parents show a less rigid devotion to the old mores than the Chinese do. They, more commonly, work out a compromise according to which the son gets the girl of his own choice while the old ceremonies are used. More often the Chinese parents insist on exercising full authority and hence the sons get their way, if at all, by open defiance.

The circumstances of the coming of the Japanese to Hawaii were more favorable to the maintenance of social organization than were the circumstances of the Chinese, the Koreans or the Filipinos. There were very few who came before 1886 and when they began to come, they came in pretty large numbers. While there was some social disorganization among the Japanese, especially in the years before 1900, this did not become chronic. Most of the earlier laborers left the Islands after a few years and nearly 90 per cent of the present foreign-born Japanese population came after the date of annexation, 1898.

While the majority of the Japanese laborers came as single men—or, at least they were not accompanied by their wives

—there was never so great a lack of women as among the Chinese. About 20 per cent of the men had their wives even before the end of the nineteenth century and by 1920 the ratio of women to men was higher than for the general population. There were several things that favored this result. There was no exclusion law applicable to the Japanese before 1924. Ocean transportation had become safe, comfortable and low priced. According to an old custom it was possible for a Japanese man to be married without being personally present at the ceremony. The Japanese women did not practice foot-binding and they were accustomed to work in the fields. They were, therefore, able to help their husbands earn the family living in Hawaii and large numbers did work in the cane fields. Unlike the Chinese, the Japanese could afford to bring brides while they were poor.

Because of their superior numbers not only in Honolulu and Hilo, but in nearly all the rural districts as well, they are able to maintain a Japanese social life everywhere. Nowhere do they suffer from social disorganization merely from paucity of numbers or from the lack of family life, or of social institutions of their own. Japanese Buddhism seems to be more highly organized than any of the ancient religions of China. Buddhist temples are found where there are Japanese and they have contributed to the maintenance of old-country moral standards. So also have the language schools. More promptly than the Chinese have the Japanese created numerous organizations for business, charitable, social and political purposes. All this means that, to an unusual extent, the Japanese in Hawaii have maintained morale. At first this was based almost wholly on old-country tradition, but as time goes on their organization tends to respond to the need for adjustment to the conditions of life in Hawaii. By reason of their superior morale the Japanese have made an exceptionally good record in Hawaii. Relative to numbers there are fewer arrests and convictions, there are fewer juvenile delinquents, fewer who receive charitable aid, fewer insane, fewer who are mentally defective. It is the effectiveness of Japanese group control that causes their out-marriage rate to be so low.

Certain developments in Japanese marriage practice throw light on their attitudes and on the changes that are taking place. Most of the picture brides came between 1910 and 1920. At this time nearly all the men of marriageable age were foreign born. While the picture brides were married before sailing from Japan, a second ceremony was required in Hawaii, usually at the immigrant station. Most of the few Hawaiian-born Japanese girls who reached marriageable age during these years were married to foreign-born men.

But about 1920 there began to be a considerable number of Hawaiian-born young men whose parents desired wives for them. It was supposed that a real Japanese wife, one born and educated in Japan, would be better than the local Japanese girls whose more or less Americanized ways were not liked by the older people. Some Japanese girls were brought over to be the brides of the native-born sons, but with disappointing results. Commonly, a family that had resided in Hawaii for twenty or more years had undergone some changes. Its members had fallen away from the strict observance of the Japanese code of etiquette. The young people were more individualized and even the mother had achieved a wifely status that is not Japanese. When the son's wife, direct from the old home village, came into the partially Americanized family there was a clash of culture.

But this was not all. It might be very well for the mother of a son to say that she preferred a real Japanese wife for her son, that the local Japanese girls were inferior in training, that is, it was all right if she did not have a daughter also. It was a parental responsibility to find husbands for their daughters as well as wives for their sons and not for long could they afford to talk their daughters down. The very prompt abandonment of this sort of bride importation is a tribute to Japanese intelligence and to their comparative freedom from the control of fixed ideas.

The way immigrant parents are influenced by their children is very interesting. Rarely is it possible for immigrants to bring their children up so that they seem to be well trained from an old-country point of view. At a certain point in the life of a child he responds to influences that come from the larger community. Despite parental teaching the child comes to hold in light esteem some of the old country customs and he is attracted by things that the parents find hard to tolerate. Sometimes there is real moral deterioration, but even when there is not, when there is just the growth of a different set of values, there is for the parent, a sense of spiritual separation. This is as true of immigrants from Europe as it is of those who come from Japan.[1]

The adverse sentiment of the Japanese and also of the Chinese toward the out-marriage of their sons and daughters calls for some special consideration. It does not seem to be quite in the same class with the sentiment of white Americans toward marriage with non-whites. An American middle class family would be profoundly humiliated if a daughter were to marry a Negro or even a man of one-quarter Negro blood even if he were acknowledged to be a man of the best

[1] In a small Iowa city there was an immigrant of superior education and character—a leader of more than local prominence among his people. He was unfavorably impressed with much that he saw in American life and, for a long time, his influence was for the maintenance of old-country customs and standards. He saw to it that his children learned to read and write his native language and they were expected to use this language in the home. But the influence of the local public schools and the playgrounds was too strong. More and more English became the language of the children at home. Finally the father appears to have realized that his children were bound to be Americans and that it was necessary for him, too, to be an American if he would not be spiritually isolated from them. The parents yielded and as they all sat around the table they spoke the English language. Long years after, when all the children had gone, the father and mother continued to speak to each other in English. When the father realized that his children were to be Americans he began to hope that there were things of real value in American tradition. When he looked for such things he found them. In his later years, he changed his message to his people, encouraging them to be Americans, but to find the things of genuine worth in American life.

personal character and of demonstrated ability. That is, the American sentiment against such marriage seems to rest solely on the fact of Negro ancestry irrespective of personal traits. But among the Japanese and the Chinese in Hawaii the opposition to the out-marriage of their sons and daughters appears to rest wholly or mainly on considerations of a practical character. That is, the opposition is not based on color but on an unfavorable forecast as to the actual success of the marriage.

Always when two people marry there are some personal adjustments to be made and if they live more or less in contact with their respective families these adjustments extend to the broader family relationships. A wife should establish friendly relationships with her husband's people and he with hers. Where there are important cultural differences, differences in social rank or in religion, these adjustments are less easily made. There is more hazard, more probability that the marriage will turn out to be a failure. Now if the parental opposition is based on the fear that the out-marriage will not turn out well, that the wife will not be the kind of a wife their son needs, their objection is not so rigidly maintained in the face of experience. Assuming that they have a disapproved daughter-in-law, there is the actual experience to serve as a basis for the modification of opinion and attitude. Maybe she will be a good wife after all and, if so, the objection is gradually withdrawn. It is not as it would be if the objection were based merely on ancestry, an irremediable thing.

For example, there is the Chinese father who admits that the Japanese wife of one of his sons is better than the Chinese wives of the other sons. He was opposed to the marriage, but he was convinced by the performance of the Japanese daughter-in-law. She actually made his son a good wife according to the Chinese conception. She was industrious, she managed the money matters well so that the son might hope to improve his economic status, and she treated her parents-in-law with the respect due them. A certain Japanese father is really appreciative of his son's white wife. Whatever his misgivings may have been before the marriage, they seem to have been dispelled by the fine behavior of the wife. This white wife was a woman of education and refinement and she knew what was expected of a Japanese son. She wanted her husband to maintain the respect of his own people. When her husband's mother died, she and her husband invited his father into their home. The husband, who understood the American tradition of family life, realized how finely his wife was acting and, on his own initiative, built an extra room to the house so that the family privacy would be protected. A Japanese girl married a Chinese young man and, despite the misgivings of the young man's parents, was taken into their home according to custom. Here the young wife so discharged her duties as daughter-in-law that she won the affectionate regard of the mother, and after some years, when she lay dying it was the Japanese daughter-in-law whom she preferred to care for her and whose hand she held in love at the last.

One might distinguish between the attitude commonly manifested by Americans and that of the Chinese and Japanese by saying that in the one case the opposition to interracial marriage rests on a code of race relations that is ritualistic in character while in the other it tends to be determined by considerations relating to the probable success of the marriage as affected by differences in religion and other things that belong to culture. For a time the one type of attitude may be about as effective as the other in preventing out-marriage but if a period of sufficient duration to permit of fundamental culture change is considered, it will be found that the attitude supported by a ritualistic code is more permanent in character. Where there is no prohibitive code, the parents, while they will not arrange for the out-marriage of a son, may find it easier to be reconciled to a marriage made against their will. Where such reconciliation is pos-

sible there is a better chance that the marriage will turn
out to be happy and successful.

The Japanese are numerous in most rural districts as well
as in the cities and they are well organized almost everywhere. Social control adverse to out-marriage is effective
almost everywhere, but the rate of out-marriage in very recent years appears to be a little higher for the rural districts.
For the two years, 1932–34, the rate for Honolulu was 4.1
per cent and for all other districts 5.9 per cent.

Until about 1916 the Japanese sex ratio was more highly
abnormal than the average for the general population, but
as a result of the continued immigration of women up to
1924 their sex ratio is now more nearly normal than average.
In their out-marriage practice they have followed the usual
rule of Hawaiian experience. When women were unusually
scarce, out-marriage was mainly by the men, there being,
1912–16, 31 cases of Japanese men marrying out to 12 cases
of women. But since 1920 the Japanese have had a higher
than average proportion of women, and a majority of those
who have married non-Japanese in the more recent years
are women. In the years, 1930–34, 161 Japanese women,
but only 144 men, married out of their own race.

In the preceding chapter attention was called to the fact
that Chinese marriage practice in Hawaii has not been according to the pattern set by American immigrants from
northwestern Europe. But the Japanese in Hawaii have
conformed to pattern up to the present time, in the sense
that there was very little out-marriage at first but an increasing amount when the Hawaiian-born reached marriageable age. The actual marriage practice of the Japanese
comes close to what the Chinese practice would have been
had it been as convenient for them to secure wives from
their native land.

The very low rate of out-marriage among the Japanese
affords no very satisfactory evidence as to the preferential
relations. A majority of the men who have married non-

ANCESTRY, JAPANESE

Japanese have taken Hawaiian or part-Hawaiian wives and after these follow the Chinese and Portuguese. But among the Japanese women the tendency is to marry Caucasians, Filipinos and Chinese, fewer marrying Hawaiians and part-Hawaiians. Probably the actual marriage practice is influenced more by opportunity as affected by numerical factors and territorial distribution than by racial preference. For example, in Honolulu where the whites and Chinese tend to be concentrated, nearly two-thirds of the out-marrying Japanese women, 1932–34, married whites and Chinese and only 13 per cent, Filipinos. But in the rest of the Territory, including the districts in which the Filipinos are concentrated, only 28 per cent married whites or Chinese and 39 per cent, Filipinos.

TABLE XXVI

Marriage of Japanese Men and Women

Brides of Japanese Men	Number to 1000			
	1912–16	1920–24	1924–28	1930–34
Hawaiian	3	7	8	6
Caucasian-Hawaiian	1	3	7	8
Asiatic-Hawaiian			8	11
Portuguese and Spanish	1	2	3	5
Other Caucasian		2	1	3
Chinese		1	5	9
Japanese	995	985	968	957
Korean				1
Filipino				
All other				
Total	1000	1000	1000	1000

Grooms of Japanese Women				
Hawaiian			2	3
Caucasian-Hawaiian	1	3	4	6
Asiatic-Hawaiian			2	4
Portuguese and Spanish		1	2	4
Other Caucasian		4	12	9
Chinese		2	5	7
Japanese	998	983	963	952
Korean	1	2	1	1
Filipino				
All other		5	9	14
Total	1000	1000	1000	1000

There is one aspect of the marriage practice that is not adequately presented by a mere reference to the race classifications. Within each racial group, commonly, there is some sort of distinction of status, of dialect or of religion and these distinctions are of importance as affecting marriage practice. Among the Japanese there are several thousand Okinawans who came from some little islands several hundred miles southwest of Japan proper. The Okinawans are said to differ a little in stature and in features from the other Japanese and, until recently, they did not use the Japanese language. While the Japanese government has adopted a policy of cultural assimilation the Okinawans are still a separate people. There is some evidence of a degree of social disorganization among those in Hawaii. They do not enjoy the full benefit of membership in Japanese organizations and their behavior tends to follow the pattern followed by other groups too small to maintain effective organization. Naturally there is little, if any, intermarriage between them and the other Japanese, and it is probable that they marry non-Japanese in higher proportion than do the ordinary Japanese of Japan proper.

There is, among the Japanese, a class of inferior privilege known as the eta. In Japan, before the abolition of the feudal order, the members of this class were restricted to certain occupational activities and no ordinary Japanese would marry a member of this lower caste. While the eta status was legally abolished two generations ago, only a little progress has been made toward their social acceptance.

In Hawaii the marriage of eta to ordinary Japanese is rare. The eta are not organized as a social group and it is said that they marry non-Japanese in much higher proportion than others do. Possibly out-marriage is regarded as advantageous,—a means of escape from a caste of inferior status. In view of the probable influence of these two special classes on the out-marriage rates of the Japanese in general, it is easy to see that the rates for the ordinary

Japanese are extremely low,—lower even than the figures of Table XXVI indicate.

Any forecast as to the future marriage practice of the Japanese in Hawaii must take into consideration their further acculturation to the American pattern and the rising influence of the younger people, born and educated in Hawaii. As long as the Japanese family system is influential, so long will its mores affect marriage practice. What is the outlook for the acceptance of the American family system by the descendants of the Japanese immigrants?

While the Japanese are uncommonly successful in the maintenance of old-country traditions they are not wholly successful. Even the immigrants slip a little and the young people of Hawaiian birth who are educated in American schools and who enjoy wider social contacts than their parents, sometimes find it difficult to conform to the standards that their parents try to maintain. Perhaps one might say that the conduct of the Japanese is pretty well up to the old-country standard so far as the more important matters are concerned and that the obvious shortcomings relate to the little things. Even among the immigrants the forms of Japanese courtesy are rather loosely observed. The status of women is being changed. In Japan the husband is in full control of the family money, but when a Japanese woman in Hawaii earns money herself she may insist on her right to do what she pleases with it. The young people are educated in the forms of courtesy in the Japanese language schools, but their sentiment commonly favors the freer American ways. Young married couples prefer to set up a home of their own instead of living with the husband's parents and they do so if they can afford the extra expense.

In the education of the Japanese boys and girls in Hawaii there is a competition between two ethical systems which differ considerably in emphasis. Through the home and the language schools comes the old Japanese tradition. Through the public school and the literature to which the public school introduces the children and through their broader social contacts comes the European-American tradition. There is something very fine in the loyalties taught by the Japanese but the young people are more attracted by the freedom, the opportunity and the romance that go with the American way of life. So far as the interest of the young people is concerned, democracy and chivalry win as against ancestor worship and *Bushido*. When young people build air-castles they tend to be of the Occidental sort.

This changing cultural situation cannot fail to involve conflict, more or less. The older people tend to be apprehensive and the younger, restive. But commonly the conflict is not very severe. Both sides seem to be willing to compromise. The parents, despite their mistrust of American ways, recognize that their children are to be Americans and that they must adjust themselves to the practical situation. In a good many cases they begin by enforcing Japanese custom and end by yielding to their children. For example, in a certain family, the parents selected the husband of the oldest daughter; the second daughter rebelled, and the third was free to accept the man she might like. In one case a father advised his son to become a Christian, saying in effect, "I am a Japanese and I will remain a Buddhist. But you are an American and the Christian religion is the religion of America. You should be a Christian."

The outlook is that the parental influence in the choice of brides and grooms will not survive the passing of the immigrant generation. Gradually the Japanese family system will be forgotten and this will be favorable to a rising rate of out-marriage.

But there is still another factor soon to count on the side of a higher out-marriage rate. At present the number of part-Japanese of marriageable age is negligibly small, but a small liaison group will soon come into existence. In the two years, 1931–33, 428 part-Japanese children were born. Within ten or fifteen years the number of adult part-Japanese will be large enough to influence the out-marriage rate of the pure Japanese.

If one considers only the obstacles to out-marriage that have been effective in the past, it is clear that a gradually rising rate of marriage with non-Japanese may be expected. If the event shall not warrant this forecast it will be because of some new sort of obstacle, not because of the permanence of the old. The consideration of this is postponed to Chapter XV.

CHAPTER XIII

THE FILIPINOS—CHRISTIAN ORIENTALS

AFTER the emigration of Japanese laborers to Hawaii was prohibited by the Japanese government in 1907, the planters depended on the Philippines as the chief source of labor supply. At first the employment of Filipinos was of a small and tentative character, but after they had demonstrated their value for plantation service their numbers increased steadily so that by 1930 they surpassed all other racial groups in the number of adult males in the general population. But there were only a few women and children. In 1930 there was a population of 63,052 Filipinos. Of this number, 10,380, mainly children under 15 years of age, were Hawaiian born and 52,672 were immigrants. Of the latter number 47,336 or nearly 90 per cent were males.[1] The actual number who immigrated 1907–1930 was much larger than is indicated by the above figures, since about forty-two thousand immigrants had left the Territory before 1930, going to California or returning to the Philippines.

On account of the departure of so many and their replacement by new immigrants there are comparatively few Filipinos who were (1930) more than middle-aged, the great majority being between eighteen and thirty years of age. Nor do many become old residents. The majority of

[1] The lack of a sufficient number of women is a source of demoralization for both men and women. The high rate of convictions for assault and for murder among the Filipinos is due mainly to the too active competition for the few available women. Naturally, sex crimes are numerous. Divorce has been extremely common and the divorced women ordinarily remarry promptly. In some years the majority of the Filipino brides have been divorced women.

174

the men resident in 1930 had been in the Islands less than six years.

About forty per cent of the adult Filipino men were reported as married but nearly three-fourths of the married had left their wives in the Philippines. A man comes to Hawaii alone and sends his savings back to his wife who pays for a small piece of land and when this is accomplished he goes home to join his family. In 1920 about 17 per cent of the men had wives of their own race in Hawaii and the percentage increased during the next four years. But since 1924 the number of women has decreased while men continued to come in uncommonly large numbers for the rest of the decade. In 1930 only about 11 per cent of the men had Filipino wives in Hawaii.

Most of the Filipino men came to Hawaii with a definite intention of returning when they have saved a sufficient amount of money. Commonly they are able to make the savings according to plan, for the plantations give them steady employment throughout the year and their necessary expenditures are small. The Ilocanos, who make up the main body of the present population, are thrifty. The planters have made it easy for the men to return to the Philippines by paying their passage if they wish to go after completing a three-year contract. This means that the behavior of the men has been controlled largely through old country interests and social relations. Such control is, of course, adverse to out-marriage. It would not do to take a non-Filipino wife back to the old home village.

As newly arrived immigrants, the Filipinos suffer from a certain inferiority of social status. Each of the immigrant labor groups has had a similar experience in its turn. Parents who belong to the earlier immigrant groups, such as the Chinese and Japanese, look with marked disfavor on the marriage of their daughters to Filipino men. Some of the earlier Filipinos were not steady workers and they tended to be spendthrifts. While most of the more recent immigrants are industrious and thrifty, they suffer from the reputation made by the former residents.

On the other side, it must be said that Filipino men are rather popular with women. Maybe a Filipino man is not as good a prospect, so far as providing for his family is concerned, as is the typical Chinese man, but his courtship has more of the spirit of chivalry and romance in it. Spain did carry something to the Philippines. Perhaps it was the Catholic Church that served as a carrier of chivalry. The apparent freedom of the Filipino from typical Asiatic forms of social control may count toward a higher crime rate, but it makes him seem more human and likable to the non-Asiatic peoples of Hawaii.

In the case of an immigrant group, most of the members of which have resided in the Territory for so short a time, it is hardly necessary to say that they have not made much progress toward the creation of a social organization of their own. The intention of most to return to their native land at an early date deprives them of the motive to organization. The fewness of women is an adverse factor. Commonly when immigrant groups begin to develop a social life of their own, it takes largely the form of a religious organization. The Filipinos are, for the most part, Catholics in religion but they are not very much interested in their church relationship. They are not the prominent members of the churches to which they belong and the church does not serve as an organizing center for a developing segregated social life.

More than 92 per cent of the resident Filipinos were outside of the city of Honolulu, chiefly on the plantations, in 1930. Those on the plantations have their activities organized in a way, but the organization is not of their own making. In Honolulu the numbers are relatively small and their residence has been too brief to permit of the development of a social life of their own. There is an observable tendency on the part of those of more extended residence

A FILIPINO

to come to Honolulu, and a larger proportion of the men in Honolulu have their families with them. In 1930, only 5.7 per cent of the Filipino men of the Territory lived in Honolulu but, of the Filipino women, 12.2 per cent were in the city and, of children, 10–14 years of age, 18.3 per cent. This growth of a family population of some degree of stability in the city tends to favor the development of organization. In recent years there has been a considerable number of organizations of a charitable, religious, recreational or social character. While such organizations may be accepted as evidence of the development of group morale, allowance must be made for the unstable character of most organizations. As the number of families increases and as some of the men achieve a better economic status, there will be a development of leadership and the organizations will acquire greater prestige. When this happens, the conduct of the Honolulu Filipinos will be controlled more by group sentiment and their status as a racial group will rise.

No new racial group in Honolulu can create for its members a satisfactory social life or give them a satisfactory status in the larger community unless its members are bound together by common interest and sentiment. The members must be loyal to the group, must conform their conduct to group standards and the standards must be of such a character as to advance their more important interests. The attitude of the rest of the community toward any unstabilized group of immigrants such as the Filipinos is such that they are not able to win recognition in any other way. True it is that when they begin to develop group solidarity they will be charged with clannishness and there will be efforts to convince them that the narrow group loyalty is foolish and harmful to their interests. The mistakes of inexperienced leaders will be seized upon to discredit them and their cause. This will mean that the conflict inherent in the situation is coming out into the open. If mistakes are made they are corrected by the trial and error method. Loyalty is promoted by conflict. Of course there is a development of ill will and fear, but what is, in the long run, more important is the creation of a more genuine respect. Respect is akin to fear. On the basis of the new respect achieved through conflict, an accommodation becomes possible, an accommodation in which the group of inferior privilege achieves a better status.

The main point, from the standpoint of the present interest, is that when the Filipinos in Hawaii shall have made considerable progress in the development of social organization,—group solidarity,—there will be sentiment adverse to marriage with non-Filipinos. If a man would stand well with his group he should avoid marriage outside. Such marriage will be felt to be a sort of disloyalty and its practice will tend to be confined to those who have not won a good status within their own racial group. But this lies in the future. For the time being, a Filipino is quite free to marry out so far as his own people are concerned. Such obstacles as there are come from the side of the Hawaiian or the Portuguese parents whose daughters the Filipinos marry. This is true among the Honolulu Filipinos who have been away from their native land a long time. Such adverse attitude toward out-marriage as there is among Filipinos in the rural districts represents merely a continuing influence of their old home community from which they came recently and to which they expect to return soon.

The Filipino men who work on the plantations have a more dependable income than most of those who live in Honolulu. Doubtless this favors a higher rate of out-marriage in the rural districts, but the actual rates are higher in Honolulu. In the two years, 1932–34, 39.5 per cent of the Filipino groups of Honolulu married non-Filipino women, while only 36.1 per cent of those in the rest of the Territory so married. Apparently the intention of most of the men to return to the Philippines has been the more important factor.

Table XXVII shows the trend of in-marriage and out-marriage among Filipino men and women for the period, 1912–1934.

TABLE XXVII

Marriages of Filipinos

Brides of Filipino Men	Number to 1000			
	1912–16	1920–24	1924–28	1930–34
Hawaiian	66	78	85	73
Caucasian-Hawaiian	1	16	25	30
Asiatic-Hawaiian	3	10	20	54
Portuguese and Spanish	101	65	48	64
Porto Rican	35	52	51	38
Other Caucasian	8	3	2	17
Chinese		4	4	3
Japanese		12	21	33
Korean				5
Filipino	782	758	744	673
All other	4	2		10
Total	1000	1000	1000	1000

Grooms of Filipino Women				
Hawaiian and part-Hawaiian	2	1	4	1
Portuguese, Spanish and "other Caucasian"	15	4	6	8
Chinese, Japanese and Korean	7	3	3	1
Filipino	973	990	987	988
Porto Rican and all other	3	2		2
Total	1000	1000	1000	1000

The marked difference between the out-marriage rate of the men and that of the women is the consequence of the abnormal sex ratio. For the four years, 1930–34, 32.7 per cent of the Filipino grooms were married out of their own race, while among the brides only 1.2 per cent were so married. Now that Filipino immigration seems to be about at an end, it is probable that the sex ratio of the marriageable will gradually approach the normal and that the out-marriage rate among the men will fall while that of the women will rise. In this case the Filipinos will be following the Chinese pattern.

If preference in marriage in Hawaii were based largely on racial similarity, as that is defined by physical anthropologists, the out-marriage of Filipino men would be mainly with Japanese women. In stature, color, hair texture and other physical race traits the Japanese resemble the Filipinos much more than Europeans do. Indeed there are Japanese anthropologists who hold that the dominant people of old Japan came from the south and that it was of a racial character much like that of the Filipinos. Moreover, in Hawaii the Filipino young men live mainly in the rural districts where nearly half of the marriageable young women are Japanese.[2]

But in practice the Filipino men who have married out of their own race have not married many Japanese or other Orientals. Largely they have married Portuguese, Porto Rican and Spanish and also Hawaiian and part-Hawaiian. Most of the Portuguese, Porto Rican and Spanish and possibly a fourth of the Hawaiians are of the same religious faith as the Filipinos. Even though the Filipinos, for the most part, seem to be not very faithful to their obligations as members of a Christian church, their attitude and also the attitude of the other Christian peoples seem to be modified by the fact that they are Christians. The Filipino men intermarry very little with the women who most resemble them in physical race traits, but they intermarry pretty freely with those who profess the same Christian faith.

[2] Kauai County has no city and most of its population is found on or near plantations. The following table shows the numbers of males and females 15–29 years of age in 1930.

	Male	Female
Population 15–29 years of age	9,129	2,871
Filipino	6,521	425
Japanese	1,500	1,363
Portuguese, Porto Rican and Spanish	518	474
Hawaiian and part-Hawaiian	328	380
All other	262	229

CHAPTER XIV

SOME SMALL RACIAL GROUPS

THERE are in Hawaii a few small immigrant groups, such as the Porto Rican, the Spanish, the Korean and the Russian, which commonly receive little attention because of their smallness. Behavior that would be considered to be highly significant in the case of a large group such as the Japanese tends to pass unnoticed if it relates to the Koreans. Nevertheless, these small groups have a role of some importance in Hawaiian life. One of their roles is to modify the conditions of interracial contact in such a way as to reduce tension and increase good will. In no small degree is Hawaii's reputation for interracial good will dependent on the multiplicity of its peoples and to the fact that no one of them is in a position of dominance.

Sometimes it is said that the white people or some group of white people are dominant in Hawaii. But this is not true excepting in the sense that the Congress of the United States might abandon its traditional policy in relation to territories, depriving the people of Hawaii of the rights they have enjoyed hitherto or, in the sense that the military authority might assume control in case of war. While most of the positions of the highest power and dignity in the political, professional and business fields are held by white men, the tendency is to justify this on grounds of merit, not on grounds of race. The white men, or some of them at least, have a tradition of education and of successful business and professional experience and they own more than an equal share of the property. Naturally there is prestige. But the other racial groups are utilizing educational opportunity. Men of other groups are acquiring property, executive experience, and prestige.

While prestige and property are important, so also is mass or number. This is especially true where there is popular education and, among citizens, political equality. In the general task of social co-ordination in Hawaii white men may for a long time play an important part if they aim not at domination but at influence in a co-operative arrangement.

The smaller minority groups will never be under suspicion of seeking dominance. Their interest is inevitably on the side of a co-operative system in which a man may hope to rise to a position of power and dignity on the basis of personal merit. When a young university graduate set up as a printer the fact of his being a Korean was no help. He had to find his business in the general business community. If he got it at all, it was because he was a good printer not because he was a good Korean. When a Negro was elected to the legislature in a district in which there were probably not more than a score of Negro voters it was necessary for him to advocate things that were of general interest to the peoples of his district, not racial issues. Should one of the minorities of superior size or influence undertake to acquire a position of dominance the opposition of all of the small minority groups would be certain, and this is one of the reasons for the belief that there will be, on the basis of local leadership, no such undertaking. If there were just two or three peoples in Hawaii, it is probable that one would be fully dominant or that it would aspire to dominance. Or at least there would be suspicion of such intention. But in Hawaii where there are eleven statistically recognized racial and mixed racial groups beside a few too small to win recognition and where all are, in fact, minority peoples, it is clear that no one of them can aspire to dominance. Where there is no majority people the minority peoples have a different status. If one racial group were dominant but with numbers too small to assure future dominance merely as a consequence of superior mass, there would be an effort on the part of such dominant group to stabilize its position through a system of discriminatory policies designed to limit opportunity for the races of inferior status. There would be, almost necessarily, a denial of political, educational and occupational equality and, in order to make such discriminations effective, in the long run, it would be necessary to prohibit interracial marriage.

South Africa furnishes an interesting example. The Cape Colored are mixed bloods with a comparatively high proportion of European ancestry. Being more or less isolated from the African natives and in contact with a European population, the tendency of mixture has been toward the light side. While intermarriage of Europeans and Negroes is prohibited by law, there is no legal bar to marriage between the Cape Colored and Europeans and there are such marriages. But separate schools are maintained for the Cape Colored. There is a degree of occupational discrimination and, commonly, the Europeans of superior status have no intimate social contacts with them. But some of the Cape Colored look so much like Europeans that they send their children to the schools designed for Europeans only and they are not detected. Doubtless, such children, educated as Europeans and mainly of European ancestry will, in their social relations, be Europeans for life and through marriage will carry over into the European population a little of the blood of the darker race. In this way the color norm for Europeans will be changed a little and without observation. That is, a little modification of color and features due to African blood will seem to be normal for Europeans and hence the passing over of Cape Colored of darker hue will be facilitated. Given sufficient time and continued intermarriage between the Cape Colored and the Europeans, there will be no pure Europeans and none who will be called Cape Colored. They will be one people; but long before the process shall have been completed it will be found impracticable to administer any of the discriminatory laws effectively. Where interracial marriage is permitted by law and public opinion it will be practiced and where it is practiced all other sorts of relationship,—political, economic, educational,—tend to be on the basis of equality.

The need for some sort of organization under which the various minorities in Hawaii may co-operate is too obvious to require argument. Men of affairs, if they have lived in Hawaii for several years, always recognize this. The more important merchants seek the trade of all the peoples. Banks are glad to accept deposits from all. Employers may show some racial preference in relation to the more desirable positions, but this is not carried so far as to prevent competent men of all races from being advanced to positions of superior responsibility and compensation. The publishers of newspapers seek subscribers where they may be found and, hence, in their news and editorial columns they aim not to offend any considerable group of subscribers. Politicians need the votes of men of all the minorities and this necessitates the cultivation of an attitude of respect and good will.

To some people this tendency on the part of the people of each race to cultivate friendly relations with the people of all the other races seems to involve a certain insincerity. To treat people with respect because it is advantageous so to do does not seem to be quite in a class with the spontaneous expression of a genuine sentiment. Perhaps these people who outwardly show respect will give expression to contrary sentiments when they are in the small circle of intimate friends where they can speak freely without jeopardizing their business or political interests. Or perhaps there will be an inconsistency between a man's ordinary behavior, which symbolizes respect, and his behavior in time of crisis when considerations of advantage are forgotten. The reaction under the influence of strong emotion seems to be so much more genuine than the considered behavior dominated by one's conception of interest or advantage.

But on the other hand it is just this tendency of behavior commonly to be dominated by considerations of advantage that is the best guarantee as to the character of conduct in the long run. We may suppress our genuine sentiment for reasons of expediency but it is not pleasant so to do. We do not like to think of ourselves as too weak or too cowardly openly to avow our real attitudes. Hence we tend to bring our attitudes into harmony with the behavior that we believe to be advantageous. Finally we come really to have the sentiment of respect that our conduct symbolizes. Perhaps most people are just at some stage of progress in this general direction and hence there are inconsistencies in behavior depending largely on the situation and the way personal interests and feeling are enlisted. At one time a man may be a sincere and strong supporter of the doctrines and the code of race equality and at another time, with equal sincerity, he may resent the tendency of the men of some racial group to do things that imply equality.

In general, the difficulties that lie in the way of a small immigrant group when it begins to develop local organization are uncommonly great. In the beginning its members are sure to be so widely scattered over the Territory that they are too few in any one place to maintain organization. They are too few to support by their patronage those who might want to start in business, nor can young doctors and lawyers get a start through services to clients of their own race. Prestige and leadership within the group fail of development and the men of enterprise are under the necessity of establishing their status through their relations with the people of other races. If other things are equal, the old country mores of the smaller immigrant groups are quicker to lose their influence. The process of acculturation goes on more rapidly, and this may be associated with social disorganization and a higher rate of crime and juvenile delinquency.

If they are strongly disposed toward the creation of a social life for themselves they may, as rapidly as economic conditions permit, concentrate in some one place such as Honolulu. For example, the Spanish show a greater tendency to concentrate in Honolulu, length of residence considered, than do the more numerous Portuguese. Likewise, the Koreans are more highly concentrated than the Japanese. Doubtless it is the social rather than the economic situation that motivates this.

Unless for some special factor in the situation, the out-marriage rate for the smaller groups is especially high. This is particularly true if there is another and a larger group whose religion is such as to facilitate intermarriage. An abnormal sex ratio works to the same result. Cultural similarities may be important.

Excepting that the sex ratio is not far from normal, the conditions seem to be favorable to a maximum degree to the out-marriage of the Spanish. They are few, they are culturally and racially much like the Portuguese. While ancestor worship does not facilitate intermarriage between two peoples such as the Chinese and the Japanese, a common Christian faith seems to remove barriers that might otherwise exist between two peoples. All told, there are more marriages of Spanish to Portuguese than of Spanish to Spanish. The forecast is for an early disappearance of the Spanish by amalgamation, mainly with the Portuguese. In the four years, 1930–34, there were 5 Spanish men who married Spanish women, 10 persons in all who married within the group, but there were 13 Spanish men and 11 Spanish women who married Portuguese.

The position of the Porto Ricans is much like that of the Spanish. They are few. They are more or less of the Catholic tradition. They have very little in the way of an organized social life among themselves. There is considerable intermarriage between the Porto Ricans and the Portuguese, but still more with the Filipinos. There is some ground for the belief that there is a growing attitude among the Portuguese adverse to marriage with Porto Ricans, many of whom have African ancestry. In spite of the smallness of the Porto Rican group and in spite of such influence as may come from their being of the same faith as the Portuguese and the Spanish, their amalgamation seems to be destined to go on much more slowly than that of the Spanish.

Here is a suggestion of race prejudice as operating especially against intermarriage with persons of Negro ancestry. In this connection certain things are to be considered. (1) The Porto Ricans are not called Negroes or mulattoes. (2) When they came to Hawaii over thirty years ago they were a socially disorganized people and they were without the traditions of industry and thrift such as characterized the other immigrant peoples. They have, therefore, made uncommonly small progress toward a better economic status. Lacking any tradition of education, they have been indifferent to school opportunities and their school rating is low. They have, among the peoples, a low economic and social status and this is a factor in the adverse attitudes of the other peoples toward intermarriage with them. (3) The Portuguese in particular are coming into such relations with the *haole* population that they are gradually coming to share *haole* attitudes as they relate to race, especially to Negroes. The attitude of new immigrants from the mainland is much like that of mainland people, and that of the old residents while different, is not uninfluenced by mainland sentiment. It appears, therefore, that in so far as there is, among the Portuguese in Hawaii, an adverse attitude toward intermarriage with Porto Ricans on account of their having Negro blood, it is a consequence largely of mainland influence, not wholly a direct response to contact with the Porto Ricans.

The Koreans as a small group are exceptional. In some respects their behavior has been according to expectation. For example, they have made more rapid progress in the acquisition of the English language than have the more numerous Japanese. Because of their fewness it was necessary for them to make a greater use of English, but there is a developing myth that they are superior in native linguistic ability.

It is claimed that nearly all of the Koreans have become Christians. Their churches serve largely as organizing centers for a strictly Korean social life. Membership in the Korean Christian Church does not create bonds of fellowship with the Japanese Christians. In a very important sense the Korean Christian Church has become a means to the expression of national spirit. Just as the Catholic Church in Ireland served for the development of solidarity among the Irish and strengthened their protest against English domination, so in Hawaii the Christian Korean Churches count for the maintenance of the sentiment for Korean independence and against Japanese domination in Korea.

In so far as the Koreans are exceptional in the maintenance of social organization it seems to be the result of their intense national patriotism. As representatives of an oppressed people they have a cause,—a cause that commands their allegiance even more fully than would be the case if they were living in Korea. While there is much controversy relative to policies and leadership there is a common loyalty to their cause. It is this loyalty that gives unity to the group and, incidentally, it creates a sentiment adverse to marriage with non-Koreans. To marry out is to desert the cause. Perhaps one should add that among some of the Hawaiian born there is a tendency toward indifference to Korean nationalism. Since Korean organization is largely confined to Honolulu and its vicinity, the influence of sentiment adverse to out-marriage is relatively weak in the rural districts. In the two years, 1932–34, 36.8 per cent of the Korean brides and grooms outside of Honolulu married out of their own race, but in Honolulu the per cent so marrying was only 18.5.

ANCESTRY, KOREAN

There are only a few statistical data relative to the Russians, but these may be supplemented by case studies. The Russians are still fewer than the Spanish, but their religion does not facilitate intermarriage with the members of any other group. While the immigrants would like to see their sons and daughters marry within the group they cannot do much in the way of creating for them a Russian social environment. Too few to maintain churches, some do maintain family worship. In one such family the father daily gives thanks that his son's new wife is Russian. The records for the most recent year show that while there were 11 Russian grooms and 6 Russian brides there was no case of marriage between two Russians. The forecast is for the early disappearance of the Russians by amalgamation, mainly with other Caucasians.

Chapter XV

PRACTICE AND PREFERENCE IN MARRIAGE

THERE appears to be a widespread interest in the attitudes of the various peoples of Hawaii toward the out-marriage of their members. Commonly this is because of a desire to forecast future marriage practice and the future racial and interracial character of the population. It is sometimes supposed that attitudes furnish the one needful clue. For example, the Territory was, several years ago, visited by the ex-governor of a populous eastern state. Apparently he was supplied with data for a somewhat earlier period and, on the basis of these data, he reached conclusions which were published on his return home. They were to the effect that, in Hawaii, the attitude of the Chinese was favorable to amalgamation and assimilation and that their descendants were destined to become a part of the general Hawaiian mixed-blood population, but that the Japanese would remain permanently of pure Japanese stock since the "men rarely and the women never" married non-Japanese.

If one accepts the marriage practice of the various racial groups for some selected period as furnishing an adequate indication of attitude, if he assumes such attitudes to be permanent as if based on innate racial traits, and if he takes for granted that future marriage practice will be determined solely by the attitudes manifested in the past he has a theoretic equipment for many interesting, but erroneous forecasts that may win wide acceptance if they run with prevailing prejudice.

The situation is not so simple as such forecasts imply. Marriage practice among the peoples of Hawaii is not de-

190

termined wholly by attitudes, but in part by such things as relative numbers, differences in sex ratios, territorial distribution, and even by other factors which affect opportunity. Past marriage practice taken by itself does not, in all cases, reveal attitude, but the complex resultant of attitude and opportunity. Moreover, attitude is not a constant factor, but one that undergoes constant and important change and, with some exceptions, the changes have been in the direction of decreasing sentiment adverse to out-marriage. The modification of out-marriage rates is a resultant of so many factors that it is necessary to be cautious if one tries to use them for the purpose of forecasting future trends. One may not take it for granted that trends will continue at a constant rate or even that they will move in the same direction all the time.

The marriage practice of the members of some racial groups in Hawaii is affected measurably by two things that are not directly matters of attitude and that are capable of statistical statement. There is the relative size of the various groups and the sex ratios among the marriageable. The larger the group the higher the per cent of in-marriage, irrespective of any sentiment relative thereto. For example, if, in a community of as great homogeneity as can be found, the people were to be divided into three alphabetic groups, one with sixty per cent of the population, one with thirty, and one with ten per cent, one would find that the rates of in-group marriage would vary directly with the size of the group. Assuming that the alphabetical grouping involved no preference factor and that the three groups were normal in their age-sex ratios and otherwise, one would expect that, in the sixty per cent group, about sixty per cent of the men would marry women of their own group simply because sixty per cent of all the women would be of that group, while in the ten per cent group, only about ten per cent of the men would marry women of their own alphabetic group and this for a similar reason.

If the groupings were of similar relative size, but based on race and associated culture, an in-marriage preference would be indicated, for the sixty per cent group, only to the extent that the number of men to marry women of their own group exceeded sixty per cent, while, for the ten per cent group, the in-marriage of a number exceeding ten per cent would be evidence of a preference factor. Applying this principle to the situation in Hawaii one would say that for recent years there is evidence of in-marriage preference among the Japanese only to the extent that more than eighteen per cent of the Japanese brides and grooms are married within the group. In the case of the Chinese, a smaller group, the excess of in-marriage above seven per cent would be evidence of a preference factor and in the case of a very small group such as the Spanish, one per cent would be sufficient to indicate preference. If one seeks, by the use of marriage statistics, to determine the relative strength of sentiment among the various racial groups favorable to in-marriage, or, what amounts to the same thing, adverse to out-marriage, he must make proper allowance for this numerical factor.

Then another allowance must be made for abnormal sex ratios. It is evident that if there is, among any of the peoples, such as the Chinese or the Portuguese, a strong sentiment favorable to marriage within the group, the actual practice may be pretty much according to sentiment if the marriageable men and the marriageable women are about equal in number. But if there are only about seven women to a hundred men, if the seven women are already married, and if further immigration is prohibited, what are the ninety-three bachelors to do? This was about the numerical and legal situation of the Chinese at the beginning of the century.

By making an allowance for these two numerical factors,—relative group size and abnormal sex ratios,—one is able to establish indexes of in-marriage preference that are not so inaccurate as to be misleading if used mainly to establish the rank of the various peoples and the trends.[1]

An index of in-marriage *practice* for any group is found by dividing the number of brides and grooms who marry within their own group by the total number, the quotient showing how many were in-married to 1000. The rank of the various races in relation to the process of amalgamation through marriage may be found by arranging the indexes in order. When the indexes for the four periods are compared they show the trend of *practice*.

In the case of four groups, the Hawaiians, the part-Hawaiians, the Portuguese and the Japanese, the sex ratios were nearly normal and the numbers were so large that marriage practice was fairly indicative of attitude. That is, for these four groups, the indexes of in-marriage practice show approximately the relative strength of sentiment favorable to marriage within the group. And in each case the downward trend of in-marriage practice corresponds to a downward trend of in-marriage preference. But in the case of the other groups this is not true because practice at certain times was too much influenced by factors affecting opportunity. When immigration ceases the sex ratios gradually become normal so that practice can be more according to preference. While there is a falling index of in-marriage preference there may, therefore, be a rising index of in-marriage practice due merely to increasing opportunity. But this opposition of trends cannot continue for more than twenty or twenty-five years because that is enough time to enable the sex ratio of the marriageable to become nearly normal. Previously rising indexes of in-marriage practice take an opposite trend when this point is reached. For this reason the index of preference is at certain times more dependable for the purpose of making forecasts.

[1] For method of computing indexes of preference see Appendix, pages 327–330.

TABLE XXVIII

In-Marriage Practice and In-Marriage Preference

	1912–16	1920–24	1924–28	1930–34
The Portuguese				
Indexes of Practice	773	679	620	615
Indexes of Preference	792	716	627	634
The Chinese				
Indexes of Practice	721	817	796	745
Indexes of Preference	940	895	850	780

A comparison of the indexes of the Chinese and the
Portuguese will make this clear. It will be noted that the
Portuguese indexes of practice never differ greatly from those
of preference and that the trends are nearly parallel. But
in the case of the Chinese the index of practice in the period
1912–16 was far from representing preference. It was not
what they *preferred* to do but what they were *able* to do.
Some married the few available Chinese women in Hawaii
and some made a trip to their native land where they married and then returned to Hawaii to earn the support of the
wives they could not bring. Such marriages in China should
have been used in computing the indexes of preference, but
since the data were not available I have made an estimate,
adjusting the indexes for the first three periods. Now that
the sex ratio of the marriageable has become more nearly
normal for the Chinese their index of in-marriage practice
is higher than that of the Portuguese and it would have been
higher at all times had the sex ratios been as nearly normal
as those of the Portuguese. It may be seen that between the
first and the second period the trend of in-marriage preference among the Chinese not that of practice had predictive
value.

Table XXIX shows the indexes of in-marriage practice
and Table XXX, the indexes of in-marriage preference for
four four-year periods extending over a total 22 year period,
1912–1934. For the period, 1930–34, the indexes of in-
marriage practice are in order of rank, the Japanese having

the highest rate of in-marriage and the Spanish, the lowest. As between the first and the second periods there was only one group, the Japanese, that kept its rank unchanged. As between the second and the third periods there were no changes in rank, but as between the third and the fourth there were three interchanges of position involving six groups.

TABLE XXIX

Indexes of In-Marriage Practice

	1930–1934		1924–1928		1920–1924		1912–1916	
	Index	Rank	Index	Rank	Index	Rank	Index	Rank
Japanese . . .	954	1	948	1	982	1	996	1
Filipino	800	2	848	3	858	3	867	2
Korean	790	3	877	2	910	2	846	3
Chinese	745	4	796	4	817	4	721	7
Other Caucasian	721	5	666	6	694	6	708	8
Porto Rican . .	668	6	670	5	732	5	745	6
Portuguese . .	615	7	620	7	679	7	773	4
Part-Hawaiian* .	486	8	458	9	470	9	396	10
Hawaiian . . .	426	9	588	8	603	8	688	9
Spanish	125	10	280	10	437	10	764	5
Total	715		722		782		858	

* Because of a change in the classification of some of the part-Hawaiians who were of a three-way mixture,—Caucasian-Asiatic-Hawaiian,—the data relating to the Caucasian-Hawaiians and the Asiatic-Hawaiians are not comparable for all four periods. The difficulty is avoided by combining the two groups into one,—the part-Hawaiian.

In some of these cases the change in the rate of out-marriage was due mainly to a modification of attitude and in others it was due wholly or mainly to numerical factors. For example, from the first to the second period the rate of Chinese in-marriage rose from 721 to 817 to 1000, and the rank of the Chinese was lifted from the seventh to the fourth place. These changes did not correspond to any change in the attitude of Chinese or in those of the other peoples toward the Chinese, but merely to the increase in

TABLE XXX

Indexes of In-Marriage Preference*

	1930–1934		1924–1928		1920–1924		1912–1916	
	Index	Rank	Index	Rank	Index	Rank	Index	Rank
Japanese . . .	955	1	971	1	986	1	996	1
Filipino	954	2	951	2	949	2	944	3
Korean	799	3	938	3	948	3	950	2
Chinese	780	4	850	4	885	4	940	4
Other Caucasian .	774	5	787	5	792	5	809	7
Porto Rican . .	718	6	687	6	775	6	835	6
Portuguese . .	634	7	627	7	716	7	792	8
Part-Hawaiian .	545	8	531	9	519	9	418	10
Hawaiian . . .	517	9	574	8	659	8	722	9
Spanish	287	10	325	10	462	10	868	5

* The preferences are not merely the preferences of the people under consideration but they involve also the preferences of the other peoples with whom they are in contact. There is an organization of preference and its opposite as affecting the marriage practice of the representatives of any one race.

the number of eligible Chinese women. Hence the opposition of trends. While the trend of sentiment favoring in-marriage was decreasing in strength the actual rate of in-marriage was increasing. The trend of Chinese marriage practice since 1924 has corresponded to the trend of sentiment, not to the trend of practice, for the preceding period. In this and similar cases the trend of attitude not that of practice, has value for forecasting.

Between 1912 and 1920 the majority of the Spanish immigrants emigrated to California and those who remained were too few to maintain a social life of their own. More and more they find their social life among the Portuguese and this involves a modification of attitude favorable to intermarriage with Portuguese. This also helps to explain the rising rates of out-marriage of the latter group, but for this group there is another important factor. By 1920 most of the marriageable Portuguese were Hawaiian born and educated and their acculturation had reduced sentiment adverse to their intermarriage with "other Caucasians." The falling rate of in-marriage practice among the Hawaiians has been the result, largely, of a change in their numerical status relative to the part-Hawaiians. In the first period there were more than twice as many Hawaiian brides and grooms as part-Hawaiian, in the last period, less than half as many. Never has there been any strong sentiment adverse to intermarriage between the two groups and there has been no significant change in sentiment since 1912. Practice has responded merely to opportunity as created by a relatively larger group of part-Hawaiians. This is significant of what will take place in the marriage practice of all other racial groups when their mixed blood liaison groups become larger.

Similarly one could account for the other changes in the rate of in-marriage and in rank by reference to the facts of the developing situation. Suffice it to state certain generalizations. In the case of any of the racial groups in Hawaii the rate of in-marriage and, therefore, the rate of out-marriage depends on:

1. Numerical factors including sex ratio and numerical size in the Territory and in its various districts.

2. The strength of sentiment favoring marriage within the group; that is, sentiment adverse to out-marriage.

If the sex ratio is highly abnormal there is a high out-marriage rate in the beginning and when the sex ratio of the marriageable approaches the normal, there is, for a time, a rising rate of in-marriage. Later the downward trend is accentuated by the existence of a considerable number of mixed-bloods descended from the early men who married out of their own race. The examples are, pre-eminently, the Chinese, the Koreans and the Filipinos, but this is at least a minor factor in the case of several other groups including the Caucasians. Since the Koreans came at a later date than the Chinese, and the Filipinos, still later, the curve of

Chinese experience may be used in forecasting that of the other two groups.

The smaller population groups such as the Spanish, the Porto Rican and the Korean tend to amalgamate with the other races through intermarriage the more readily because they are too small to maintain a satisfactory social life of their own. This is true even of the rural part of the population of other groups such as the Chinese and the "other Caucasians." The earlier stages of amalgamation are at only a moderate rate but, after one or two generations, such groups hasten on to their extinction as pure groups on account of the number of mixed bloods.

During the first generation of Hawaiian residence the strength and effectiveness of sentiment adverse to out-marriage depends mainly on the traditions and on the existence of a family population. Peoples like the race-conscious Americans and British tend to maintain a high rate of in-marriage if they are real members of a society of their own race—a society of families. The initial racial attitude of the Portuguese and the Spanish was less favorable to marriage within their respective groups. Where two peoples such as the Portuguese and the Spanish have the same Christian faith it tends to facilitate intermarriage. It counts even as between the Portuguese and the Catholic Filipinos who differ considerably in racial traits. But having the same type of religious tradition does not have a similar effect if the tradition is one involving ancestor worship. Peoples such as the Chinese, the Japanese and the Koreans with a tradition of familialism including ancestor worship tend to marry within the group almost entirely for a generation if women are available. This is the result of the family authority or influence in the selection of brides and grooms. As the acculturation of such groups proceeds there is, more or less, a weakening of tradition and when the brides and grooms are of the native born generation a moderate increase in the out-marriage rate may be noted.

In the case of the Japanese there was a large group; its sex ratio became nearly normal at an early enough date to prevent the development of any considerable out-marriage practice. Their family traditions are highly adverse to marriage with non-Japanese. Naturally the development of a part-Japanese liaison group is retarded, and hence the second stage in amalgamation will go on more slowly than for any others.

The traditions adverse to out-marriage are not highly effective in the case of individuals who have no family relationship. Much of the interracial marriage in Hawaii has been by European, American and Asiatic men who were free from tradition mainly because they were away from home. The largest liaison groups, the Caucasian-Hawaiian and the Chinese-Hawaiian, owe their existence mainly to the presence of numerous Caucasian and Chinese men of this type at an early date.

For one or two generations the acculturation of the various racial groups to a common pattern is the most important factor tending to reduce sentiment adverse to out-marriage. Modifications of economic status are associated with this. But there comes a time, early or late, when further acculturation is conditioned by amalgamation. Only as racial contacts come to involve family relationships does acculturation go on to its completion on the side of the more subtle interests and attitudes. The rising mixed-blood group is the symbol of the more advanced acculturation as well as of the progressive amalgamation. In relation to any long distance forecast the information relative to the growing mixed-blood groups is of the utmost importance.[2] The best ground for the belief that the later stages of amalgamation and assimilation will go on at an increasing rate is the increasing number and size of these liaison groups.

Sentiment adverse to out-marriage is not necessarily

[2] Information relating to this may be found in the Appendix, pages 346–347.

based on the fact of difference in physical race traits. Indeed in Hawaii such differences appear to have a subordinate role. The sentiment of Koreans against intimate social relations with Japanese is nationalistic, not racial. The relative freedom of Filipinos to marry Portuguese as compared with Japanese has a religious rather than a racial basis. The tendency on the part of Americans and Europeans to marry Hawaiians rather than Chinese or Japanese cannot be accounted for on the basis of color. Neither can the fact that both the Chinese and the Japanese marry Hawaiians more frequently than they marry each other be credited to race.

The system of race relations in Hawaii has not been such as to create a strong feeling on the part of the various peoples that they must maintain group solidarity at whatever cost. Since there is open to them increasing opportunity as they make progress toward acculturation there tends to be a weakening of the narrow group loyalties and a development of a more inclusive loyalty to the general interests of Hawaii.

The code of race relations based on the assumption of social equality makes possible an increasing economic opportunity, excellent educational advantages open to all irrespective of racial antecedents, and full political participation by the citizens of every ancestry. Since attitudes are, in the long run, based on the realities of life there is a gradual weakening of sentiment calling for the maintenance of separate group loyalties according to ancestry and as this decreases there is a lessening of sentiment adverse to out-marriage.

For some of the people in Hawaii this weakening of the influence of the traditions has not gone far enough to facilitate their interracial marriage, but among all there is a measure of departure from the old standards and forms. Since the actual marriage practice is a sort of compromise between the old and the young it is easy to see that the attitudes of the younger and more Americanized part of the population will prevail more and more. As the influence of old country family systems is weakened, as the members of the third and later generations come to have a more individualistic outlook on life and as the choice in marriage comes to be made by the persons most directly concerned there may be expected to be an increasing proportion of out-marriage on the part of the members of the racial groups that have, in the past, given most evidence of strong sentiment adverse thereto.

The most general statement that can be made relative to group sentiment adverse to out-marriage is that it is related to all of the things that tend to create or maintain a desire for group solidarity or that contribute to the achievement of such solidarity. Man is essentially a social being. All of his purposes and aspirations are defined in relation to his situation in society. One wants good status within his group and inevitably he wants his group to have a satisfactory status in the larger society. Now, the strength of a group, and hence its status, depends largely, on the loyalty of its members. In disunity there is weakness. Moreover, one must be loyal in order to maintain good personal status within the group.

The members of a social group whether it be nationalistic, linguistic, religious, or racial cannot afford to be indifferent to the maintenance of group solidarity unless they have a good prospect for acceptance on terms of equality into some larger, more powerful or otherwise more desirable group.

The members of a social group have common memories, common sentiment and common interests. Otherwise they do not constitute a social group. In the case of an immigrant people in America the memories of the ancestral land, its history, its traditions, legends and myths rich in sentiment, and its festivals, rituals and religious faith are important among the things that give them a sense of belonging to each other and a sense of separateness from the other members of the larger community. Commonly their inability to speak the language of Americans or to speak it easily and effectively tends for a time to reduce communication to a minimum. While there may be important economic relations on the basis of such minimum communication all the more intimate sorts of association that give rise to group consciousness and that impose a demand for loyalty are restricted. The more or less discriminatory treatment that immigrants sometimes receive from the rest of the population tends to give them common economic interests or at least to make them feel that they have such interests as against the rest of the community.

Here is an adequate basis for at least temporary group consciousness. If, within the gradual acculturation of such a group, there is a corresponding development of social relations, that is, if education is without discriminatory practices, if the immigrants or their children are admitted into the more desired occupations on terms of equality as soon as they have the qualifications, if they are able to participate in political affairs without prejudice, and if they are welcomed into the more intimate sorts of social life as rapidly as their achievement warrants such a course, there will be no need for perpetuating the original group solidarity. It is better to have a good status in the community as a whole than in a mere section of the community. If one is confident of his ability to win such status in the larger society he sees little need for maintaining the smaller group as a separate people. Under such conditions immigrants, or at least their sons and grandsons, may prefer to forget their foreign language and to lose the cultural traits that identify them with the land of their ancestors so that their acceptance as Americans may be unquestioned. Through participation in the life of the larger group one comes under the influence of a new set of traditions, he defines his interests in relation to the larger society and exchanges an old loyalty for a new.

It may be, of course, that the members of an immigrant

group feel themselves or something in their culture to be superior. If purity of blood or loyalty to their religion or anything else in their old country culture seems to be very important they may prefer for a time to maintain themselves as a separate group with its special loyalties. To be a member of a minority group, especially of a weak group, has obvious disadvantages, but, according to group sentiment, there may be values that are worth the cost. Nevertheless, such small groups tend to disappear if the members are fairly treated by the rest of the community, and if there is no strict code determining the character of social relations.

But if the members of an immigrant group meet with sharp discriminatory treatment in economic and political affairs and if, on the basis of cultural fitness, they are not admitted to the more intimate sorts of social relationships, and if this state of things continues beyond the early period of contact, the immigrants are under the necessity of maintaining their separate organization on a more permanent basis. They must achieve and maintain an effective group solidarity. To this end it is necessary to emphasize the importance of things that unite them and at the same time separate them from others,—language, religion, nationalistic ideals and, possibly, ancestry or race.

But it makes no difference what is the cause of the desire for group solidarity; if there is such a desire there must be a corresponding sentiment adverse to marriage outside of the group for such marriage is bound to work against group morale. If there is much out-marriage there is a tendency to develop intimate social relations with outsiders. Through such marriage the group may lose some of its members or it may gain members who are not wholly sympathetic toward its traditions or loyal to its interests. The very fact of out-marriage tends to subject the group customs and standards to outside criticism and when such criticism is tolerated the group is headed toward dissolution. And then there is the influence of the increasing number of marginal people, the mixed-blood descendants who share in two sets of traditions and who are likely to be of divided loyalty. If sentiment within the group is too weak to prevent marriage to the members of other races, sects, nationalistic or linguistic groups, how much the more will it fail to prevent further mixture by marriage to those who are half or three quarters of their own blood?

The way the practical circumstances of life and social sentiment work jointly to determine marriage behavior in Hawaii is a matter of considerable interest. In the first century of interracial contacts in Hawaii, 1778–1878, there were practical conditions of such a character that foreign men, mainly white and Chinese, desired Hawaiian wives. At the same time they were freed, in some measure, from the control of their group mores adverse to out-marriage. Largely it was distance that freed them. In the total situation the fact that considerable numbers of foreign men did marry Hawaiian women and the fact that gradually there came into existence a considerable body of descendants of mixed racial ancestry were important factors toward the creation of a special pattern of race relations which tends to harden into a code. This code, based on the assumption of racial equality, sanctions the marriage practice and gives to the descendants of mixed ancestry a satisfactory social status.

The special conditions of the past, such as abnormal sex ratios and the conditions that tend to emancipate men from social control, may pass away; but as the number of men and women of mixed ancestry increases at the expense of all the groups of pure racial stock the sentiment that supports the code will be more and more effective and, barring some radical change in government, the sentiment adverse to racial equality and freedom in marriage will continue to decrease and interracial marriages will increase.

CHAPTER XVI

INTERRACIAL MARRIAGE AND DIVORCE

THE present interest in divorce relates mainly to its racial and interracial character. Are the hazards to an enduring family life greater in the cases of some races than in the cases of others? Under Hawaiian conditions are they greater or less for those who marry across race lines than for those who marry within their own group? In the study of marriages it was assumed, tentatively, that the marriage data supplied a fairly satisfactory indication as to the increasing number of families of the various racial and mixed racial kinds and consequently, as to the future number of children of each kind. But if marriages of some sorts are, with uncommon frequency, followed by early divorce the assumption calls for some qualification. It is the purpose, first to determine the facts statistically as nearly as may be and then briefly to consider the more theoretical aspects.

Whether the divorce rate is high or low among any people depends on whether many people make so great a failure of their married life that they want to be freed from it, and on their ability to secure a divorce if they so desire. Touching this second point, it may be said that in Hawaii, commonly people can secure divorces if they want them. There are seven different legal grounds and they are liberally interpreted by the courts. In many cases there is no contest or only a formal contest and the granting of a divorce is almost certain in such cases. Public opinion is tolerant. Relative to the ability of the husband to pay, alimony is liberal. In more than three fourths of the divorce cases the wives are the applicants. There were, in 1930, more than twice as many adult males in the Territory as adult females and because of this abnormal sex ratio most of the divorced women find it easy to remarry if they so desire. During the ten years preceding 1930 there were granted 5,883 divorces, but there were reported for census purposes only 934 divorced women and a considerable proportion of these were so young and so recently divorced that their early remarriage could be considered probable.

The family failure that makes people want divorce is, directly, just a matter of the personal adjustment of the husband and wife, but the maladjustment is related to the general social situation in which they find themselves. In a society that is characterized by little change the whole pattern of life comes to be standardized. The role of the husband and also that of the wife are perfectly well known and both, supported and controlled by the unquestioned standards of their community, tend to carry on as expected. Under such stable social conditions there is commonly only a small demand for divorce or, if there is a demand, it is on account of something such as barrenness that makes it, among some peoples, one's duty to be divorced. Moreover, in such a society, law, religion, and public opinion may prohibit divorce or interpose serious obstacles to it.

But in a region of high social mobility it is otherwise. In such a society there is much disorganization. The individual tends to be emancipated. He follows a course of his own choice—maybe a course that is all the wiser because untrammeled by tradition, maybe a foolish course, a mere following of impulse or whim without control from the standpoint of any consistent scheme of life. A degree of freedom from social control may mean opportunity to achieve a better way of life and one can find men and women who have used their freedom wisely. But it may mean opportunity to fall below customary standards so that there is personal as well as social disorganization. Family disorganization in Hawaii may be regarded as an incident to the temporary social disorganization that results from migration and from the association of several peoples who differ greatly in tradition. Under conditions of personal emancipation for many, there is no standard pattern of family life. The tendency is for each family to set its own standards and it may be that husband and wife fail to agree. Each marriage tends to be an experiment and when the experiment fails there is freedom to secure a divorce and try again. Sometimes the second marriage seems to be more successful.

The situation in Hawaii is such that one would expect to find a high rate of divorce. The immigrant population has come to the Territory so recently that it is only partially adjusted to the conditions of life in Hawaii. Old country family customs tend to fall into decay and the old standards tend to become ineffective for the control of conduct. The new standards require time for their achievement and, in the meantime, large numbers suffer from the lack of effective standards.

Many of the immigrants to Hawaii came from countries in which there is comparatively little divorce. For all immigrant peoples the rates in Hawaii are much higher than in their respective homelands. Even the Portuguese, who, as a Catholic people, had little experience with divorce prior to their immigration, are now divorced at a rate that is only a little below the average for the rest of the population. The high rates for immigrants generally do not represent a transplanting of old country customs and standards but rather the decay of such customs and standards.

Certain changes in family status that may be regarded as a part of the Americanization of immigrants tend to increase divorce. A woman, who was economically dependent on her husband and, in the old home village, willing to play a subordinate role, begins to be self-assertive in Hawaii when she earns a personal income. She insists on freedom to spend her own earnings as she pleases and this involves other sorts of freedom. Moreover, since there are plenty of single men and only a few unmarried women, a husband dare not try to discipline his wife lest she leave him for another man. One old immigrant man, reflecting on our laws relating to divorce and alimony and on the changed status of women, said, "This is a woman's country. I prefer a man's country. I am going back." Another immigrant who had married unhappily and had been divorced criticized America for giving the wife the advantage. "The courts protect the woman ninety per cent and the man ten per cent. It ought to be fifty-fifty."

Certain temporary conditions that have been important in the recent past are becoming less important. When the Japanese men were securing wives by the picture bride method, the parents making the selection, it often happened that there was a lack of personal compatibility. In addition to the ordinary matrimonial risks there was the fact that commonly the grooms were older than was customary in Japan and that they had lived in Hawaii for several years, undergoing changes which tended to make the problem of adjustment more difficult. When such was the case it might be easy for the bride to secure a divorce and get a new husband more to her liking. In many cases she had the benefit of the presence of a brother who represented the family in arranging for the new marriage. During the height of the picture bride movement, 1912–16, the divorce rate among the Japanese was more than twice as high as it has been in the more recent years.

In the case of the Filipino immigrant women a somewhat different procedure yielded similarly high divorce rates. During a few years immediately preceding 1925 the number of Filipino female immigrants was exceptionally large. They were encouraged to accompany their husbands who were coming as plantation laborers, their passage being paid by an organization representing the plantations. It is said that among the women who came there were some

who had a ceremony of marriage in the Philippines primarily in order to secure transportation and that as soon as
possible after arrival they sought divorce. Since Hawaiian
law requires two years of residence for the libelant in a
divorce case, the highest divorce rates came two or three
years later.

If there were some sort of insurance to cover the family
hazards that result in divorce the premium rates would
fall after the third year of married life and after the tenth
year they would be comparatively low and still lower in
later years. Since the divorce rates are much higher for
recently contracted marriages it follows that, other things
being equal, the rates will be higher for any racial group
in which an unusually large proportion of the married are
young and near the beginning of their married life. During
and soon after the period of maximum immigration of Japanese women, 1912–16, this was an important factor in
their high divorce rates and likewise for the Filipino women
in the more recent years. Now that Filipino immigration
seems to be at an end one may forecast an early and marked
fall in Filipino divorces.

Among the native Hawaiians it was, of old, the custom
for husbands and wives to separate freely and without
formality when they were dissatisfied, and remarriage was
expected. Probably such separation was greatly increased
as a result of the social disorganization that followed the
coming of foreigners. Only gradually did they, in practice,
accept the present law which requires formal marriage and
a legal divorce before remarriage. Their increasing divorce
rate during the first quarter of the present century probably means an increasing tendency to take their troubles
to court rather than an increase in actual separations.

The presence in Hawaii of a relatively large number of
men in military and naval service tends to increase the
divorce rate in the county in which they are stationed and,
in particular, the rate for the racial group to which they

belong. Enlisted men in the army and navy are commonly expected to be unmarried. Their marriage is not encouraged by the military authorities, but it is permitted. In the year, 1926–27, a year that may have been exceptional, more than one per cent of the men stationed in or near Honolulu did marry. Commonly, the men are stationed in the Territory for only two or three years and, while some take their discharge in Hawaii in order to remain with their families, many desert their wives when they are transferred or discharged, and the wives then apply for divorce. While the number of men involved is small compared to the whole number of enlisted men, it is large enough measurably to affect both marriage and divorce rates for the white people.

Aside from the military population, the white people in the Territory may be divided into two classes according to the stability of their residence. On the one hand, there are the families that have resided in Hawaii for two or three or more generations and other families whose residence has been of so extended a character that they have social relations with the old families. On the other hand, there are those who live in the Territory a few years for business or professional purposes but who, excepting for their business, have little social contact with the more stable part of the population. The high divorce rate for white people is mainly on account of the men in military service and the civilians of unstable residence, but the data as to this point are not so nearly complete as to warrant a statistical statement.

The comparatively low rate of divorce among the Chinese is associated with a stable residence. Only a few Chinese have immigrated since 1897. They have made greater progress toward social adjustment than the people of more recent immigration. Very small groups such as the Porto Rican and the Korean tend to experience a higher degree of social disorganization than do the larger groups and their divorce rates are correspondingly high.

It is well known that divorce rates in the United States are exceptionally high as compared with those of other countries.[1] But the rates for Hawaii are higher even than those of Continental United States. Table XXXI gives the average annual number of divorces to the 1000 married

TABLE XXXI

Ratio of Divorces to Married Population

	AVERAGE MARRIED POPULATION 1925–1931	AVERAGE ANNUAL NUMBER OF DIVORCES 1925–1931	NUMBER OF DIVORCES TO 1000 MARRIED POPULATION
Continental United States	50,165,440	188,429	3.55
Divisions:			
New England . . .	3,303,079	7,842	2.37
Middle Atlantic . .	10,766,172	15,664	1.45
East North Central .	10,816,057	49,620	4.59
West North Central .	5,594,910	23,238	4.15
South Atlantic . . .	6,041,577	14,794	2.44
East South Central .	3,894,758	15,411	3.95
West South Central .	4,846,893	30,502	6.29
Mountain	1,487,325	10,411	6.99
Pacific	3,916,175	21,079	5.38
Territory of Hawaii . .	106,398*	596	5.60

* A considerable number of the Chinese, Japanese, Korean and Filipino men in Hawaii who were reported as married at various census dates did not have their wives in Hawaii. Such men commonly remain in Hawaii for a time and then return to their old homes and their wives so that they do not appear to constitute a factor of any importance in the local divorce situation. They are not, therefore, included in the numbers estimated as married.

[1] Divorces to 100,000 Population (adapted from Reuter and Runner, *The Family*)

	Census Year	
England and Wales	1928	7.3
Belgium	1927	31.0
France	1927	45.0
Germany	1925	54.0
Denmark	1927	55.0
Switzerland	1927	62.0
Japan	1927	79.0
Austria	1927	85.0
Continental United States	1928	160.0

population for Continental United States and its principal divisions and also for the Territory of Hawaii for the seven years ending December 31, 1931. It will be seen that Hawaii's rate is equalled or nearly equalled by those of the three most western sections,—sections which have in the last generation trebled their population, largely by immigration from the more eastern sections of the country and from foreign countries. The similarity between the rates in Hawaii and those of the sections of Continental United States to which there has been the greatest movement of population suggests that the high rate in Hawaii is causally related to its high rate of population increase rather than to the special racial character of its peoples.

Table XXXII shows the rising trend of divorce rates in Hawaii, 1905–1927, and the downward trend since 1927. The marked increase for the 22 years is associated with the immigration of married women. In 1900 there were only 24,048 married women enumerated. In 1910 there were 31,380,—a gain of 30 per cent in ten years. In 1920 there were 45,550,—an increase of 45 per cent in the decade. The immigration continued at about the same average rate up to June 30, 1924, at which time there were about 53,000 married women in the Territory. After 1924 the immigration of women was practically terminated, and abruptly: that of the Japanese by the 1924 Exclusion Act, and that of the Filipino women by a change in plantation policy. In the twenty-four years, 1900–1924, the number of married women had increased by about 120 per cent, mainly as a result of immigration. During this period the largest gains were of Japanese and Filipinos, the Japanese coming in diminishing numbers after 1913 and the Filipino women, in increasing numbers up to 1924. After this date there was no gain from immigration, all sources considered, and only a moderate increase in the married population as a result of the maturing and marrying of the native-born.

TABLE XXXII

The Married Population and Divorces in Hawaii

	ESTIMATED AVERAGE MARRIED POPULATION	AVERAGE ANNUAL NUMBER OF DIVORCES	DIVORCES TO 1000 MARRIED POPULATION
1905–1908 (4 years) . .	57,396	149.50	2.60
1909–1912 (4 years) . .	65,120	264.00	4.05
1913–1916 (4 years) . .	78,250	357.25	4.56
1917–1920 (4 years) . .	87,150	507.00	5.82
1921–1924 (4 years) . .	102,150	557.25	5.45
1925–1927 (3 years) . .	105,253	630.33	5.98
1928–1929 (2 years) . .	106,438	575.50	5.40
1930–1931 (2 years) . .	107,500	563.50	5.23
1932–1933 (2 years) . .	107,000	534.00	4.98

The rate of divorce in Hawaii began to fall two years before the coming of the business depression and seems to be definitely correlated with the cessation of female immigration in 1924. Since 1931 there has been only an insignificant immigration of men and when men ceased to come from outside the movement within the Territory was greatly reduced. While the stoppage of immigration in 1931 was not unrelated to the depression, it was nearly due to come even if there had been no depression and at the present time, it does not appear to be probable that immigration will revive in any important way when prosperity returns. One may forecast for Hawaii a long term trend in the direction of decreased mobility of population and of increasing general social stability. If the theory here advanced is correct a further decrease in divorce rates will be a natural result.[2]

[2] There has been a fall in divorce rates in all parts of the United States since the beginning of the depression and it is doubtless attributable to the depression, in large measure. The experience of Hawaii suggests that the depression may have reduced divorce by reducing the movement of population,—the movement from East to West and from the rural districts and smaller cities to the larger cities. If this hypothesis turns out to be valid it will be possible to forecast future divorce trends from data relating to population movements.

While the divorce rates are high for all of the peoples of Hawaii, there are some significant differences in the rates and the trends. The differences in rates, as among the various racial groups, are not significant merely of racial or cultural differences, but largely they are indicative of the special circumstances of life in Hawaii and of the position of the various racial groups in relation to the cycle of social changes that immigrant peoples undergo. Table XXXIII shows the ratio of divorces to married population in the Territory for seven specified periods extending from 1913 to 1933, with a racial classification of libelants, the race of the libelee not being a matter of record. If the libelees also had been classified the rates of the racial groups would have been modified in a small measure.

TABLE XXXIII

Rate of Divorces to 1000 Married Population

	4 YEARS 1913–16	4 YEARS 1917–20	4 YEARS 1921–24	3 YEARS 1925–27	2 YEARS 1928–29	2 YEARS 1930–31	2 YEARS 1932–33
Hawaiian and Part-Hawaiian	5.11	7.59	7.22	8.10	6.99	5.59	5.46
White*	4.39	6.31	8.01	9.63	8.03	7.22	8.37
Porto Rican	2.86	4.01	4.95	8.37	7.05	4.72	1.53
Chinese	2.41	4.29	3.17	2.68	1.89	2.54	2.78
Japanese	4.97	4.93	3.79	2.93	2.55	2.49	2.17
Korean	3.66	7.57	8.50	10.67	7.57	6.55	5.19
Filipino	1.03	7.14	6.39	11.46	12.52	14.01	13.51
Total	4.56	5.82	5.45	5.98	5.40	5.23	4.98

* Hawaiian court statistics classify native born citizens of Portuguese ancestry, not as Portuguese but as part of the white population. For this reason the term "white" is used in this chapter, all Portuguese, Spanish and "other Caucasian" being combined in one group.

Probably the most important thing to be considered in relation to these trends is the tendency of the rates to rise soon after any considerable immigration and to fall after immigration diminished or ceased. For example, the rate for white people rose following the rather large increase of white population after the World War. The Japanese rate fell as immigration was reduced, 1916–24, and still further after it ceased in 1924. Even the admission of a few hundred Chinese women in the five or six years following the World War seems to have influenced Chinese divorce rates. Most of these women were admitted, not as immigrant aliens but as citizens. It appears that some Chinese men divorced their native wives in order to marry the newly arrived women of their own race. The number of married Filipino women more than doubled in the four years, 1920–24, the divorce rate went up correspondingly in the next period, 1925–27, and only in the most recent period has it begun to fall. In part, some of the rising rates are to be accounted for by the movement of people from the rural districts, where divorce rates are low, to Honolulu, where they are much higher. In the case of small groups like the Porto Rican and the Korean it is probable that the trends at some points are not significant.

On the basis of Chinese experience a further hypothesis is suggested and later this may be tested by the experience of the Japanese. It will be noted that the Chinese rates reached a low point, 1928–29, after which they, contrary to the general trend of all races, began to rise. During the earlier period, the married Chinese were mainly immigrants, the Hawaiian-born being for the most part too young to marry. More recently the situation has been reversed, most of the married, especially of the recently married, are native born. Their Americanization involves a decadence of ancestor worship, of the Chinese family system, and of the sentiment associated therewith. Not improbably this is a factor toward a rising divorce rate, the members of the second and third generations being mainly responsible therefor. Since the Japanese immigrated at a later date than the Chinese they have not reached the same place in the cycle of change as have the Chinese and their rates of divorce are still going down.

A special and more detailed study of marriage and divorce was made for the County of Honolulu, each for a single year: for marriage, the year ending June 30, 1927, and for divorce, the year ending December 31, 1927. The County of Honolulu had (1930) 55 per cent of the population of the Territory and 59 per cent of the married population. The City of Honolulu had 67 per cent of the population of Honolulu County and 75 per cent of the married. During the decade, 1920–1930, the population of the City of Honolulu increased by 65 per cent, the growth being mainly on account of the coming of people from the rural districts. The population of the rural part of the County increased by 62 per cent or, excluding enlisted men in military service and the officers and their families, by about 37 per cent. A considerable part of the rural population of Honolulu County including the military is so near the City of Honolulu that its social relations tend to be urban or at least to be affected by proximity to the city. It will, therefore, involve no great inaccuracy so far as the present purpose is concerned to regard the whole County as urban.

Commonly when cities grow rapidly they experience a considerable measure of social disorganization and Honolulu has been no exception to the rule. The presence in the city of large numbers of rural people involves serious problems. The activities of plantation workers are pretty fully organized by the plantation. There is little idle time and that little is, to some extent, planned for by social workers, —amusement, recreation, and education. The work is steady throughout the year and the income is dependable and large enough, commonly, to permit of some saving. Residents of non-plantation rural districts have their customary round of activities. There is little planning, but the traditional procedure is somewhat favorable to social stability and to stability of family life. But when rural people come to the city they find that employment is irregular and there is no employer to organize more of their activities than are utilized in the work directly. The customary round of rural life is impossible. The wages, while at a higher rate for the time in actual service, may be lower for the year or for some months, but city life calls for increased expenditures. People not much experienced in planning are suddenly called upon to take the initiative in securing employment and in planning expenditures and the use of leisure time under unfamiliar conditions.

Under the circumstances one might expect to find that some of the more fortunate people or those of greater enterprise and more stable character would make pretty satisfactory adjustments while others of less ability or with less good luck would suffer from lack of adjustment and from irregularity of employment. This is what has happened in Honolulu and it is reflected not only in charitable, police and court statistics, but also in higher divorce rates. For example, in 1927, the divorce rate for Honolulu County was 9 to the 1000 married population while in the rest of the Territory it was 2.5 or less than a third as high.

The marked difference between the city rate and the rural rate tends to confirm the view that the high divorce rate in Hawaii is not in any important measure explained by reference merely to the racial character or the cultural traditions of its peoples, but rather by a consideration of the special circumstances of life in Hawaii, the circumstances incident to the mingling of several peoples who differ in cultural traditions and who are living under economic and general social conditions to which they are not yet adjusted. If it were largely a matter of traditional backgrounds the city rates and the rural rates would be more nearly equal, for the city population is made up of the same racial types as are found in the country and the proportions are not such as to suggest any marked difference in the rates.

Some of the rates in Table XXXIV do not mean quite what they seem to mean. For example, the rate for the part-Hawaiians is higher than that for the Hawaiians which is

TABLE XXXIV

Divorce Rates in Honolulu County, 1927*

	MARRIED POPULATION	PERSONS DIVORCED	PERSONS DIVORCED TO 1000 MARRIED POPULATION
Hawaiian	4,830	99	20.5
Part-Hawaiian	3,925	102	25.9
White — all	15,924	424	26.6
White — civilian . . .	12,324	224	18.1
Porto Rican	940	38	40.4
Chinese	5,600	40	7.1
Japanese	23,520	147	6.3
Korean	1,080	21	19.4
Filipino	4,552	145	31.5
All others	150	12	
Total	60,521	1,028	16.9

* This study was begun by Mr. Shih Po, a student from Peking, China, in 1927, but on account of his death early in 1928 the study was not completed until in 1929. In the meantime some of the libelees who, apparently, were not very well known locally could not be found or identified as to race. Out of 544 divorces granted, the race of only 514 libelees was determined. For the purposes of the study of Honolulu County divorces, the 30 cases in which the race of libelee is undetermined are omitted.

contrary to what would be expected by people who are acquainted with them. It is a matter of recency of marriage. A comparatively large proportion of the married part-Hawaiians are young and they have been married recently and it is among the recently married that the rates are highest. If the numbers were large enough to warrant computations for groups according to the duration of marriage it would be found, doubtless, that, for the various duration groups, the part-Hawaiian rates would be lower than the Hawaiian. This would be in accordance with general observation and with the other indices of social disorganization. From a similar cause the Filipino rates are exceptionally high.

But after making all appropriate allowance for differences in the recency of marriage for the various racial groups, it is apparent that divorce is much less frequent among the

Chinese and the Japanese than among the others. To one familiar with these peoples this is not surprising. The importance of the family relationship among people whose religion includes ancestor worship is a stabilizing factor. To the extent that this is the cause of the low rates one must acknowledge the influence of tradition. But one may ask, "Why are Chinese and Japanese traditions maintained more adequately than those of other immigrant groups?" The answer to this question involves a consideration of the special social situation in Hawaii of the different racial groups. One important factor relates to the relative size of the groups; a large group like the Japanese, or a medium sized one like the Chinese, is able to maintain social organization much better than the smaller groups. Moreover, the attitude of the influential *haole* population is important. For example, in the case of another white group such as the Portuguese, there is so much contact including inter-marriage and so much prospect of further development of intimate social relations between these two white groups that the Portuguese tend to be indifferent to the maintenance of customs and standards that identify them as Portuguese or even to be definitely opposed to such maintenance. Hence there is, for the time being, so much the greater social dis-organization. But there are greater obstacles to the develop-ment of the intimate social relations between *haole* and people of Oriental ancestry, this largely on account of *haole* attitudes. The Chinese and Japanese, therefore, tend, so much the more, to maintain organization on the basis of their traditional cultures. That is, they suffer less disorganization and this is evidenced not only by the divorce data but also by the other indexes of social disorganization. The divorce rates among civilian whites are more than double the rates for the Chinese or the Japanese and a little above average for all civilians.

In Table XXXV is given the racial distribution of the grooms and brides of Honolulu County for the year ending

TABLE XXXV

*Men and Women—The Number Divorced to 1000 Wedded,
Honolulu County, 1927*

RACE	WEDDED			DIVORCED			DIVORCED TO 1000 WEDDED		
	Grooms	Brides	Total	Husbands	Wives	Total	Men	Women	Total
Hawaiian	90	138	228	39	60	99	433	435	434
Part-Hawaiian . .	162	256	418	36	66	102	222	257	244
White (civilian) . .	397	423	820	123	121	244	310	286	299
White (service)* . .	216	83	299	113	67	180	523	807	602
Porto Rican . . .	38	41	79	17	21	38	447	512	481
Chinese	147	131	278	22	18	40	149	137	143
Japanese	450	456	906	74	73	147	164	160	162
Korean	22	22	44	10	11	21	454	500	477
Filipino	134	103	237	77	68	145	574	660	611
All others	4	7	11	3	9	12			
Total	1,660	1,660	3,320	514	514	1,028	309	309	309

* The rates for the service men and their wives are affected by their special circumstances. In most cases where the men were libelants the wives had never been residents of Hawaii and, in most cases where the wives were libelants, the men had ceased to be residents of the Territory. The data for the service men are segregated in order that those of the civilian population may appear separately.

June 30, 1927 and of the husbands and wives divorced in the calendar year 1927. In the last three columns are the ratios of the numbers of men and women granted divorce to the numbers united in marriage for the year. It will be observed that the ratio of persons divorced to persons united in marriage was extremely high on the average, being 309 to 1000, or nearly twice as high as the rate for Continental United States which was for that year 160. For the part-Hawaiians, the civilian whites, the Chinese and the Japanese the rates are below average and for the others above average.

As in Continental United States, the initiative in divorce proceedings in Hawaii is usually taken by the wife. This is true even in the case of peoples like the Japanese among whom there was an opposite tradition. Of the 514 divorces included in this study, the wives were libelants in 399 or 77 per cent of all cases, the percentage being even higher for those of Oriental birth or ancestry than for the others. Table XXXVI shows the number of libelants by sex for each racial and interracial type of divorce.

Of the divorced women, 54.5 per cent had no living minor children, whereas in Continental United States nearly two-thirds are childless.[3] Probably the presence of children more commonly in the families of the divorced in Hawaii is in considerable measure the direct consequence of a higher divorce rate. While, on the mainland, there are under two children to the family for those that have children, the number is slightly in excess of two in Hawaii. As would be expected the average number is largest where the average duration of marriage preceding divorce is greatest, that is, among the part-Hawaiians.

More than two-thirds of the women and nearly half of the men who are divorced in Hawaii marry again. During the eight years, 1920–27, there were 224 divorces to 1000 marriages. According to information supplied by applicants for marriage licenses in the year 1926–7, 15.3 per cent of the brides and 10.5 per cent of the grooms had been divorced. The average age of the brides who had been divorced was 28.5 years.

For Continental United States, 1930, the number of divorced women in the population exceeded the number of divorced men by 17 per cent but in Hawaii the situation was reversed, the number of divorced men exceeding the number of divorced women by 73 per cent. Evidently remarriage is more common for women and this would be expected in a population in which there are twice as many men as women.

Several competent students are in substantial agreement that in Continental United States only about one-third

[3] Cahen, *Statistical Analysis of American Divorce*, p. 112.

TABLE XXXVI

Divorces—Libelants Classified According to Race and Sex, *
Honolulu County, 1927*

RACE OF DIVORCED HUSBANDS	Sex of Libelant	Hawaiian	Part-Hawaiian	White	Porto Rican	Chinese	Japanese	Korean	Filipino	All Others	Total
Hawaiian	Male	9									9
	Female	22	6	1		1					30
Part-Hawaiian	Male		8								8
	Female	6	16	3		3					28
White (civilian)	Male	1	3	25						1	30
	Female	6	17	66	1	1				2	93
White (service)	Male		1	31					1		33
	Female	6	8	56	1	2	1	1	1	4	80
Porto Rican	Male				6						6
	Female			1	10						11
Chinese	Male		1	1		1					3
	Female	1	5	2	1	10					19
Japanese	Male						17				17
	Female	2		1			54				57
Korean	Male							1			1
	Female							9			9
Filipino	Male	2		1	1				3		7
	Female	5			1		1		63		70
All others	Male		1								1
	Female									2	2
Total	Male	12	14	58	7	1	17	1	4	1	115
	Female	48	52	130	14	17	56	10	64	8	399
Total (Civilian)	Male	12	13	27	7	1	17	1	3	1	82
	Female	42	44	74	13	15	55	9	63	4	319

* To read this table note the titles at the left and top. For example the pair of numbers in the second column, third line, is read as follows: There were three plus seventeen or twenty divorces of white civilian men from part-Hawaiian women, the husbands being libelants in three cases and the wives in seventeen.

of the divorced remarry and that divorce for the purpose
of remarriage to a third party is not an important factor in
the motivation of divorce actions.[4] The exceptionally high
rates in Hawaii seem to warrant a different inference.
There is an absence of evidence as to the number of cases
in which divorce is sought in order to marry an already
selected third party, but when so many of the women do in
fact remarry, it is possible for any woman who contemplates
divorce proceedings, if she is not too old and if she is ordinarily attractive, to be pretty confident that, in case of
divorce, she will be able to marry again if she so desires.
Not improbably such prospect tends to encourage women
to seek divorce.

Among the various racial groups the rate of remarriage
seems to be affected largely by economic factors. If a
husband and wife who separate have no property and only
a small and precarious income neither may think a divorce
worth the cost unless he or she expects to remarry. Among
such people the remarriage rate is extremely high; for example, 85 per cent of the Hawaiian divorced women remarry. But if there is considerable property or income,
divorce may be sought irrespective of any intention to remarry. Among such people the remarriage rate will be
lower. For example, among white women only 56 per cent,
and among Chinese only 39 per cent, remarry.

We now come to the question relating to the relative
frequency of divorce among those who marry within their
own race and those who marry outside of their race. For
two or three reasons one is not able to give a perfectly
accurate answer to the question involved. There are the 30
cases in which the libelee could not be racially identified.
It was necessary to estimate the married population for the
year 1927. The data are for one year only and those of the
next year would not be in quite the same proportions.

---

[4] These views are summarized in Cahen's *Statistical Analysis of Divorce*, in
the chapter on remarriage.

Nevertheless, the probable errors are not so great but that some conclusions of value can be drawn.

TABLE XXXVII

Divorce Rates of the In-Married and the Out-Married,
Honolulu County, 1927

	IN-MARRIED			OUT-MARRIED		
	Married Population	Persons Divorced in the Year	Divorces to 1000 Married Population	Married Population	Persons Divorced in the Year	Divorces to 1000 Married Population
Hawaiian . .	2,896	62	21	1,934	37	19
Part-Hawaiian	1,954	48	25	1,971	54	27
White (service men included) .	13,462	356	26	2,462	68	28
Porto Rican .	660	32	49	280	6	21
Chinese . .	4,474	22	5	1,126	18	16
Japanese . .	23,094	142	6	426	5	12
Korean . .	962	20	21	118	1	9
Filipino . .	3,868	132	34	684	13	19
All others . .	48	4		102	8	
	51,418	818	16	9,103	210	23
All but the Japanese and the Chinese . .	23,850	654	27	7,551	187	25

In the case of the in-married—all races—there were 16 persons divorced to 1000 married population as compared with 23 divorced in the case of the out-married. A more detailed examination of the table raises a question as to the meaning of this difference. It may be noted that for the Hawaiians, the Porto Ricans, the Koreans and the Filipinos, the rate of divorce was higher for the in-married than for the out-married, very much higher for the latter three. In the case of the white people, there was only a small difference between the two rates, while for the Chinese and the Japanese there was a marked difference, the divorce rate being two or three times as high for the out-married as for the in-married.

The following generalizations seem to be warranted:

1. The out-marriage rates are highest for the racial groups that are most disorganized,—for those that have the least effective control over their members.

2. The divorce rates are highest among those who are most disorganized, that is, among the members of the racial groups that out-marry most.

3. Among the more disorganized racial groups, the divorce rates are about equally high, on the average, as between the in-married and the out-married.

4. There is so little intermarriage between the Chinese and the Japanese that there is no statistical test as to their permanency but it is probable that they will be as enduring as those of the in-married.

5. To the extent that there is intermarriage between members of a disorganized group and members of a well organized group there is a tendency to lower the divorce rates of the members of the disorganized group.

6. Since there is a considerable difference in the divorce rates among the various racial groups, it is necessary to make allowances if one uses marriage data in forecasting birth trends.

The high rate of divorce in Hawaii does not appear to be the result of interracial marriages but of the circumstances that tend to free people from their traditional control.

It is true, doubtless, that the marriage of men and women who differ considerably in racial traits and cultural backgrounds does involve some extra problems of adjustment. There may be clashing habits and standards. The difficulties in the way of understanding are greater. There is also the question of the wider social relations. Do husband and wife wish to maintain social relations with his people or with hers or with both? Do they agree in their desires and are they able to win social acceptance according to preference? Do they find themselves more or less isolated socially? The way these questions are answered is important from the standpoint of the happiness of married life and the prospect for its permanence. It is not difficult to find interracial marriages which have failed notoriously in almost every way and some have been terminated almost immediately after the wedding.

When a man and a woman of very different cultural backgrounds marry there is an uncommon need for imagination, sympathy and intelligence on both sides. If one of them stupidly assumes that it will be possible to go on living according to the customs of his or her ancestors and with indifference toward the customs to which the other is habituated, the outlook for a happy family life is far from good. If both are stupidly self assertive there is no hope at all. A man, speaking of a woman not of his own race from whom he had been divorced, said, "She always disconsidered me."

On the other hand, the very fact of out-marriage in the face of family sentiment against it may indicate that, as between the two, there is some unusual attraction, something favorable to the working out of a personal adjustment. Moreover, among those who marry out of their own race, there are some who reflect upon their situation more than is common. Probably they realize more fully the nature and importance of their problems than do most other brides and grooms. The necessity for mutual forbearance may be more definitely recognized. Stupid blunders may be fewer than is common among married people. Moreover, there is the challenge of the situation. If one's friends and "in-laws" look askance at the marriage it is necessary to convince them, to demonstrate the wisdom of one's decision. A young Japanese woman who married a Chinese man is very proud of her success in winning the good opinion of her father-in-law who, in spite of his former disapproval, now says that she is the best of his daughters-in-law. These compensatory factors are important. Apparently they are sufficient to counterbalance the unfavorable factors. It is not difficult to find interracial families of a happy and stable character.

CHAPTER XVII

THE CHARACTER OF THE MIXED–BLOODS

THERE is a continuing interest in the character of the men and women of mixed racial ancestry. It is probable that after two or three hundred years nearly all of the resident descendants of the peoples now living in Hawaii will be of mixed blood. It may be supposed, therefore, that knowledge about the present mixed-blood population will afford a clue for the forecasting of future social conditions when the mixed-bloods play a more important part in the total situation. The present writer has some doubt as to the sort of conclusions likely to be drawn but believes that a very cautious use of the data may go a little way toward the creation of a better understanding of the situation and of probable future social trends,—or, if not a better understanding, then, of a healthy skepticism relating to unsolved problems.

What of the traits of the mixed-bloods so far as they are socially conditioned? What of their social status and of the relation of such status to character and achievement? What of their cultural inheritances and the relation of such inheritances to behavior and attitude? What of their biological inheritance and of its importance from the standpoint of social efficiency? What of their personality traits as conditioned by any and all factors? What will be the character of society when the population is mainly of mixed racial ancestry representing the various peoples now resident of the Territory?

At the present time the only mixed-bloods who are statistically recognized as mixed-bloods are the two groups of part-Hawaiians,—Caucasian-Hawaiians and Asiatic-Hawaiians. But there are statistically unrecognized mixed-bloods of many varieties in small but increasing numbers. If recent trends in marriage continue, all the pure racial groups will become more and more involved and the population will gradually become one of a very complex mixture of Japanese, Chinese, Hawaiian, Filipino and Caucasian mixed ancestry mainly, but with minor influence from still other racial groups. After a time it will come about that most of the mixed-bloods will be unable to trace their ancestry and then they will gradually come to think of themselves as a race,—the Hawaiian or Neo-Hawaiian.

There are, in Hawaii, hundreds of varieties of mixed-bloods if one takes into consideration not only the several parent races but also the various sorts of fractional mixture. Miscegenation involving at least three racial groups has been going on for more than a century and at the present time one can recognize at least eight peoples who may be considered as differing enough in physical traits to involve genetic differences of possible importance.

Considering only the miscegenation that has taken place in Hawaii, nearly all of the mixed-bloods who are not part-Hawaiian are still children. So far, the mixed Caucasian-Chinese, Chinese-Japanese, Filipino-Portuguese and others without Hawaiian blood are so few or so young that they have not become the object of much interest and they are officially classified as persons of pure racial character according to arbitrary rules. There are few social data relating to them and, while the case study method is available it has been used only to a limited extent. For these reasons this chapter is mainly concerned with part-Hawaiians, who are relatively numerous, fairly well represented in the adult age groups and separately classified for general statistical purposes.

For census purposes the part-Hawaiians are divided into two groups which are defined somewhat arbitrarily. The

Caucasian-Hawaiians are those who combine Caucasian with Hawaiian ancestry in any fractional proportions, and among the ancestors recognized as Caucasians are some Porto Ricans, most of whom have American-Indian and Negro as well as Spanish blood. The Asiatic-Hawaiians are those who combine Hawaiian with Asiatic ancestry,— Chinese, Japanese, Korean, Filipino,—in any proportions. About a third of them have some Caucasian blood also, but this is ignored in the official classifications. A boy whose mother is half Chinese and half Hawaiian and whose father is English is counted as Asiatic-Hawaiian. Nearly all of the Asiatic-Hawaiians past thirty years of age have Chinese ancestry, but, among the younger, there are increasing numbers who trace their ancestry to the Japanese, Koreans and Filipinos. The census data are defective in considerable degree because facts of ancestry are not always reported correctly. The chief deficiency comes from a tendency on the part of dark part-Hawaiians to report themselves as pure Hawaiian. Also some Asiatic-Hawaiians who have more white than Chinese blood prefer to escape from the arbitrary classification by claiming only the white and the Hawaiian ancestry.

It may be seen that the three groups, Hawaiian, Caucasian-Hawaiian and Asiatic-Hawaiian, as enumerated for census purposes, are not sufficiently well defined to warrant the use of any refinement of statistical method in testing hypotheses relating to relative ability. In this chapter comparatively little use is made of statistical data and the conclusions based on them are for the most part negative.

Since the character of a population group is affected by its age constitution, it is well to note peculiarities of the age constitution of the part-Hawaiians. There is a small part-Hawaiian population in the fifth and the sixth generation of mixture and there are even a few aged men and women who are of the third or the fourth generation of mixture. But since the large immigration of foreigners belongs to the last sixty years, the mixed-blood population is predominantly young, and this is especially true of the Asiatic-Hawaiians.

TABLE XXXVIII

Population by Age Groups (1930)

AGE	NUMBER TO 1000				
	Hawaiian	Caucasian-Hawaiian	Asiatic-Hawaiian	Total	Native White of Native Parentage U.S.A.
Under 21 years .	437	639	764	580	457
21–44 years . .	343	272	198	285	344
45 years and over	220	89	38	135	199
	1000	1000	1000	1000	1000

Sometimes statistical data are used in an effort to show that Caucasian-Hawaiians are superior to Asiatic-Hawaiians or *vice versa*. If one makes a list of prominent leaders among the part-Hawaiians, it is found that, proportionately to population, there are more Caucasian-Hawaiian than Asiatic-Hawaiian men of prominence. This may be taken to indicate superiority on the part of the Caucasian mixture. But, in considerable measure, this prominence in leadership may be interpreted as a consequence of the age distribution. It is obvious, that, other things being equal, the group made up most largely of children will have more pupils in the schools and fewer men of an age at which professional or political leadership could be expected. According to the 1930 census, there were about four-fifths as many Asiatic-Hawaiians as Caucasian-Hawaiians, but in the case of persons 45 years and over there were only a little over a third as many. Another thing that works to the advantage of the Caucasian-Hawaiians is the property and social status inherited from their ancestors.

The argument for the superiority of the Chinese-Hawaiians is maintained by a somewhat different procedure. It is held that Chinese-Hawaiian boys make a somewhat better record for steady application in the schools and that in later life they show greater stability of character. They are said to be more dependable in business positions. But, aside from any possible question as to the adequacy of data, there is the fact that when one compares young part-Hawaiian men of Chinese and of white ancestry, he is more or less comparing those of different generations of mixture. A large proportion of the Chinese-Hawaiian young men are the sons of Chinese, while more of the Caucasian-Hawaiian are the grandsons or more remote descendants of their white ancestors.

While it has not been definitely established, one may suppose that the personal disorganization incident to the coming into existence of a group of mixed cultural backgrounds does not reach its maximum point until about the second or the third generation of mixture. On account of the influence of the parent of the better cultural adjustment, many of the boys of the first generation of mixture enjoy the advantage of a pretty good home training and their labor and social relations, generally, tend to be organized in harmony with the traditions of the group to which such parent belongs. But in the second and the third generations of mixture, the tendency is toward emancipation from the control of both ancestral groups and toward the development of control by the mixed-blood group itself. But it has not had sufficient time to develop adequate standards on the basis of experience or to make them effective in practice. Later generations may be expected to enjoy the advantage of a progressive reorganization involving not only the particular mixed-blood group but also the larger society with which it is more and more identified.

If the above hypothesis is found to be valid it may appear that the superior steadiness and dependability of Chinese-Hawaiians over Caucasian-Hawaiians is explainable by reference to their different position in the cycle of social change. One may doubt whether the evidence indicates any superiority of inborn traits on the part of the Chinese-Hawaiians.

It is always difficult to characterize a people without some falsification. The individuals are not all alike. One tries to say what is true or nearly true of large numbers, thus failing to characterize the important few who are unusual. Readers commonly expect this and so they are not much deceived if the writer is reasonably careful to say what he means concerning a group that is fairly homogeneous in its physical traits and in its social character. But the part-Hawaiian group is more heterogeneous than the Hawaiian, or any of the immigrant peoples. On the side of biological heredity, some are nearly pure Hawaiians, some are mainly of Chinese, Portuguese, British, German or American ancestry. A few claim descent from four or five races,—Hawaiian, Chinese, Nordic, Jew, Negro. Nevertheless, most of them are at least one quarter and not over three quarters of Hawaiian blood. Considering adults only, the ancestry on the other side is mainly Chinese or white. Those of the more complex mixture are mainly children. On the side of social relations there is a similar diversity. Some part-Hawaiians find their society mainly among the Hawaiians and others mainly among the Chinese, the Portuguese or the *haole*. There is a tendency among some to create a social life within the group, but never do they draw strict social lines on the basis of race. On the side of education, there are some who have studied successfully in leading American universities, while at the other extreme, there are those who, in their intellectual outlook, are more like their Hawaiian ancestors of a hundred years ago. But the majority have made definite progress in the direction of Occidental culture. They are found in nearly all occupations, but, relatively to whites and Chinese, there are fewer in professional work or in the more responsible positions in business. In the case of pretty large numbers there is a considerable inheritance of the old Hawaiian traditions. Largely they work with modern tools and they use the foods and clothing materials made available by modern commerce, but in relation to things affected with sentiment they may be much like Hawaiians.

A volume in preparation by Dr. E. B. Reuter and Dr. Doris Lorden presents evidence to show that in many respects the Chinese-Hawaiians are intermediate between the Chinese and the Hawaiians. In school the Chinese-Hawaiians are retarded more than the Chinese, less than the Hawaiians. They enter the professions in smaller proportion than the Chinese, in larger than the Hawaiian. Mental tests made by Dr. Porteus [1] and others show a similar intermediacy of Asiatic-Hawaiians. Physical measurements made by Louis R. Sullivan indicate a similar intermediacy as to physical traits such as stature, growth curves of children, nose height, nose width and head length.[2] The evidence of this fact of intermediacy of the mixed-bloods as between the parental races in relation to physical traits, behavior, and certain sorts of achievement is so unquestioned that it is not necessary to labor the point. It may be added that commonly it is not merely the statistical average that is intermediate, but also, that the individuals are personally intermediate. If some of the half-and-half Caucasian-Hawaiians were as dark as Hawaiians and others as light as Caucasians the average complexion would be intermediate. This is, approximately, what one might expect if color were a Mendelian unit trait. But commonly the color of each person is intermediate and also his behavior and social status. But if one is seven-eighths Hawaiian he might pass as pure Hawaiian or, if seven-eighths white, as pure white. A few of the nearly pure white part-Hawaiians live on the mainland where they are regarded as white and marry freely among whites, some of them in families of great social prominence.

Probably the Chinese-Hawaiians are, on the average, a

---

[1] Stanley D. Porteus, *Race and Social Differences in Performance Tests.*
[2] Clark Wissler, *Growth of Children in Hawaii, Based on Observations by Louis R. Sullivan.*

little darker complexioned than the Caucasian-Hawaiians, but this does not serve for identification since the actual color depends mainly on the fractional mixture and on the complexion of the Hawaiian ancestors who differed among themselves. Nevertheless one who is widely acquainted can, on the basis of appearance, classify the part-Hawaiians, if they are not over half of Hawaiian ancestry, as part-Chinese or part-white and be right most of the time unless they have both Chinese and white ancestry. Commonly, one depends more on the name than on appearance. But even this method is not always dependable because of names like Lee and Young which may be either Chinese or English.

Practically, the somewhat doubtful line of social cleavage as between Chinese-Hawaiians and Caucasian-Hawaiians is drawn on the basis of family connection. That is, they are identified as to race mixture by their relationship to a known Chinese or white father or grandfather. When most of the part-Hawaiians come to be of a generation more remote from their non-Hawaiian ancestors, this means of identification will not serve so well. The difficulty of classification is still further increased by the fact that several thousand are of a three-way mixture, having Caucasian, Chinese and Hawaiian ancestry and this group is growing more rapidly than any other.

The facts relating to the intermediate character of the part-Hawaiians on the side of color, features and body build seem to be pretty adequately explained by reference to the theories of the more recent genetic studies. Their intermediacy in relation to behavior and social status is more problematic. Are they intermediate mainly because of intermediacy in relation to native intellectual capacity and to temperamental traits or is their intermediacy mainly a consequence of their special cultural inheritance and their social status?

If one's interest is merely in the present situation the way one answers this question may be of very little importance.

The important thing is merely that they are intermediate. But looking forward one or two hundred years, the theory one holds assumes considerable importance. This is because changes in tradition may take place more rapidly than changes in the biologically conditioned race traits.

The white people of Hawaii are, for the most part, superior to the Hawaiians in certain ways. They are able to make adjustments to the requirements of a modern commercial society more promptly and more satisfactorily than the Hawaiians. Doubtless one could add that the Hawaiians are superior in certain ways. But they are living in a commercialized society and the sorts of superiority that do not help in that kind of society are, for the time being, less important as affecting status. Similarly the white people are superior to the Caucasian-Hawaiian mixed bloods who, in turn are superior to the Hawaiian. Now if one believes that the inferiority of the mixed-bloods as compared with the Caucasians is a consequence, merely, of a failure to participate fully in the traditions of the white people he will tend to look for the disappearance of such inferiority in the course of a few generations as the mixed-bloods gradually become possessed of different traditions. On the other hand, if one believes that this inferiority of the mixed-bloods is due mainly to the inheritance of certain traits that belong to the genetic constitution of Hawaiians, he will forecast a continuation of such inferiority into the indefinitely remote future.

The one theory is favorable to an attitude of indifference toward interracial marriage and race-mixture. One might even consider an early amalgamation of races to be desirable. At worst, any defect on the side of social efficiency is regarded as a matter of only temporary concern. Any social problems resulting from race-mixture are to be solved by education and by the creation of a system of social relationships of such a character as to facilitate the reorganization of the peoples on the basis of a common culture.

The other theory supports the policies advocated by the racial purists. When once the race considered to be superior has lost its purity there is no help excepting through the slow processes of biological evolution. Some believe that selection in our time is dysgenic and that, consequently, this hope is unwarranted unless there shall be some fundamental change in the social conditions affecting survival. If one accepts this theory he tends to look upon race mixture as an evil of the first magnitude. It is the chief duty of a superior race to preserve its purity and, to this end, social policies should be such as to prevent interracial marriage. Since legalized interracial marriage involves social approval of such a union, it is favorable to a complete amalgamation involving both or all races concerned. It is, therefore, more to be deplored than mixture through illegitimate unions, which under certain conditions may be held to have merit in that it tends to improve the race considered to be inferior while it maintains the purity of the superior.

The questions at issue are considered under three heads: (1) The social status of the mixed-bloods; (2) their cultural inheritance; and (3) their biological inheritance.

There are some regions of the world such as India where the mixed-bloods are looked down upon by people of both parent races and where there is a ritualistic code which symbolizes for the mixed-bloods social inferiority. There are a good many regions like Java, Jamaica and the United States where the mixed-bloods have an intermediate status, where they constitute a class inferior to the one parent race and superior to the other. In a few places such as Hawaii the mixed-bloods have a status of equality with both parent races in the sense that there is professed a doctrine of equality and that the social code symbolizes equality. Such equality is not a matter of measurement, but of law and of ideal. It is not that the members of one race are, on the average, held to be equal to the other or to the mixed-blood descendants in stature, in native intellectual capacity, or in the temperamental qualities that are important from the standpoint of achievement, but that individuals of equally good character and ability have a right to equal opportunity irrespective of race. The code calls for equal educational opportunities, equal political rights and recognition according to personal achievement.

An unpublished study by Dr. Everett V. Stonequist develops the idea that the way the mixed-bloods carry on in any society is largely determined by the character of their status. Where their status is inferior to that of both parental races their lot is a hard one. They have little opportunity to rise and hence little incentive to try. They seem, through lack of character and ability, to justify the status inflicted upon them.

Where the mixed-bloods have an intermediate social status there may be, among them, considerable discontent because they are denied the status of the race of superior power, but there may also be considerable compensation in the superior status they enjoy as compared with the other parent race. They may be more or less segregated from both parent races but recognized by the dominant parent race as superior to the other, enjoying a preferred political and economic status. If, however, they are not so recognized by the race of superior prestige they may be, nevertheless, the leaders of the race of inferior status. In any case the intermediate status conditions their personality traits in such a way as to seem to justify the status they actually have.

Where the social code is based on the ideal of racial equality there is, so far as the law and the ideal are concerned, no intermediate position for the mixed-bloods. The code gives them a status of equality with both parent races and their personality traits are correspondingly conditioned. A person's success is a matter depending on his individual ability and character rather than on his racial classification. Here too the outcome seems to justify the social policy in that individuals of all groups tend to rise or fall according to personal merit.

The experience of the part-Hawaiians is consistent with this theory and it supports the view that the behavior and the social efficiency of mixed-bloods are determined largely by their social status. They have equal political rights and some of them win political positions of importance. They have equal educational opportunities and some win honors in school and college. They have equal occupational privileges and some rise to positions of dignity in the professions and in business.

The favorable status of the part-Hawaiians was possible because of the special character of the code of race relations. Since race relations were based on the principle of equality, interracial marriage was not socially condemned. Hawaiian women and white and Chinese men of high standing in their respective racial groups intermarried and did not sacrifice their standing by so doing. Because of the character and prominence of some of the men and women who thus inter-married the pattern of social relations involving their children symbolized a social status that was not reduced on account of their mixed ancestry. It is a matter of great importance that a large proportion of the mixed-bloods recognized as such were born in wedlock.

Some of the part-Hawaiians are the inheritors of considerable wealth. In some cases the inheritance came from the business enterprise of the non-Hawaiian father and in some cases from lands belonging to the Hawaiian mother. The social position of these wealthy part-Hawaiian families tends to maintain the general status of part-Hawaiians by what it symbolizes.

The good status of part-Hawaiians is maintained also by their record of achievement. One might refer to the wife of one of the later kings, to a former manager of the Inter-Island Steamship Company, to a lawyer of high standing, to a former pastor of a large Protestant church in Honolulu, to the one-time treasurer and also to the auditor of the Territory, to at least two former mayors of Honolulu, to a young man, half-Hawaiian, who won honors at Yale, and to many others who have had the ability and the opportunity to win positions of trust, responsibility and honor.

It is not the contention that the part-Hawaiians are successful in as high proportions as the whites and the Hawaiian-born Chinese in respect to these sorts of achievement. Not so large a proportion of part-Hawaiians reach the positions of power and dignity. The main point is that when a part-Hawaiian has the ability and the sort of interest that make such achievement possible he is not, on account of inferiority of status, denied the opportunity necessary to the winning of a legitimate success. The fact that considerable numbers of well-known men, and also some women, do win such success is an important factor in the maintenance of the good social status of part-Hawaiians. A good status tends to perpetuate itself through its influence on achievement.

But it is not wholly a matter of social status. Traditional culture is an important factor. When, through contacts between two peoples, there comes into existence a mixed-blood population, it is probable that the mixed-bloods will inherit something of both traditions, but the way the traditions are shared is variable. In Hawaii a good many white men and also a good many Chinese tried to bring up their mixed-blood children as much as possible according to their own culture and in some cases they met with a considerable degree of success. But the success was more certain in relation to matters of technique than in relation to matters greatly affected with the sentiment which are more important from the standpoint of values and interests. For example, a certain Hawaiian woman who married an Englishman about 60 years ago was proud of her husband and was disposed to co-operate with him in the education of their children. The children were taught to live pretty much like white people and they spoke English almost without accent. They wore clothing such as white people wore and acquired white skills of many sorts. They were Christians. But through community and home contacts the children all came under the influence of the old Hawaiian traditions which are so important in the conditioning of attitude and behavior at the deeper level. These partly westernized mixed-bloods inherited old Hawaiian beliefs,—superstitions we call them. Their fears and interests were largely conditioned by Hawaiian tradition. If the mother and the Hawaiian relatives thus educated them unintentionally they did it all the more effectively for that reason.

During the nineteenth century the part-Hawaiians tended to marry back into the Hawaiian race more than in the opposite direction. More commonly the social influences affecting the second generation of mixture were predominantly Hawaiian. For most part-Hawaiians the subtle influence of sentiment is mainly on the side of the old Hawaiian tradition. Even in the case of some part-Hawaiians who are mainly of white blood, there is a tendency to draw heavily on old Hawaiian tradition for the enrichment of emotional experience although they utilize pretty freely the things that belong to Caucasian technique.

Because of the persistence of so much that belongs to the old Hawaiian culture, so much of what is affected with sentiment and hence important in relation to values and interests, the part-Hawaiians are not so well able to compete successfully in a modern industrial society as are white people or the Chinese. Because of the lessening influence of the old Hawaiian tradition and because of an increasing participation in the traditions of western civilization, they are more successful than the Hawaiians. If one will explore a little further into the cultural backgrounds of the Chinese, on the one hand, and of the Hawaiians, on the other, the reasons for this view will appear.

The Chinese have been familiar with a competitive commercial economy for thousands of years and they have lived under conditions that have emphasized the importance of family solidarity even to an extent that involved a certain callousness toward the rest of the world. Much of the time persistent toil, extreme thrift and determination to hold on to the family possessions were the conditions of survival. Naturally the mores developed in harmony with the way of life. Values of all sorts were involved and the organization and direction of interests tended to be according to practical needs. Likewise there was a development of skills. Business technique is so far freed from the mores that a Chinese man may go far in a course that is financially advantageous without doing violence to his moral standards and without jeopardizing his social status. At the same time some of their standards, such as those relating to partnership responsibilities and to the payment of debts, are favorable to business success. Moreover the Chinese know the value of property as a means to power and prestige. One might say their whole outlook on life is greatly affected by the special circumstances under which they have lived and by their organization of economic and social relations and that the outcome is favorable to success in a competitive commercial economy. Largely the business efficiency of the Chinese and also their success in the various fields of intellectual endeavor is a consequence of their traditions.

The nature of the Chinese superiority can be stated more specifically. In general, they work more steadily and they are more persistent in seeking opportunity. They are more thrifty and they keep such property as they acquire, not being easily cheated or easily induced to give disproportionately to ability. In business they are shrewd, buying at the most favorable prices and selling at about the price that yields the maximum net profit. They extend credit judiciously and usually they are able to collect. They enjoy good credit because they meet their own financial obligations faithfully. They are good at planning in the sense that when they make far-reaching plans they are likely to be workable,—

they are consistent with the realities of the situation and there is internal consistency. They carry out plans with more vigor and persistence than do the Hawaiians. More generally, one might say that the Chinese scheme of life is one in which the acquisition and possession of property is important. They are more interested in earning in order to save, in saving in order to invest, in investing in order to secure a profit, in holding, in spending and in giving in order to enhance prestige. Attention is directed more steadily and consistently toward economic success and consequently they know much more about the business situation and are superior in their business technique.

Associated with such superiorities are corresponding types of behavior in school. Chinese children attend school more regularly, they win higher grades and there is less retardation. More of them complete high school and college courses and prepare for the professions. There is a more systematic effort in the home to bring up the children so that they will possess definite standards,—standards of courtesy, standards of taste, moral standards and standards of achievement. If a youth does unusually well in school he reflects honor on the whole family including ancestors and he is himself honored by the family. Among the Chinese there is a very strong traditional motivation to intellectual endeavor.

When the Chinese first came to Hawaii their social status was low. They were inferior to white foreigners in wealth and in education and they were inferior to the Hawaiians in numbers. Brought from China mainly to serve their white employers in a humble capacity, they lacked the prestige that they might otherwise have possessed on account of the character of their culture. On account of the brevity of their residence in Hawaii there had been comparatively little development of understanding and of sympathetic attitudes such as existed between whites and Hawaiians. For these reasons the early Chinese were, in spite of such virtues as they possessed, looked down upon by both whites and

Hawaiians, sometimes with contemptuous indifference and sometimes with fear and hatred.

But in so far as their status was in consequence of their being newcomers it was bound to undergo change. Gradually they made their adjustment to the situation, first winning an improved economic status and finally an improved status in relation to matters more affected with sentiment. In the earlier stages of their economic advancement there were sharp conflicts and there was a development of fear and hatred, but when an accommodation had been worked out, unfriendly sentiment tended to disappear and now it is the fashion to speak of the Chinese in terms of respect and appreciation. While there has been no corresponding development of ill will toward the Hawaiians the fact of their inferiority to the Chinese and their descendants in respect to the matters heretofore mentioned is recognized by both the Chinese and the Hawaiians and also by all the other peoples.

On the other hand, the old Hawaiians had no commerce and probably not even barter, unless mutual present making can be called barter. In the making of presents one does not avow his desire for a return present as motive nor is there any haggling about conditions. The return gift is made as a moral obligation, not in consequence of a contract. Such gift exchange belongs to the mores. The introduction of profit seeking trade by foreigners brought from the outside world certain commodities that the Hawaiians greatly desired and hence they, under the tutelage of foreigners, did gradually enter upon a commercial economy. But, so far, they have not brought their mores into full harmony with such an economy.

Commonly they do not feel that it is important to keep on working when they have enough for the near future. They are willing to work some of the time for a living, but they want to take some time to live,—some time for activities that are valued for their own sake. These enjoyable activities are not postponed to old age nor until one has acquired wealth. A man takes his enjoyment as he goes, even at the risk of not being financially prepared for an emergency.

To an old-fashioned Hawaiian, the practices of the hard boiled business man are immoral. One would be ashamed to drive a hard bargain based on another man's necessity, to refuse credit to a man in need merely because payment is improbable, to embarrass a debtor by urging payment, or to avow so much interest in making money or in keeping it when others are in need. Commonly an Hawaiian man cannot make even a start toward economic competence because if he accumulates some property his moral standards compel him to share it with his needy relatives and friends. They "eat him out." Occasionally there is the exception that proves the rule. I am acquainted with an Hawaiian man of considerable business ability who is accumulating property, but he is not well liked by his people. As a leader of a group of about a dozen Hawaiians he was helping them to acquire larger incomes than they had known before, but he lost his position as leader. He urged the men to work too much of the time and they thought that he was grasping. His conduct was not determined by motives that were respectable from the standpoint of the old moral order. From the standpoint of a different and, possibly, superior sort of society, the Hawaiian traits, so far as conditioned by the old ethical standards, may appear to be superior to those of the Chinese. Superiority is relative to the situation.

The outstanding traits of the Hawaiians today, i.e., the traits that are more or less peculiar to them and important from the standpoint of social efficiency in the existing society do not seem to be wholly and perhaps not even mainly a direct consequence of the special character of their old culture, but rather, of the fact that the old culture was disorganized through the coming of foreigners. To the student who is reasonably free from ethnocentric tendencies it is apparent that the old Hawaiian culture was fairly well related to the practical situation of an isolated people living under the conditions that prevailed in Hawaii. Their social organization was so effective that the Islands were able to support a comparatively dense population. Their economic system was, for a stone age culture, one of much merit. Their mores served as a basis for such planning as was necessary in a society governed mainly by tradition. In the execution of their plans they often showed a resoluteness of character that is impressive. In general their conduct seems to have had adequate motivation, and sentiment found artistic expression. Life was interesting and attention was directed toward actual interests in a fairly adequate way. In short, there was an effective social organization and, for individuals, a reasonably consistent life organization, this being mainly a matter of tradition but, in part, a matter of planning,—of creative activity.

In so far as Hawaiian culture and Hawaiian personality traits were modified in consequence of contacts with foreigners who came to the Islands, such modification does not appear to have been the consequence of forcing by the foreigners. There was comparatively little harshness or cruelty and the more important modifications were not intentional on either side. Important was the subtle change in values that resulted from the new contacts. The technical superiorities of the foreigners,—superior weapons and tools, superior ships, superior clothing materials, superior means of communication, superior trading methods and superior skills of many sorts—were impressive. They gave the foreigner prestige. Prestige always has something in it akin to magic. To the extent that the Hawaiians acquired the new techniques and used them effectively for their purposes they placed themselves upon a plane of equality with the foreigners. But to the extent that their efforts to acquire such techniques fell short of success or to the extent that they were inhibited even from making trial, there was prestige for the foreigner. He was a wonder-worker, a superior sort of being not capable of being wholly understood. The important thing in relation to the undermining of the old Hawaiian moral order was the desire on the part of Hawaiians for the comforts, the power and the prestige that might be expected to result from the acquisition of the new foreign goods and skills. It was this interest in foreign things that induced them to modify their conduct in ways that were contrary to the old mores. Through the violation of their old standards the old moral order was undermined so that it became less and less effective for the regulation of personal behavior and of social relations. Customs, interests, standards, values were disorganized. The most sacred things of the old tradition came to be held doubtfully and while they continued to affect practical behavior they did not regulate it adequately.

One consequence of the inferiority of technique on the part of the Hawaiian was that he lost the initiative to foreigners. He lost confidence in himself,—in his ability to carry out plans, especially plans of a far reaching character. The whole situation was being modified so much by foreigners that Hawaiian ideology did not serve for effective planning. Such plans as were made might be impracticable under the new conditions and hence the making of plans was discouraged. One tended to wait for something to turn up or for a white man of prestige to take the initiative and the responsibility.

Under these conditions affecting outlook and motivation, the Hawaiian has tended to become a man of short vision, unsure purpose, irresolute, vacillating, irresponsible, —a man without clearly defined standards relating to the modern sort of situation. He tends to live from day to day without a consistent scheme of life. His activities are disorganized and he acquires the more effective technique needed in a modern society only at a slow rate.

It is clear that, in relation to success in a modern commercial society, the Chinese have an important advantage over the Hawaiians on the side of tradition. Partly it is a matter of technique, but the disadvantage of the Hawaiians is in consequence mainly of a defect of interest and of self-confidence. So subtly are these defects related to the old primitive mores and to their disorganization that they are not greatly subject to modification through rationally devised plans. They must just be outgrown and, for this, time is required. There is no record in world history of a people of a stone age culture achieving an advanced commercial civilization in a century or two. The Nordic race used two thousand years.

The important fact from the standpoint of the present interest is that the part-Hawaiians are, in relation to tradition, intermediate between the parent races. They benefit from the better adapted culture of the white and the Chinese ancestors and they suffer from the persistence of features of the old Hawaiian culture and from its disorganization. Some of them seem to be just like Hawaiians and, at the other extreme, there are some who appear to have the efficiency of the whites or the Chinese, but the great majority are intermediate. For the most part the darker complexioned are the more like the Hawaiians, but personal acquaintance and case studies suggest that the cause is to be found largely on the social side. For example, a part-Hawaiian young man of only one-fourth Hawaiian blood was brought up, not by his non-Hawaiian father, but by his mother's people in a rural community in which the population was largely Hawaiian. Later in life he enjoyed excellent educational advantages, but in his ideas, interest and attitudes he impresses one as being predominantly Hawaiian. On the other hand a young woman, with a larger share of Hawaiian ancestry, lived with her white grandmother when she was a little girl. While her color is evidence of the Hawaiian ancestry, her mannerisms, her thinking and her efficient ways make one feel that she is white.

Some of the facts relating to physical traits are known. For example, the death rates of the Hawaiians are exceptionally high, age considered, and those of part-Hawaiians are lower, but above those of whites or Chinese. Probably their intermediate position in respect to death rates is in part a matter of biological heredity. The isolation of the Islands had protected the Hawaiians from several infectious diseases to which they are now exposed. They have not been subjected to the long selective action of such diseases and presumably they are not so well immunized as the peoples who have come from less isolated regions.

But, on the other hand, the bad conditions under which they live are important. They no longer have the dietetic habits of the olden time and they use the foods made available by modern commerce unwisely. The old Hawaiian theory as to the causes of disease survives, more or less, even to the present day and, because of it, the Hawaiians and, to some extent, the part-Hawaiians, tend to expose themselves needlessly to diseases that are highly fatal to them. For example, the families of lepers often try to conceal the presence of the disease and to keep the afflicted one at home. The physicians and nurses who serve in connection with public health agencies find it hard to persuade tubercular patients to go to the hospital in the early stages of the disease while there is a good prospect for recovery. Hawaiian mothers give their babies very inferior care and in some cases they seem to be afraid to co-operate with the public health agencies. Evidently the high death rates of Hawaiians and the intermediate rates of the part-Hawaiians are in large measure the consequence of bad living conditions and incompetency in the care of infants and the sick.

But whatever the present character of the part-Hawaiians it is certain not to be permanent. If in the past they have, as a group, been weak because few in number, they will gain the strength that comes from superior numbers. If they have been weak because of the lack of traditions and morale, they will gain these in time and through experience. It is one thing to know that one belongs to a weak minority group of uncertain status and quite another to have a sense of power and responsibility such as is possible only to a member of a powerful group. Zest for power, initiative and resoluteness come with the exercise of authority. When the part-Hawaiians shall have become a majority, when they shall be bound together by common loyalties, when they shall exercise authority, they will manifest the personality traits natural to their situation.

CHAPTER XVIII

CULTURAL DIFFUSION AND INTELLIGENCE

THE assimilation of peoples is, in one of its aspects, a diffusion of knowledge and skill. To the extent that two peoples living together in the one community are separated by differences in knowledge, one of them being confined within the limits imposed by its special state of ignorance, assimilation is incomplete. Not only must there be common information and common skills of the more directly practical sorts but, even more important, is a common language and a common technique for the acquisition and organization of information. There must be, in a sense, intellectual parity if there is to be full assimilation.

There are at least two distinguishable meanings of the word "intelligence." On the one hand intelligence is information and the technique through which information is secured, organized and utilized. In this sense intelligence is something that is acquired through experience and study. It is social inheritance. It is education. On the other hand intelligence is inborn capacity to acquire, organize and utilize information. It is a matter of biological inheritance. If a person is superior as to inborn ability he acquires the information more easily and he may go farther in the acquisition of techniques of the more difficult sort, but it remains true that such techniques have to be acquired. A man must learn a language before he can speak it and he cannot perform the operations of calculus until he has studied the higher mathematics.

It may or may not be true that a people of inferior knowledge is also a people of inferior native capacity. But whether it is true or not it will seem to be true. A person's actual ability to learn depends not only on his inborn traits, but also on his organization of interests and on what he believes about himself and the world. For example, the white people in some sections of the mountainous South lived under conditions of such isolation and without schooling for so long a time that their illiteracy and associated traits became traditional. When some of them came to a northern state they escaped from their traditions pretty slowly. I have known boys, the grandchildren of some of the poor whites of "Old Virginny," who, after four or five years in a northern country school, were unable to read. They were not stupid, if one may judge from their behavior at play or when rabbit hunting, but reading did not run in their families. They did not believe that they could learn to read and in support of this disbelief they had the fact that their fathers and mothers and older brothers and sisters did not learn. And besides they did not care to learn. The teachers began by teaching the names of the letters of the alphabet without doing anything to reveal to the child what it was all about so that it could seem to be worth while. If the home did not do this it was not done. Their folks did not read, and why should they bother about learning? They suffered from no serious native defect, but from the character of their family traditions. I knew two or three of these supposedly stupid children who, when they were ten or twelve years old, seemed to undergo some change of attitude. I do not know the history of their experiences well enough to know what was cause and what was effect, but certain things were associated. They discovered that they could learn, they made rapid progress in learning and they manifested an interest in the opinions of the teacher and of the children of literate parents. They began to conform to standards that did not belong to their families and their social status was improved. In any case there was ambition, an intellectual awakening, and their activities seemed to be more a matter of purpose and plan. Something like this happens frequently, one might say, typically, when a people of inferior intelligence, that is, of inferior knowledge and skill, comes into contact with a culturally more advanced people.

Under the contact conditions heretofore mentioned, there is for the people of inferior culture, an incentive to acquire some part of the superior culture and this part belongs typically to the field of knowledge and technology, but the incentive may be much less effective than a man of the superior culture would suppose. If a new sort of tool is desired it must be because it is obviously useful toward the accomplishment of existing purposes and useful on the basis of existing skill or skill that can be acquired without too much difficulty or delay. The Hawaiians were eager to secure from Captain Cook little pieces of iron fashioned somewhat like cold chisels. They were able to use these in place of sharpened stone tools in operations with which they were familiar and the advantages were easily seen. They could use them with little or no special training.

This double requirement affecting the desirability of superior knowledge by a people of inferior culture may serve to reduce very greatly the incentives to learning, and especially is this true if there is great cultural disparity. The purposes of a people are such as develop within the limits of their existing culture and a good many of the contrivances of civilization would serve no purpose among peoples of less advanced technical development. Of what use would a knowledge of calculus be to an Indian hunter and what would an Hawaiian fisherman do with a knowledge of algebra? Where there is no obvious value there is no incentive. Only as the people of a simpler culture come to participate in the more complex activities of modern life and only as they discharge functions of a more specialized and technical sort can incentives become adequate in relation to the more specialized sorts of knowledge.

The difficulties involved in the acquisition of knowledge and technique depend largely on the existing cultural inheritance. Where there is a rich cultural inheritance and where children are customarily provided with opportunities and incentives for the acquisition of a considerable body of common knowledge it requires only a little of the spirit of adventure to carry a youth some distance beyond this and far enough to bring him within sight of attractive occupational opportunities that call for specialized knowledge. When a young man belongs to a family and to a social class where college education is traditional he does not necessarily give evidence of unusual intellectual ability or of highly disciplined character when he prepares himself for a profession. But among preliterate or even illiterate peoples the social inheritance is of a different character. Customary home education does not reveal the value of the school disciplines. When an Oklahoma Indian severed his tribal connection, learned a trade, came to Honolulu and carried on successfully as a steamfitter he was doing a very difficult thing and was giving evidence of superior intelligence and character.

In the case of peoples who are not far from the cultural level of the preliterate and precommercial peoples there may be especial and very serious obstacles to their acculturation on account of sentiment of a religious character. Some of the matters involved may be purely secular to the more advanced people while for the less advanced they belong to the mores, that is, they involve things that are held to be sacred. For example there is, near Honolulu, a little river whose lower course near the sea is navigable for small craft. But access to the sea was made difficult by a big stone in midstream and near its mouth. The owner of a glass-bottomed boat designed to carry tourists wished to have the stone removed. He employed a few Hawaiian men and took them to the spot. But they were horrified. The stone was sacred. They feared the wrath of a god and refused to do the work. The owner then employed some Japanese but the Hawaiians communicated their fears to them and they also refused to do the work. Not until the owner found white men to do the work did he succeed in having the stone removed. Now the Hawaiians are more fully convinced than ever that they were right for, soon after the stone was removed, the god sent a storm so that the mouth of the stream was wholly obstructed by a huge bank of sand. This so worried the boat owner who needed an income to pay his debt that after a time he became insane. One may not show disrespect to the gods and escape their wrath. What was merely a secular matter to white people was related to a sacred tradition of the Hawaiians.

The rate at which a people acquires the special knowledge and skills of a people of more advanced cultural development depends largely on its existing state of culture. If there is great disparity of culture the people will advance slowly and they will seem to be stupid, but if there is only a moderate degree of cultural difference, progress will be more rapid and the people will be considered to be more intelligent and, no matter whether it is true or not, they will be considered to have an innate superiority by biological inheritance. The present interest relates to the intellectual response of the various immigrant peoples to the situation as it exists in Hawaii.

It is probable that the raw experience of life that is not controlled by outsiders in the interest of education is educationally the most valuable of all for those who are in a position to utilize it. If one has the appropriate background of tradition and of personal achievement he turns not only the favorable but also the seemingly unfavorable circumstances to good use. But this raw experience of life does not so well serve the need of some others. What serves as an inspiring challenge to one man saps the courage of another. Not everyone is qualified to win honors in the University of Hard Knocks.

Social relations in Hawaii have been affected by its code of racial equality in a way favorable to the creation of incentives for considerable numbers of men in all the racial groups. In the absence of sharp lines of racial discrimination a man of any race might hope, on the basis of personal merit, to reach a position of a desirable sort. Enough men belonging to all of the racial groups have won so high a degree of success that many others have been stimulated to try. But in this respect the races have not all responded in the same way.

When people live in a stable society where a man's role is determined almost wholly by his family relationship and by tradition all normal men may seem to be pretty much alike. If there are important differences in their inborn capabilities the circumstances do not furnish opportunities or the testing experiences through which such differences are manifested in full measure. But when, in a foreign land, cultural diffusion is going on, there appears to be a wide variability of intelligence. Not only are original differences revealed more fully, but the varying sorts of experience and incentive affect individuals in manifold ways. New knowledge and new skills in a changing social situation and one characterized by much freedom are highly significant of opportunity. Power and status come to be determined by competition rather than by tradition and a premium is placed on intelligence and the courage of adventure.

Pretty generally the immigrants who came to Hawaii have become more intelligent than their relatives who remained in the old home villages. It is not only that they have acquired more knowledge and especially more knowledge of the things that relate to the activities of a more complex economic system but that there has been a shift in the organization of interests, that is, in the attitude toward new information. Their outlook tends to be more individualistic and a man has a greater sense of freedom to plan his own career. He can do this planning so much the better if he is better informed and he tends to value the information correspondingly. While the various individuals respond to the influences of the new culture contacts in greatly differing degrees there is a pretty general response so that it is practically true to say that the peoples in general are more intelligent because of migration.

So fundamentally are these things related to the personality of individuals that they are manifested in the unconscious mannerisms and in the facial expression of immigrants and especially of their children. I spent some time in a certain rural district in Japan from which many of the Hawaiian Japanese had come. I met uncles, aunts and cousins of those I had known in Hawaii, was entertained in the homes of some of them, and visited the schools attended by their children. One could not fail to be impressed with two things: (1) The greater degree to which the Japanese who remained in their old village homes have their behavior regulated by tradition. Commonly, the sons follow the occupations of the fathers and, most of them being farmers, they cultivate the identical fields that were cultivated by their ancestors and with almost identical methods. The ritual of respect, that is, the traditional ways of being polite, are known to all and are everywhere observed. The moral control is so effective that, on an island with a population of about sixty thousand, there is no jail because there is no need of one. (2) The mannerisms of the old country villagers seemed to an American to show a constraint not characteristic of the Hawaiian Japanese. There was less self-assertiveness, less expression of individuality. Their faces, especially those of girls, were less expressive. It seemed that the numerous little muscles about the eyes and the mouth that have to do with facial expression were relatively undeveloped from lack of use. These were the impressions one had from people in the mass and they were confirmed by a comparison of cousins. Under the freer conditions of Hawaiian life where personal incentives are more adequate and where there is a decided tendency toward a more individualistic outlook on life there has been a modification of mannerisms and facial expression in a direction that may be called American. It is not so much that they have been taught by Americans or that they have copied from Americans as it is that they have been exposed to a social situation of a certain sort and that there has been an inner transformation natural to the situation and a corresponding outward expression.

The intellectual awakening incident to migration and acculturation is made manifest in all the activities of life but it is especially observable in economic and educational activities and sometimes in political. In America the immigrants often practice a thrift that their neighbors regard as parsimony. Of foreign-born farmers there has been a saying, "They sell what they can sell. What they can't sell they feed to the pigs and what the pigs won't eat they themselves eat." Commonly, it is said that such people have a low standard of living. But this is not true. Their saving is for a purpose. The purpose is forward looking and it involves the welfare of the family on the side of social status as well as on the side of comfort and physical efficiency. They sacrifice immediate comforts and, may be, physical efficiency, in order to achieve a higher standard of living which is not defined mainly in terms of food and shelter. For example, about seventy-five years ago a poor immigrant woman, a widow, worked as a servant to support and educate her little son. We can only infer what her standard of living was, but the boy grew up to be a man and, after achieving distinction in a profession, he was made Governor of his state, possibly the most distinguished governor that his state has ever had. One does not rise above his standards. The immigrant standard of living is one that involves the future position of his family in society. It may be more important to be respected than to be well fed.

Through industry and thrift the immigrant secures the means wherewith to buy a home, or he may establish himself in business. In the latter case he must plan an enterprise to be conducted under conditions that are not wholly familiar and he has every incentive to execute his plans successfully. There is no other sort of experience as valuable educationally as planning and executing one's own far-reaching plans.

If one uses the statistics relating to the economic progress of an immigrant people or relative to their response to educational opportunity and if he considers such data against a background of old country life he will, if he has insight, find plenty of evidence of an intellectual transformation. In reading the following tables relating to savings bank deposits and the value of real estate and of personal property assessed for purposes of taxation, one should see what such savings and property mean to the rank and file of the people. In the earlier years of their residence some immigrants expect to use their savings to re-establish themselves back in their former homes, but in a better position than they had formerly. Their average bank deposits do not grow large because the older and larger accounts are being closed all the time as some of the men return to their old village homes. While such men continue to be dominated by old country interests they have little concern about their status in Hawaii. Not only do they undergo physical privation, but, what is more significant, they refuse to expend their income in ways that would tend to raise their local status. They hold single-minded to their original purpose, that of acquiring as soon as possible, the funds necessary to the improvement of their status when they return to the old home village. But even at this stage they are acquiring an individualistic point of view in that they purpose not to accept their traditional status in their home land, but to achieve a better, and they are working to a plan. A good many, on their return, find that their aspirations and habits of thought have been so modified by five or ten or twenty years of life in Hawaii that they do not fit well into the life of the old home village and they are not as happy as they had expected to be.

From a certain district in Japan about six thousand people or one-tenth of the population came to Hawaii. Including their Hawaiian born children, a third as many have returned to their old home villages and, with their Hawaiian savings, they have competed for the ownership of land. They have been willing to pay for the land more than it is worth for productive purposes because its ownership confers a higher social status. This competition has raised the price of land to about twice that of similar grades of land in districts from which there was no important emigration. But most of the returned men who were interviewed seemed to be more or less disappointed and they expressed regret that they were not living in Hawaii. This was, in part, because Hawaiian wages are higher, but some spoke of their preference for the freer life of Hawaii. To them the Japanese forms of social intercourse had become burdensome. The returned Filipinos have had a similar experience. Mr. Kilmer O. Moe has interviewed many who, after a return to the Philippines, have come to Hawaii a second time. For the most part they were disappointed with their old home villages. Some had tried to introduce new ways of living which were not appreciated by their old friends.

But no matter what the attitude of new immigrants, they, if they remain a long time, gradually develop an interest in the things that are important to their comfort and their status in Hawaii. This is true, more particularly, of the family population. The children have only a second-hand knowledge of the old country. Hawaii is their native land,

and for them sentiment is organized around the local situation that conditions their own experience. Through the influence of the children the parents undergo an almost unobserved change of attitude which they sometimes discover when they return to Japan. If immigrants postpone their return until their children are grown and married they find it very difficult to leave Hawaii.

The subtle change that takes place in the mind of a man as he comes to feel that Hawaii is his home affects the use of his income and savings. At first he spends almost nothing for the sake of its effect on the mind of others. But, by the time his Hawaiian born sons and daughters are old enough to marry, the question of local status is highly important and the family income is expended largely for things that may be expected to enhance prestige. Household furniture, education, gifts to friends on such occasions as weddings and birth festivities come to be important. Of outstanding importance is the daughter's wedding outfit for which the family pays much more than Americans would regard as reasonable.

The savings are, for a time, regarded as a means to an improved status in the old home. A man sends his savings home or, may be, he deposits them in a savings bank so that he can take them with him when he returns. But after a somewhat extended residence in Hawaii he may use his savings to pay for a home or he may invest them in a business enterprise. While such investments do not prevent the return of the immigrant, they do serve to postpone such return. They tend to raise his status not only in the immigrant community but, generally, among all the peoples so that life in Hawaii is increasingly satisfying.

In Tables XXXIX–XLIV information is given relative to the ownership of property by the native Hawaiians and by four of the larger immigrant groups. There has been a little Korean property credited to the Chinese and a little Porto Rican and Spanish credited to the Portuguese. This

TABLE XXXIX

Savings Bank Deposits

	MAIN PERIOD OF IMMIGRATION	NUMBER OF ACCOUNTS TO 1000 POPULATION		
		1911	1920	1930
Hawaiian and part-Hawaiian		70	235	415
Portuguese	1878–1886*	105	222	454
Chinese	1876–1897	49	203	612
Japanese	1898–1924*	9	126	401
Filipino	1915–1931*			235

* Considerable numbers of immigrants have come at dates other than those mentioned but so many of them have left Hawaii that the present population owes little to them.

TABLE XL

Average deposits per capita of population

	1911	1920	1930
Hawaiian and part-Hawaiian	$ 7	$19	$ 36
Portuguese	43	88	116
Chinese	15	57	150
Japanese	1	18	64
Filipino			49

TABLE XLI

Number of Persons Owning Assessed Personal Property to 1000 Population

	1911	1920	1930
Hawaiians and part-Hawaiians	50	46	67
Portuguese	50	70	96
Chinese	85	76	104
Japanese	28	35	56
Filipino			1.5

TABLE XLII

Average Per Capita Value of Personal Property, as Assessed, for the Entire Population

	1911	1920	1930
Hawaiian and part-Hawaiian	$34	$57	$64
Portuguese	21	36	56
Chinese	99	95	99
Japanese	21	50	57
Filipino			1.17

TABLE XLIII

Number of Persons Owning Real Estate to 1000 Population

	1911	1920	1930
Hawaiian and part-Hawaiian	151	152	161
Portuguese	73	102	143
Chinese	23	53	113
Japanese	5	9	22
Filipino			.7

TABLE XLIV

Average Per Capita Assessed Value of Real Estate for the Entire Population

	1911	1920	1930
Hawaiian and part-Hawaiian	$290	$400	$468
Portuguese	108	236	545
Chinese	41	176	570
Japanese	3	20	92
Filipino			1.67

was inconsequential before 1920 and not of much consequence since that time. Much personal property is unassessed and the valuations are not necessarily accurate for either real or personal property. Bank deposits are not taxable and they are not assessed. The period of immigration is given for the main body of immigrants now resident or represented by children so that the relation of length of residence to economic achievement may be seen.

The generally rising numbers of bank depositors and the increasing per capita amounts deposited are easily seen for all five groups. In part this is the consequence of an increase of banking facilities in the country districts and of a growing familiarity with and confidence in banks as places for the safe keeping of money, but, beyond this, there is evidence that interests, financial and other, tend more and more to center in Hawaii.

Similarly one may note the increasing numbers of all immigrant peoples who own personal property and real estate and the rising per capita values. An interesting comparison may be made between the Portuguese and the Chinese both of whom immigrated almost wholly in the nineteenth century. The Portuguese, in 1911, had on the average more money in the savings banks than the Chinese and, if one looks to the real estate table, it is evident that they were saving, typically, in order to buy homes. But the Chinese owned more personal property,—a larger proportion were owners and the average value was higher. This points to a different pattern of behavior. The Chinese more commonly used their savings in business and the Portuguese in securing homes. But in 1930 they were not so dissimilar and, not very strange, the average per capita values, all three sorts of property combined, were, for the two groups, not far from equal.

The smaller figures for the Japanese are reasonable, considering the later date of their coming. Probably when they have relatively as many grandchildren as the Portuguese have now they will make an equally good showing as to property ownership. The Filipinos, as the latest comers, have only recently achieved the distinction of separate classification and only in the case of bank deposits are the numbers of much significance.

The more stable position of the Hawaiians and part-Hawaiians in relation to the total value of property owned is significant of two things. They are not immigrants. Their old culture, still somewhat influential, was not so well adapted to the needs of a modern economic organization as that of the immigrants. Because of their continued residence in the land of their old traditions they require more time for the necessary reorganization.

The way the various immigrant peoples have responded to educational opportunities in Hawaii is also significant of the intellectual awakening. The figures of school attendance for the lower grades may indicate little as to the attitudes of either parents or children, for attendance is compulsory for children under 15 years of age and over 6. But the attendance of boys and girls 16 and 17 years of age is free from compulsion and is, therefore, indicative of the personal attitudes of parents and children and also of group sentiment.

The increase of percentage of school attendance for children of this age, in the twenty years, 1910–1930, is attributable to three things. (1) On account of the multiplication of high schools, the movement of population and the improvement of transportation, more of the people are located conveniently for high school attendance. (2) On account of improving economic conditions there have been more parents who could afford to keep their children in school to this age. (3) But most important has been a growing popular appreciation of schooling and the figures of the following table are mainly significant of the developing attitude of the various peoples.

At the earlier dates there was a considerable amount of retardation in the grades, mainly on account of the fact that large numbers entered the primary grade without a speaking knowledge of English. On account of this retardation most of the children of this age were, in 1910, in the elementary grades but by 1930 they were mainly in high school.

The response of the various immigrant groups to educational opportunity in Hawaii has been influenced in part by their old country ideas and customs and in part by their situation in Hawaii, the local situation gaining in importance as time passes. The Chinese, the Japanese and the Korean had ancient traditions highly favorable to schooling. Many of them, especially of the Chinese, had enjoyed very limited advantages in the old country, but under the easier economic conditions prevailing in Hawaii they were quick to give their sons superior educational advantages and, when they discovered that an educated daughter could earn more than an unschooled one they gave their daughters the advantages also. Considering the incomes of most Chinese families it is easy to see that the advantages were often secured at the cost of considerable privation and that for many the acquisition of property was delayed considerably in the interest of education. How the fathers and mothers did toil and skimp in order to give the oldest boy his chance, and how he helped his younger brothers and sisters! The solidarity of the Chinese family made Chinese educational policy possible.

The Portuguese did not at first send their children to school much beyond the age of compulsory attendance and the truant officer who enforced the compulsory attendance law was responsible for a considerable part of the actual attendance. The more common view among the Portuguese was that the children did not really need schooling unless as a part of the training for special occupational activities and that it was a mark of refinement and of a superior status to which the children of most common laborers could not reasonably aspire. They wanted their children to help to earn their own living. Since the families tended to be of about maximum size these earnings seemed to be necessary if the family was to achieve its ambition for an owned home or for the ownership of a business enterprise.

One may compare the Chinese and the Portuguese educationally. The one represents a culture based on Asiatic familialism, the other a culture based on European Christianity. The Chinese sought to educate their children in order that they might contribute the more effectively to the improvement of the family status. The Portuguese sought first an improved economic status in order that they might enjoy such advantages including education as money may secure. Perhaps the most important comment is that both policies, as gradually modified in the light of experience, seem to be working fairly well. Apparently immigrants in their effort to improve their status are not confined to a single pattern of procedure. They may start, each utilizing the old country traditions, and, provided they work out a fairly consistent organization of behavior, they will succeed. The test is internal consistency and consistency with the situation, not conformity to some outsider's theory. Learning from experience, both Chinese and Portuguese have modified their educational practice in the direction required by the situation. For a while a disproportionately large number of the Chinese high school graduates were expecting to secure types of positions that are associated with a superior social status and their educational programs were dominated by such expectations. Only after suffering some disillusionment are their educational practices and occupational plans coming to be more consistent with the realities of the situation. The Portuguese, who at first seemed to regard schooling as not very important, except for the few, are coming to realize that boys and girls in general are able to benefit from good educational advantages and there is a corresponding change in their practice. The Chinese and the Portuguese do not differ so much in educational practice as they did a generation ago.

Comparatively few of the school children were foreign born at any of these dates. The important distinction is between the older children of immigrants and the younger, and between the children and the grandchildren. Naturally the older children, born soon after the immigration of their parents, were, in their childhood, less exposed to the influences that tend to Americanize the family. They entered school commonly without a speaking knowledge of English and with comparatively little evidence of cultural change toward the American pattern. But their younger brothers and sisters born, maybe, twenty years later grew up in a different social environment and in one that was characterized by wider social contacts. Commonly the younger children had learned to speak English, in a way, from their older brothers and sisters and from their playmates and, in other respects, they were more like American children. Later the grandchildren of the immigrants entered school at a more advanced stage of acculturation. Associated with these various stages of acculturation there have been corresponding types of attitude and behavior.

The interest at this point relates to intelligence, that is, to the growing individualism of the peoples and to the redirection of their interests as reflected in the school attendance of children 16 and 17 years of age. When there is an increase in personal ambition and in self-confidence there is, under Hawaiian conditions, a higher appreciation of schooling. In the public mind success in school has been associated with later success in the world of affairs. When there is a rising interest in education the children not only come to know more about the things taught by the schools, but also seem to have superior learning ability. When a boy, with or without the encouragement of his family, seeks to rise to a status above that of his family he makes and executes plans. In this way he gains in ability and after a time, it seems as if his superiority were native born.

For example, about fifty years ago a Portuguese boy of school age was required by his parents to work in the cane field. If he had superior intellectual ability it was not manifest. Physically he was inferior in the sense that his strength and endurance were insufficient for the work. In order to permit him to rest and recuperate after an illness the parents sent him to school for a time. Here he attracted the attention of the teacher because of his superior learning ability. The parents were persuaded to let him remain in school with the result that he became a successful member of one of the learned professions. Recently his son won a professional degree from one of the leading American universities and people are predicting for him a brilliant career. The importance of the achievements of exceptional men of this kind comes largely from the fact that they are widely known and that comparatively large numbers of Portuguese young men are, on account of them, acquiring new interests and a new confidence in their ability.

From Table XLV one may see that in 1930 the majority

of the native born Portuguese were of native parentage. The 16 and 17 year old children were, for the most part, the grandchildren of immigrants. Even among the Chinese there were some grandchildren, but as for the Japanese and those of still more recent immigration the boys and girls of this age were of the first native born generation and in many

TABLE XLV

	The Native-Born Popula-tion, 1930, According to Nativity of Parents. Number to 1000		Number attending school To 1000 Children 16 and 17 Years of Age		
	Both Parents Native Born	One or Both Parents For-eign Born	1910	1920	1930
Hawaiian and part-Hawaiian . . .	884	116	458	488	482
"Other Caucasian" .	717	283	638	640	702
Portuguese	613	387	155	258	356
Chinese	232	768	573	691	767
Spanish	190	810	65	197	218
Japanese	47	953	299	351	543
Porto Rican* . . .	44	956	84	93	152
Korean	29	971	531	654	680
Filipino*		1000	217	176	242
	379	621	359	401	514

* Estimated. For the present purpose, persons born in the Philippines or in Porto Rico are considered to be foreign born.

cases among the Japanese and Filipinos they were the older children of the family.

Two things in this table deserve attention. There is the relatively high percentage of school attendance among the 16 and 17 year old children of the Chinese, the Japanese, and the Koreans. But for all groups there is a rising rate of attendance that runs parallel to their economic progress and their acculturation. The main purpose of the table is to show the rising rates of voluntary school attendance in the upper grades for all immigrant groups as they more and more respond to the intellectual stimulus of the Hawaiian social environment.

In education there is always a need that the actual situation be considered. There are the children of various types of ability and ambition representing homes of the different economic classes and of the varied racial and cultural backgrounds and they all need to be educated with considerable reference to their probable future places in society. One of the functions of the schools is to assist pupils so to educate themselves that they may find an appropriate place in society. This is true at least in a society where one's place is not fixed by his family relationship. Then there is the economic, political and general social organization of society that for the time being seems to set pretty rigid limits to the total opportunity and to condition the distribution of such opportunity in an important way. Everywhere family connection and property inheritance are important factors affecting opportunity. But superior ability and character always tend to overcome such handicaps as may inhere in the social organization. Some people born in humble homes rise to positions of distinction while some born to superior privilege move in an opposite direction.

On account of certain factors in the historic situation it has come about in Hawaii that most of the positions of highest power and dignity have been occupied by white men of American and Northern European ancestry,—the *haole*. While the other peoples suffered from the disadvantages incident to inferior education the right of the *haole* to hold the positions of leadership and authority was not seriously questioned. But as the other peoples benefit from education the reasons for this arrangement are less obvious. Gradually, for forty years, the Chinese and Portuguese have been achieving a better position than they had at first and by 1920 they were so well established in their better positions that no one questioned the reasonableness of their ambition. But the Japanese had immigrated more recently and, in

1920, they were nearer the beginning of their struggle for status. Because of Hawaii's approach towards a condition of closed resources many of the Japanese had remained longer, on the average, at about the level of their first position than had the Chinese or Portuguese, so that their struggle for status came more as a surprise. Since they were competing for positions that others held and desired, a conflict was imminent and the more rapidly they advanced their position the more active the probable conflict. Moreover the Japanese were much more numerous than any other people in Hawaii and hence such readjustments as they might make would tend more to disturb the general economic situation. The Koreans were making a similar effort at the same time and with comparable success, but they were so few that no one paid much attention to them.

The pattern of the Japanese struggle for status was much like that of the Chinese and it involved an extensive use of the schools. The high schools, which at an earlier period had only a few Japanese now began to receive them in large numbers and the attitude of the Japanese community was such as to warrant the expectation that the movement would continue for a considerable time.

For a time there appeared to be considerable local sentiment favorable to a school policy designed to prevent the further increase of high school attendance and to make the privilege of high school attendance more highly competitive on the basis of scholarship and other things supposed to indicate whether children are able to benefit from schooling at the high school age or not. But such policies as were actually adopted did not, apparently, tend to reduce attendance. If only 80 per cent of the graduates of the intermediate schools (grades 7, 8, and 9) were admissible to high school it is probable that only a few who would have attended high school were denied the privilege. Possibly the denial of the privilege to some caused it to be more highly valued by those who were recommended. In any case, during the four years of the new policy, 1930–34, the public high school attendance of Japanese pupils increased by 43 per cent and that of all others by 26 per cent.

The problem involved in the excessive ambition of the children of immigrants is primarily a problem for the children and their parents. If the sons of Japanese and other immigrants were aspiring to positions that, for most, were unattainable, there was no other school so well able to make them understand this as the school of experience. A good many white-collared white men attempted to point out to them the disadvantages of aiming at a "white-collared" position and the advantages of jobs of the humbler sort but they were unable to escape the suspicions of the advised. Why was not such advice used by the people who gave it? But experience did teach the lesson. For the most part, boys, after aspiring to high position, took such jobs as they could get, and if the older boys had indulged in extravagant expectations their younger brothers were more likely to keep their feet on the ground.

Perhaps, too, the wise people feared too much on account of the high aspirations of these young people. On the whole, is it not a good thing that youth shall have visions that are beyond realization? Others besides Rabbi Ben Ezra might say:

> "For thence,—a paradox
> Which comforts while it mocks,—
> Shall life succeed in that it seems to fail:
> What I aspired to be,
> And was not, comforts me:
> A brute I might have been, but would not sink i' the scale."

The discovery of attainable and worthy goals of endeavor and the making and carrying out of suitable plans is the most important discipline of life. If men generally were to write their confessions, it would be surprising how many, after aspiring greatly, have made a virtue of second or third choice —and, doing this, have lived usefully and happily. With age, too, there may come another sort of change in purpose. Purpose may be defined in a less narrow personal way. One may say with America's elder statesman that, "The longer I live the more clearly do I see that life consists not in what one tries to get but in what he is able to do." What seems to be needed mainly is a social situation of such a character as to facilitate a reorganization of purpose when the time for this comes in the experience of boys and men.

The schools of Hawaii, public and private, have played an important part in the creation of the existing system of race relations. Except for the work of the schools in teaching the children of all races to speak and to read a common language, it is certain that the interracial economic and social relations would have been less favorable to the development of a sense of equality. The ability of Hawaiians to hold positions of dignity and honor in the government after the passing of the old chiefly rule was a result largely of the education received in mission and public schools. Through education, sons of the immigrants are rising to leadership in business, in the professions and in politics. If in the beginning the schools represented ideals held by outsiders and more or less imposed on the common people they are becoming more and more an expression of general public sentiment. If, in the past, the schools have contributed much to the creation of the developing mores of racial equality they are more and more coming to be supported by and controlled by the doctrines and sentiments that they have helped to create.

In a similar way one might consider the political activities of immigrant peoples as an expression of the changed intellectual outlook due to migration. Political influence like property or education may be a means to the readjustment of status. As the immigrants are individualized, that is, freed from their old-country mores, and as they come to feel strongly about their status in the new land and to reflect about their situation, their actual problems are intellectually stated. A proper statement of a problem suggests a method of solution and, to an uncommon extent, the immigrant peoples do seek a solution and they utilize for this purpose the resources supplied by their savings, their study and their political participation. In doing this they acquire more knowledge than do their cousins in the old country and they become more alert intellectually. The contact of cultures serves as an intellectual stimulus and through the resulting intellectual activities there is a fusion of cultures and an achievement toward intellectual parity.

Chapter XIX

SOCIAL DISORGANIZATION AND PERSONALITY

PERSONALITY, as defined by Park and Burgess, is "the sum and organization of those traits which determine the role of the individual in the group." A man has personality possibilities other than those that are actually realized. The actually developed personality traits of a man are what they are largely because of the character of the society to which he belongs.

For the present purpose two main types and two subtypes may be distinguished. Men tend to be either conformists or non-conformists. The conformist type is exemplified by the man who follows custom and observes the standards of his people faithfully. In a stable social organization he enjoys a high degree of security and he has the satisfactions that come from participation in family and community life on the basis of universally approved standards. The conformist lacks initiative but he is dependable. His conduct creates no problems and if there were problems he could not solve them.

The non-conformist is the man who is, in considerable measure, freed from the influence of traditional standards and codes. In a society that is undergoing great change it happens that some of the old ways are ill adapted to the situation and there is a call for invention. If the non-conformist violates the old code intelligently and in the interest of worth while and well organized practical ends he is a man of creative personality. The function of the non-conformist is to contribute to the working out of a new and consistent organization of behavior when the old organization does not work well. At best, he is the competent experimenter.

But there are other non-conformists who, lacking the support of universally approved standards, merely drift according to impulse and circumstance. They do not have a consistent system of interests and their activities are disorganized in the sense that they defeat each other.

Among non-conformists, very few are of the extreme types, but all may be placed accordingly as they are more or less near one extreme or the other. There are only a few great prophets, philosophers, poets, artists and lawgivers, but there are a good many who are of creative personality in the sense that they manage to go through a period of fundamental social reconstruction in fairly good order, modifying their practices in a successful way to meet changing conditions. Not very many become willing dependents or habitual criminals, but there are many who are so lacking in ability to solve their problems that their condition is below what would be considered as reasonably satisfactory.

The changes that societies undergo result from a variety of causes. There may be inventions or discoveries within a group and they may be sufficient to bring about social changes of some importance. But commonly such inventions accumulate slowly and their application is still more delayed so that the social changes so generated are gradual and the problems of readjustment that are faced at any one time are not very difficult. They tend to be solved by the trial and error method without there being much awareness of the problem. But if, through contacts with other peoples, the accumulated inventions and discoveries of a long period are suddenly made available for the use of a people, the rate of social change is accelerated and problems of social reconstruction of a more insistent character arise. But if such contacts are merely through commerce, travel and foreign study, there is still a moderation in the speed ɔf social change. Foreign culture, if inconsistent with tradition, tends to be rejected or to win acceptance only when there is further invention to make it consistent and this involves considerable retardation and a lessening of the intensity of the conflict.

But when, through extensive migration, permanent relations of an increasingly intimate character are established between two peoples who differ considerably in culture, the whole situation is set for social change at high speed for one or both peoples and the problems incident thereto clamor for solution. In such case the slow and muddling method of trial and error is inadequate. The problems tend to be stated intellectually and when they are stated adequately, rationally devised experiments may contribute to their solution.

Man is essentially a social being and this means that the activities of the various individuals in a community must be of such a character that, taken together, they constitute a reasonably consistent whole. The individual is not independent, but is under the necessity of playing a part in his group. When each individual knows what to expect of all the others, that is, when each acts in conformity with the general expectation, the parts do combine into a reasonably consistent whole unless there is some disturbing factor introduced from the outside. So important has this been through the ages of man's evolution that it may be supposed that he is biologically conditioned toward conformity. In fact, most men find it very difficult to do things that run counter to what is generally expected of them. The non-conformist is exceptional and needs to be explained. Men tend to conform except when on account of the intrusion of some new factor into the situation old customs fail to work successfully. This occurs typically and in its most exaggerated form when two peoples of widely differing traditions establish permanent social relations. When two such peoples begin to become one people it is certain that their diverse traditions do not combine into a consistent whole. In such a case the problem may be solved practically through an adequate modification of the customs and standards of one people so that they will be consistent with those of the other people whose customs may undergo comparatively little change. Or it may be solved through more nearly equal changes in both organizations.

Sometimes immigrants to America are able to segregate themselves and to live more or less apart from other people for a time and, in such cases, they live mainly according to their old country customs and standards. But, soon or late, some of them or of their children come into more intimate relations with outsiders so that they belong not only to the immigrant group but also to the American community. Participating intimately in the social life of two peoples they are, to use Dr. Park's term, "marginal men." They are marginal not only in respect to their position in relation to two peoples and two cultures but also in respect to their personality traits. Owing loyalty to two peoples and two more or less conflicting organizations of custom and standard, the marginal man does not yield full allegiance to either. The conflict inherent in his situation gives rise to an inner conflict and behavior tends to be disorganized. One cannot conform to the requirements of one set of standards without violating the other. Some things that he does run contrary to other things. Some of his purposes tend to defeat other purposes.

In such a situation a man does not drift to a safe harbor. He must solve his problem in the sense of working out a reasonably consistent organization of behavior involving his relations to both peoples or he tends to become a problem case. If he is a man of superior intelligence and disciplined character he has every incentive to seek a solution. A premium is placed on straight thinking and resolute action and the man who succeeds in solving his problem in this way wins a good status for himself and contributes to

278 INTERRACIAL MARRIAGE IN HAWAII

the progress of civilization. But one may fail because of overwhelming circumstance or because of defects of intelligence and character and, at the worst, the defeated may fall to a level where effort ceases. Hence the wide range of difference in personality among immigrants. Some may remain conformists for life, some become men of high creative personality, some are merely disorganized, and many are of intermediate types.

The rate at which an immigrant group in America is assimilated is related to social disorganization and to the development of marginal personality types in two ways. During the earlier period of immigrant residence in America, the more rapidly the acculturation goes on the greater the social disorganization. For the first generation or two, an immigrant people makes a better record in relation to dependency and delinquency if its progress toward Americanization is at a moderate pace, that is, if its circumstances are such that, at first, it is able to maintain order mainly on the basis of old-country moral standards. But a certain weakening of old-country tradition is inevitable and the group in time becomes culturally hybrid. At this stage there is at least a moderate degree of social disorganization even under the most favorable conditions and, from this time on, the further steps in acculturation tend to simplify the problems of adjustment on the basis of full participation in the life of the larger community. If progress is too slow in the later stages of acculturation it tends to prolong the period of disorganization needlessly and there may be a development of ill will in the rest of the community.

In its more general character immigrant experience in Hawaii conforms to the regular pattern. But the special conditions in Hawaii and in Continental United States differ in certain respects. Two of these call for attention. Culturally and racially Hawaii's immigrants have differed more from white Americans than most European immigrants to the mainland have. If the Americanization of the English or the Swedes on the mainland is accomplished rather promptly and without serious conflict it is not so much a tribute to America's ability to assimilate peoples of unlike culture as it is to the essential similarity of cultures to begin with. If the amalgamation of the descendants of the English, Irish and Germans who lived in colonial Pennsylvania is pretty fully accomplished it is no evidence of freedom from race prejudice since all were regarded as members of the same race.

In some parts of the United States there is much disorganization among Negroes and mulattoes. They are not slaves and they are struggling for a status of equality, but they have not fully escaped from the influence of sentiment, habits and doctrines that were associated with slavery. In other parts of the country there are non-whites who do not belong to the slave tradition but their status is affected by the traditional race doctrines and attitudes of the American people and these were largely a consequence of slavery. Where race differences are involved it is expected that assimilation will go on more slowly, that conflict of a more intense and persistent character will be found and that there will be a corresponding development of the more extreme types of personality.

So far as original differences are concerned, acculturation and amalgamation meet with greater obstacles in Hawaii than they ordinarily do on the mainland. Under the circumstances it might be supposed that in Hawaii there would be a more prolonged and intense cultural conflict and that, in the absence of assimilation or of a sufficiently prompt assimilation, there would be an extreme degree of social and personal disorganization and that it would persist for so long a time as to permit of a development of the more extreme types of marginal personality. But this is not the case. While one may discover the evidences of disorganization in Hawaii it is less extensive than in some areas of white immigration on the mainland. While there are individuals who occupy a marginal social position, the conflict inherent in their situation tends to be less intense than such conflicts are in some other sections of the country. While there are individuals who have developed the special types of personality that are expected they do not tend to be of the more extreme sort. Often enough a man seems to occupy a marginal position only for a certain period of his life after which he seems to have his social relations so consistently organized that there are no important conflicts or problems.

Race relations in Hawaii are not complicated by a historical background of slavery. If the problems incident to the assimilation of Hawaii's immigrant peoples are not just like those of the mainland in relation to white immigrants, neither are they like those of the mainland in relation to the various non-white peoples. Because of the difference in historic background Hawaii has a different system of race relations. The most important difference is found in the social code symbolizing racial equality and in the doctrines that support this code. Since the code was not developed in the interest of racial purity it permits of a freedom of social relations among the races that is not known on the mainland. This freedom is extremely important from the standpoint of acculturation at the level that is greatly affected with sentiment and hence important to the development of personality traits.

One may find in Hawaii men and women who possess the various sorts of personality traits that are expected in the case of immigrants and it would not be true if one were to say that racial differences do not affect the social relations that have to do with the development of personality. But the racial factor is not as important as it is on the mainland, because it does not serve in equal measure to limit the social contacts through which assimilation is achieved. In so far as the personality traits of the people of an immigrant group, including descendants, are affected by the rapidity or the slowness of assimilation the position of the Chinese or the Japanese in Hawaii is not just like that of the Germans or the Norwegians on the mainland, nor yet is it like that of the Chinese and the Japanese in California. There are on the mainland some white immigrant groups such as the French Canadians in New England and the Jews in New York who seem to be more retarded in respect to their assimilation, length of residence considered, than are the Chinese or Japanese in Hawaii. The Chinese in Hawaii are being amalgamated through intermarriage more rapidly than the Jews of New York and the Japanese, more rapidly than the French Canadians of New England. Not color difference or original culture difference but the code affecting social relations is the important thing.

There is in Hawaii a considerable difference among the various immigrant groups from the standpoint of conditions affecting the rate of acculturation, the degree of social and personal disorganization and the effect of this on personality traits. The ability of immigrants to effect a satisfactory adjustment in Hawaii, especially in Honolulu City, is affected by the cultural advancement of their homeland. Peoples like the Chinese, the Japanese, the Koreans and the Portuguese who were familiar with a pretty well developed commercial economy in their respective native lands find it easier to make and carry out business plans than do such peoples as the Filipinos or the Porto Ricans who are less advanced in commercial development.

Religion also is a factor. If the religion is not unfavorable to success in ordinary secular activities and if religious sentiment is strong enough to maintain the traditional institutions of worship, the immigrants tend to be bound together into a moral whole. That is, the conduct of such immigrants tends to be organized mainly on the basis of their old traditions. Their acculturation proceeds more slowly and hence they are exposed to less jeopardy of disorganization in the earlier period of their residence.

The numerical size of an immigrant group is also a matter of considerable importance. A large group such as the Japanese finds it easier to maintain its distinctive institutions and hence to maintain social control on the basis of the old traditions than does a small group such as the Korean or the Porto Rican. Groups like the Chinese and the Portuguese occupy an intermediate position.

Very important for at least a half century is the sex ratio of an immigrant group. It seems that the immigrants from no country are able to maintain their standards unless they establish family life. If, for a long time, nearly all of the men live outside the family relationship there is a moral slump and later, when wives are secured, it is necessary to create or re-create standards. The Chinese are having an experience like this and also the Koreans. The Filipinos, also subjected to the influence of an abnormal sex ratio, have not as yet made a full response because of the brevity of their residence and because they are still on the plantations mainly.

Since the various immigrant peoples did not all come at the same time they are not all at the same stage in the general process of assimilation. For example, the Chinese and the Portuguese are, excepting for the people over fifty years of age, mainly of Hawaiian birth and education while most of the Filipinos have arrived within the last ten or twelve years and the Hawaiian born are mainly children under fifteen years of age. The Japanese occupy an intermediate position and so also the Koreans and Porto Ricans.

The length of residence is a matter of especial importance in Hawaii because of the character of movement within the Territory. Nearly all of the immigrants spend the earlier years of their residence on the plantations, but as time goes on they have tended to leave the plantations and considerable numbers have come to Honolulu. Data relative to this movement are to be found in Chapter IV.

Because of the character of plantation life the immigrants

are not greatly exposed to disorganizing influences and their acculturation goes on more slowly than in the city. On the plantations there is an organization of activities that is planned by the manager. The plans are made mainly from the standpoint of efficiency in production, but they affect the whole life of the plantation workers and their families. On the economic side there is an extreme degree of stability and security. Commonly laborers remain on one plantation during the whole period of their plantation service. On the sugar cane plantations there is no seasonal unemployment. Men are not laid off and rarely is a man discharged. The wages have been high enough to permit of some savings by laborers and most laborers do in fact accumulate savings. Such savings are significant not only of ability to meet an emergency but also of planning and of effective execution. The man who has the sense of success that comes from the possession of a small but gradually increasing savings deposit tends to exercise self-control and to observe traditional standards.

With income so dependable and adequate in relation to living costs the workers are able to plan their expenditures untroubled by irregularities and uncertainties of income, and most of them are able to do this pretty well on the basis of their traditional economy. If a Japanese mother, in order to maintain the status of the family, wants to provide her daughter with a wedding outfit according to old country custom only more expensive, she begins two or three years in advance, saving a little from each month's income and, now and then, buying some garment so that by the time the girl is old enough to marry she is suitably equipped. The important thing to be noted in this connection is the way the steady dependable income facilitates the purpose of the family to maintain good standing in the group by conformity to the *old* standards. Incidentally this causes the standards to persist. When people feel that they enjoy a pretty good status in their community they tend to be conservative as to conduct. They have something to lose if they violate the conventions.

Favoring the maintenance of old country customs and standards is the segregation of the different racial groups on the plantation. If the children of Japanese live in a neighborhood where all are Japanese they are the more easily disciplined by their parents. Such segregation tends to reduce conflict to a minimum. To some extent the plantation fosters and controls leisure time activities of the American type such as baseball, but this does not prevent the workers from creating other sorts of leisure time activities according to their traditional interests.

After an immigrant learns a few words of what is known as "pidgin" so that he can understand orders, he need not, on the plantation, make much further advance on the side of language. The language deficiencies of many immigrants tend to limit their social contacts and the lack of contacts means the lack of opportunity for acculturation. Nearly every special condition of city life tends more to facilitate the rate of acculturation. A much larger proportion of the city people of all races are Hawaiian born and since these have attended school they all speak English more or less adequately. Economic relations facilitate the acquisition of English and make it necessary. Social life is therefore less restricted.

While the larger immigrant peoples such as the Chinese, the Portuguese and the Japanese do show some tendency to segregate themselves in special areas in the city, the areas are too small to prevent association on the part of the children who may play in the streets, on vacant lots, or on playgrounds. When the more prosperous immigrants or their adult sons and daughters move out from the areas of first city settlement they go to unsegregated or less segregated areas. The multiplication of contacts due merely to the location of one's residence is associated with a more rapid acculturation. It is not merely that one does have contacts with the people of other racial groups but that one values such contacts and seeks to enlarge his social opportunities by conforming to the necessary standards.

Coming to the city involves, for a plantation worker, a radical change on the economic side. The worker must make his own economic adjustments. Maybe he goes into some independent enterprise, in which case he must make and execute his own plans. If he is especially capable he may win, in the city, a higher economic and social status than would be possible to him in the country. If he does do this he tends to create a marginal position for himself. Probably his success is not won by strictly traditional methods and, in his business relations, he comes into contact with people of races other than his own. Then there is the question of his family's social status. There is ambition for recognition not on the basis of the traditional family status but on the basis of successful achievement. Here is one type of marginal man.

But city life is more highly competitive and there are a good many who do not meet the requirements of the situation. They find only the low wage employments and they are irregularly employed. Sometimes even the small income is expended incompetently and the more incompetently because it is irregular and undependable. At the worst such people quit trying to earn their living and willingly depend on charitable agencies or, sometimes, on crime.

One of the ways through which city life tends to disorganize the people has to do with the location of residence. When a man is reasonably prosperous he tends to select his residence in a neighborhood of good repute and this means, for the members of the larger immigrant groups, a neighborhood in which the standards of his own people are maintained. But when a man falls below a certain level of economic success he may be under the necessity of living in the area of lowest rents. In such areas a family is pretty sure to meet the poorer families of other racial groups.

Poor people have extra difficulties. There is more incentive to stealing and other sorts of delinquency and less influence of neighborhood sentiment for the maintenance of standards. Poor people are not able to choose their associates or those of their children. The families of these polyglot areas tend to destroy, each the standards of the others. The families are already beginning to be disorganized when they move into such areas, but their living together hastens the process.

Dr. Lind [1] has pointed out that in Honolulu the dependents, juvenile delinquents and criminals are disproportionately numerous in these areas inhabited by the poor of all races. Here are marginal men of another sort.

The various peoples of Hawaii may be ranked according to the effectiveness of their social organization. Various sorts of social data such as those relating to divorce, juvenile delinquency, dependency and crime serve as indexes of disorganization. In general, the ranking is about the same no matter what sort of data are used and when there are differences they are commonly explainable by reference to some special factor in the situation that makes the data unrepresentative for one or more groups. In the following parallel columns seven groups are ranked, first, according to the prevalence of juvenile delinquency in the Territory and, secondly, according to the dependency in Honolulu County in 1934 as based on employment through the Federal Emergency Relief Administration.

It will be noted that the ranking of the first column, Table XLVI, is based on data for the whole Territory while that of the second relates only to Honolulu County where the population is, in higher proportion, urban. The high rating of the Filipinos in the second column is explained by reference to two facts. Most of the Filipinos live in the rural districts where there is little unemployment. Most of

---

[1] A. W. Lind, "Some Ecological Patterns of Social Disorganization in Honolulu," *American Journal of Sociology,* Sept. 1930.

TABLE XLVI
Indexes of Disorganization

AVERAGE ANNUAL NUMBER OF CASES OF JUVENILE DELINQUENCY TO 100,000 CHILDREN 10–17 YEARS OF AGE FOR THE TERRITORY FOR THE TWO YEARS 1929–1930	NUMBER OF PERSONS EMPLOYED BY THE FEDERAL EMERGENCY RELIEF ADMINISTRATION IN HONOLULU COUNTY IN NOVEMBER, 1934, TO EACH 1000 MEN 20–54 YEARS OF AGE AS ENUMERATED IN 1930
1. Japanese 341	1. Filipino 15
2. Chinese 812	2. Japanese 47
3. White* 1250	3. Chinese 57
4. Korean 1391	4. White† 66
5. Filipino 1664	5. Hawaiian and part-Hawaiian. 122
6. Hawaiian and part-Hawaiian 1701	6. Korean 133
7. Porto Rican 2810	7. Porto Rican 298

* On account of the character of the data it was necessary to combine the Hawaiians and part-Hawaiians into one group and also the Portuguese, Spanish and other Caucasians into one group, the white.

† For the purpose of this computation the men in military and naval service, were excluded from the male population 20–54 years of age.

TABLE XLVII
Distribution of Civilian Population in Three Districts

	CITY OF HONOLULU	RURAL PART OF HONOLULU COUNTY	ALL OTHER COUNTIES	TOTAL
	Per Cent	Per Cent	Per Cent	
Hawaiian	42.7	10.7	46.6	100
Caucasian-Hawaiian	52.9	7.8	39.3	100
Asiatic-Hawaiian .	40.1	14.3	45.6	100
Total above . .	45.0	10.7	44.3	100
Portuguese	44.5	7.7	47.8	100
Spanish	47.0	18.0	35.0	100
Other Caucasian . .	70.0	8.1	21.9	100
Total Caucasian .	56.4	8.0	35.6	100
Porto Rican . . .	34.2	12.6	53.2	100
Chinese	71.1	13.7	15.2	100
Japanese	33.9	15.8	50.3	100
Korean	40.3	23.9	35.8	100
Filipino	7.5	24.7	67.8	100
All others	56.4	16.2	27.4	100
Total	37.3	15.2	47.5	100

the dependent Filipinos in the city had been assisted by the Social Service Bureau to return to their native land. Aside from the Filipinos, the two rankings are much alike, the Japanese and the Chinese making the most favorable showing and the Porto Rican the least favorable. The superior showing of the Japanese over the Chinese is due largely to the rural location of more of the Japanese.

The Hawaiians, below the Koreans in the first column, are above them in the second. Some of the Hawaiians and part-Hawaiians of the city had come from the country somewhat recently and they had friends and relatives in the rural districts. When the depression came they were able to return to their friends and to live under conditions less affected by the depression and hence they have needed relief employment so much the less.

In general, it may be said that the degree to which any of the immigrant groups is disorganized is determined in large measure by the heretofore mentioned factors: (1) culture and social organization at time of immigration; (2) the size of the group; (3) the sex ratio; (4) length of residence in Hawaii; (5) location in Hawaii, rural or urban.

The Japanese, who make so favorable a showing, constitute the largest group and they were without much delay provided with wives from their homeland. They were, in the beginning, familiar with a commercial economy and, in Japan, the people are in an exceptional degree controlled by moral standards. Moreover, they dwell mainly in the rural districts. The fewness of Japanese in the prison and jails, the fewness of juvenile delinquents and paupers, is due mainly to a persistence of old country standards. While their acculturation goes on the more slowly, it seems probable that it will be accomplished with an exceptionally small moral slump.

In so far as the Chinese fail to make as favorable a showing as do the Japanese it may be explained by reference to three factors in their situation: (1) They have never been well provided with wives and hence there has been less influence from family life. (2) They are less numerous. (3) They are more concentrated in the city, 71 per cent of the Chinese being in Honolulu in 1930 as compared with 34 per cent of the Japanese.

The Filipinos mainly enjoy the advantage of a rural residence but more than any others in recent years they suffer from a highly abnormal sex ratio. Moreover, their cultural equipment is inferior from the standpoint of the problems of economic adjustment in the city.

The Portuguese have enjoyed an advantage even over the Japanese in that they came, for the most part, as families. But they were much less numerous and a larger proportion of them are exposed to the disorganizing influence of city life. Probably the culture of Christian Europe is less resistant to the disorganizing tendencies of life in Hawaii and elsewhere in America than are the cultures of China and of Japan based as they are on familialism. This means, of course, an earlier assimilation of Europeans but also a greater moral breakdown for the time being.

The people of Korea are believed to have been better organized about four centuries ago,—before the invasion of Korea by the Japanese general, Hideyoshi,—than they have been more recently. Despite the strength of patriotic sentiment the immigrants from Korea did not seem to be, at the beginning, as well organized as those from China or Japan. Moreover, they were few in number and their sex ratio was highly abnormal. The Koreans are found in Honolulu and vicinity in larger proportions than are the Japanese. In the rural districts the Koreans are commonly too few to create an organized social life, but in the city they show considerable ability to organize themselves and they are achieving a more effective moral control. Most of the Koreans profess the Christian religion. In changing almost en masse from one religion to another they were not able to avoid the hazards incident to such a course. Not only in relation to religion but also in language and in still other respects the Koreans are undergoing a more rapid acculturation than the Chinese or the Japanese and, under the circumstances, a higher degree of disorganization is to be expected.

The Porto Ricans are at a considerable disadvantage. The general social situation in Porto Rico prior to their departure was bad and there was an adverse selection of individuals. They are few in number and widely scattered. Except for such organization as is created by the plantations they have been almost unorganized. In the city they seem to be less able than the members of any other immigrant group to work out a satisfactory economic adjustment. More than others they are found in prison and jails and in an exceptionally high degree they depend on the agencies of charity. More than thirty years have passed since the main body of Porto Rican immigrants came to Hawaii, but even in Honolulu where more than a third of them reside they have made only a slight beginning toward the creation of an organized social life for themselves and they have made little progress toward a satisfactory status in relation to the rest of the community. Nevertheless, some families are gradually working out a better adjustment.

In so far as personality traits are associated with race mixture it is necessary to characterize several types in Hawaii. In general the Hawaiian code of race relations tends to make racial status a less important matter than it is elsewhere in the United States and hence the position of the mixed-bloods is not such as to result in the development of the more extreme marginal types of personality. This is true more particularly of the Caucasian-Hawaiian mixed-bloods. In Chapter VII, I have pointed out that this group is so large and that so many of them are several generations removed from the ancestors who founded their mixed-blood families that they are beginning to develop distinctive tradi-

tions of their own. They share in the traditions of their
Hawaiian ancestors and also in the traditions of their white
ancestors. It would be going too far to say that they have
succeeded in creating a new and successful organization of
life utilizing the better parts of both cultures, but they have
at least made some progress in that direction. A good many
individuals seem to have organized some of the ways of the
old Hawaiian life and some of the ways of white people into
a fairly consistent whole. Others fall below this level of
success, but under the rather easy conditions of life as experienced by Hawaiians and part-Hawaiians, they do not
necessarily suffer from any very serious personal disorganization. If one does not succeed at the haole level of ambition
one can fall back to the Hawaiian level and, maybe, without
a sense of disappointment. Since the Hawaiians enjoy a comfortable status and since they are sure to accept a part-
Hawaiian, giving him such status as his personal character
warrants, the latter need not worry. I have known a few
nearly pure white part-Hawaiians who have, for a time,
seemed to be in a marginal position and in the way of
becoming marginal men of the more pronounced type. But
in most cases they have, after a little, won the status they
wanted or something else that was acceptable so that they
became successful and contented. There is not enough race
prejudice in Hawaii, especially not enough manifested toward
part-Hawaiians, to serve as a strong stimulus. If life were
less happy there would be more hard thinking and there
would be more men of creative personality.

What has been said of the Caucasian-Hawaiians is in the
main true of the Chinese-Hawaiians excepting that this
group is smaller, younger and nearer the beginning of its
traditions. If a Chinese father is very anxious to have his
part-Hawaiian son recognized socially in the Chinese community he may place the youth in a difficult marginal position with the natural result so far as personality traits are
concerned.

Less is known about the status of the other sorts of mixed-bloods, mainly because they are so young. There are a few children of mixed European-Asiatic ancestry and there is some ground for believing that marginal men of the more characteristic type will be relatively more numerous among them. Doubtless, they will be ambitious for a superior status and it is still uncertain what status will be accorded them either by the white people or by the Asiatic. For a long time they will be too few to create a satisfactory social life for themselves and they may not be willing to accept status among the other mixed bloods. Under such conditions they may become definitely race conscious and marginal.

It is not difficult to find cases of marginal personality,—marginal in at least a moderate degree. One looks for men and women whose social relations have been out of the ordinary. There is the case of a Japanese girl who, as a small child, was adopted by a white family and now she has the mannerisms of white people and does not want to associate with the Japanese. A Chinese girl because of the church relationship of her mother associated mainly with white people and now does not quite fit in the society of Chinese young people. A half-Hawaiian woman of a well educated and refined type was brought up by white people and she grew up with very little contact with Hawaiians and part-Hawaiians. She married a white man who took her to California where his opportunities were restricted on account of his non-white wife. She came back to Hawaii "because," she said, "I was sorry for him." In color she is much like an Hawaiian, but she is American rather than Hawaiian in her way of thinking. She does not understand the Hawaiians. A brilliant Chinese-Hawaiian young man, educated in a school mainly attended by whites and accepted in white society in his school days, now associates by preference with whites rather than part-Hawaiians, but is neglected by his old school friends. There are numerous cases of men and women who have experienced a modification of social relationships on account of marriage outside of their own group. What impresses an American most is not the fact that such people manifest the traits of marginal personality but rather that so many have reached an accommodation that is so nearly satisfactory that such traits are manifested in only a moderate degree.

The behavior of comparatively large numbers of the people of all the larger racial groups is affected by their marginal position to such an extent that it is statistically evident. For example, the great majority of Chinese and Japanese who came to Hawaii were people of humble status in their old homes. They had enjoyed scanty educational advantages and, following the ancient custom of their peoples, they married young and had large families which they were able to support more adequately than would have been possible in Asia, but less adequately than accords with the American standard. Now the sons and daughters, born in Hawaii, have enjoyed good educational advantages extending through high school in many cases and frequently through college; they have come to appreciate the advantages that come from a higher plane of living and they are seeking a higher social status.

The statistical evidence of attitudes different from those of their parents is found in the data of school attendance showing unusual persistence in the struggle for education, in the data relating to marital condition which indicate a considerable postponement of marriage while the young people are improving their economic position and in the data of births, which indicate a marked fall in the size of families. Associated with these statistical trends is a weakening of sentiment for the family system of their ancestors, and an increasing tendency to desire an organization of family life consonant with a more individualistic outlook. Needless to say, these changes are accompanied by a certain amount of conflict within the family, the older people standing more for the maintenance of traditional ways and the young contending for the right of personal choice,—for a family organization of less solidarity and one more in harmony with an American outlook.

The experience of Hawaii is too young to furnish definite evidence relating to the later stages of acculturation on the part of the peoples of Oriental origin. While immigrants cannot speak the language of the country and while they differ much in respect to manners, customs and economic status the expectation on both sides is that contacts will not extend far beyond what are economically necessary. Hence, no one is surprised or disappointed at the absence of social relations of a more intimate character. But as the children and grandchildren of the immigrants acquire an adequate command of the English language, as they acquire a better economic status and as their education fits them for participation in social life of the larger community there will be disappointment and resentment unless there is a corresponding enlargement of social opportunity. If there is a considerable retardation in the development of such opportunity the tendency will be toward the production of more men of the marginal type. Men who are fit for some sort of social recognition and who aspire to it without being quite able to achieve it tend to be distinctly and, sometimes, aggressively marginal in personality.

If one were to assume that practice in relation to interracial contacts is almost if not quite unchangeable he would forecast a period of increasing conflict and of rising race consciousness as the more obvious grounds for social separateness disappear. If one has had no experience outside of a society which has a well defined social code whose function is to maintain race attitudes and practices unmodified, he will find it hard to believe that social opportunity for the grandsons and granddaughters of Orientals can possibly be enlarged in sufficient measure to prevent the development of serious conflict. But in Hawaii there is no such code, at least not among the people who have lived in the

Territory for a long time, and there is, therefore, a fairly constant but unobserved changing of attitude to correspond to the realities of the situation. The Chinese and the Japanese did not have their social events listed in the society columns of the newspapers fifteen years ago but they do now. In 1934 they did not get into the "Blue Book" but who knows what will happen in 1940?

On the whole, the outlook is for a retardation in the development of such opportunity sufficient to permit of a beginning of conflict and there will be a start toward the development of the traits of marginality for some, but, if Hawaii runs true to tradition, there will be, at a fairly early date, an accommodation in the direction of consistency with the doctrine of racial equality. The accommodation will mark the end of the conflict and, in so far as there are marginal men, they will be of the less extreme type. As the waters of the Pacific moderate temperature changes in Hawaii, the tradition of racial equality moderates the stresses incident to the assimilation of its peoples.

Chapter XX

RACE RELATIONS AND COMMUNAL MORALE

WHERE the people who constitute the population of any definite area have economic and social relations with each other they have common interests and their behavior tends to be organized on behalf of these interests. Some of these interests are of an enduring character and they cannot be realized except by a consistent organization of the behavior of individuals. That is, the behavior of the individual must be controlled by the community and in the interest of the common good. Because the interests are enduring the control of conduct must be continuous and effective. Transient individual interests must not be permitted to jeopardize the continuing common interests.

When the conditions of life for any people are relatively constant, that is, when there is so little change that adequate readjustments are made without the people becoming conscious of any very serious problems, control is exercised by the mores. Tradition supplies a rule of behavior for all of the situations that may arise. When practically all of the social relations of a community are so controlled, they are said to be under the mores.

Tradition as a means of social control has some obvious advantages. The mores are self-enforcing. When a man conducts himself in harmony with the mores of his people he has a sense of personal freedom, since the rule is an expression of his own sentiment. There is no enforcement by external authority. If one violates the mores he suffers a penalty, but the penalty is not inflicted. It is automatic and inescapable because it is his own personal reaction.

296

But if there is a rapid succession of important changes in the conditions of life, traditional control becomes insufficient. Such changes may come as a consequence of migration, or of invention and discovery but, no matter what the cause, the changing conditions call for a modification of behavior if the common interests are to be served. Tradition is too rigid and hence a new sort of control, the political, serves a purpose. The virtue of political control is that it aims to secure a constant readjustment of behavior adaptive to the changing conditions. Under the rule of tradition one must be loyal to such standards as exist, but when rule is by the political method, there is a consideration of interests and the aim is to gain advantages. A new rule is adopted because of the expected benefits and one judges the rule by its fruits. Loyalty is not expected. The rule is repealed if it is not satisfactory. Political rule tends to be experimental.

Social control is never exclusively political. Never is a community willing to submit all of its ways of life to experimentation. Always there is a substratum of conduct that remains within the mores. Always some practices are *tabu* and their discussion is forbidden also. When moral standards are violated or when their validity is questioned one is shocked. He does not discuss the question. His response is emotional not intellectual. When matters of conduct are discussed with an open mind moral standards are decadent or non-existent.

The fact that political decisions turn on a consideration of interests is at once a source of strength and of weakness. Where there is a practical problem involving a changed situation that calls for a modification of method, a clear statement of the interests involved followed by a procedure selected because it is considered to be the most fit to subserve those interests is the shortest way to a solution. It is the way of intelligence and a people well organized for the use of this method can adjust itself to a new situation with a speed unknown to a people governed more by tradition, and, in emergency situations, it does not suffer as serious disorganization.

But where decisions are based on a consideration of interests, where some practical advantage is aimed at, it is not always the interest or the advantage of the community. Aggressive special-interest pressure-groups tend to use political organization for their own advantage and against the common interest. To whatever extent this is done the political organization forfeits its right to the loyalty of the people and there is, in fact, a decrease of loyalty. Only when such special anti-social interests are held in check by the mores can a political organization work successfully. When the political organization rests on an adequate substratum of moral control it has a sort of sanctity itself. Its methods are secular, but they are limited by the generally accepted moral standards. The political constitution of a people is this control by the mores over political action. Sometimes so-called constitutions are written, but where such written constitutions are not adequately supported by the mores they are bent to the purposes of dominant groups.

When moral standards are adequate the people have confidence in the political organization as an instrument of justice, and loyalty is unquestioned. People in general may be depended upon to do what is expected of them and there is the efficiency and strength that comes from co-ordinated effort. When one can expect confidently of people it is evidence of high morale and, under some conditions, confident expectation tends to create morale. Great leaders control their followers by expecting great things. When Lord Nelson, before the battle of Trafalgar, said to his men, "England expects every man to do his duty," he made it almost impossible for them to fall below the level of heroism, and they won a famous victory despite the fact that the enemy had the heavier guns. When General Sheridan, at the battle of Winchester, met his men in disorderly retreat he made known his expectation by continuing his course toward the enemy. The retreating army reorganized as expected and turned a defeat into victory.

But the different sections of the population of a community may be unable to agree on a body of moral standards sufficient to serve adequately as a basis for political organization. This may result from the existence of clashing special-interest groups or from the persistence of opposing traditional standards. Such a society lacks morale and the tendency is not only for political policies to come under criticism, but also for an attack to be made on the state itself. In modern communities one may find much evidence that the people are working at cross purposes. The increase in the size of armies and police organizations and the rise of dictatorships in our time are signs of declining communal morale. If men are not controlled by moral standards they will be controlled by physical force. A dictator untrammeled by courts or a law-making body may inflict more severe and swifter penalties than would be possible under a constitutional government and hence he may be able to maintain a more consistent organization of behavior. Under some conditions people prefer order to freedom. Where morale is deficient regimentation comes in.

In modern times there are two things that tend to prevent the development of an effective co-ordination of activities in the sphere of the larger affairs. First, the size and complexity of the economic mechanism has outrun intelligence. Under the conditions of the simpler old economy an ordinary man might be expected to understand the situation well enough to enable him to carry on consistently, but, for very large numbers, this is no longer true. The complication of indirect relations with remote peoples calls for an economic intelligence which the people have not yet achieved.

In the second place there is not, among the peoples involved, a sufficient basis of values and standards held in common. Things highly valued by the people of one tradition seem to be of little worth to others. Things sacred to one people are secular to another. Forms of control effective among some fail in the case of others. The problems that statesmen and others think about and talk about most commonly are not the ones that will, in the long run, prove to be the most difficult of solution. The more serious misunderstandings are those that rest on unexamined assumptions. The conflict is between things taken for granted but not granted, a conflict that is inevitable as long as conduct and thought are controlled by widely divergent mores. What makes such conflict so difficult of accommodation is that it lies below the level of ordinary reflective thought.

One of the discouraging things about so many conflict situations in our time is the tendency to work out a temporary accommodation that ignores the fundamentals of the problem. Americans tend to be satisfied with the arrangement that can be most easily effected if, by means of it, they believe that they will be able to get by for two or three years. When such temporary accommodations are worked out it is certain that new conflicts will soon develop. After a series of conflicts without intelligent accommodation one cannot be confident that there has been any real progress toward a solution of the problems involved.

At this point the writer may not take the space required for a statement of the grounds of his belief but the belief itself may be stated briefly. When there is a conflict in Hawaii the people concerned do not, in the beginning, show any more intelligence than one would expect in an ordinary American community—I think, even less, in some cases. But the terms of the problem are not so far to seek and, in the end, there is more probability that the accommodation will last for more than a few years. Not always are the fundamental problems considered openly and publicly and, in the practical accommodation, there is likely to be no formal statement of the relevant facts and principles. But what is not formally recognized in words is recognized in the conduct of affairs and in personal conduct so that there is definite progress toward a solution. When, after a term of years, there is a new conflict it is not a mere repetition. It is based on a new situation. A series of conflicts is associated with definite progress toward a workable adjustment. This is on account of the situation being understandable.

Hawaii is a meeting place of several peoples who differ considerably in their traditional backgrounds. There are the people of America and North European origin and those who represent Southern Europe, peoples whose moral standards have been influenced by hundreds of years of Christian teaching, mainly Protestant in the one case and, in the other, Catholic. There are the Chinese, the Japanese and the Koreans whose mores are those of familialism influenced by Buddhism, Confucianism and perhaps other moral systems. There are the native Hawaiians who formerly had a moral order fairly consistent with their circumstances and who are more or less suffering from the disorganization incident to their progress toward Western civilization. The Filipinos have been influenced by Catholic teachings for a considerable time but one can distinguish between the religious attitudes of Filipinos and those of European Catholics. All told, the traditional moral and religious backgrounds of the various peoples of Hawaii are sufficiently varied in character as to suggest the existence of great difficulty in the building up of communal morale. There is difficulty, but it must not be exaggerated.

On the other hand, the local organization of economic life is comparatively simple. There is agriculture and there are the commercial and other services rendered to the agricultural population by towns and cities. Because of the smallness of area and population and because of the relative simplicity of the economic organization, the economic problems have not outrun intelligence so far as they have in the larger and more complex communities. If a man does

not understand the situation well enough to have a workable
idea as to the meaning of his own service and as to what
status and reward he may reasonably expect it is not an
impossible task for him to acquire such understanding.[1]

[1] The advantages arising from the relative simplicity of the situation may
be seen if one compares Hawaii, a small and not very populous area, and
one with a simple economic organization, with a great nation including
metropolitan centers and outlying regions. In 1929 the wage rate for
carpenters in Honolulu was about twice the wage rate of agricultural laborers
in the country districts of the Territory, consideration being given to the
perquisites enjoyed by agricultural laborers. In view of difference in skill,
legitimate differences in living costs and in regularity of employment, this
ratio may be considered to be not far from reasonable. The ratio between
the wage rates of these two classes of laborers was associated with a general
organization of wage rates, profits and rentals that was not far from
consistent in the sense that it did not seriously impede the process of exchange. City services did not come at such a high cost as to restrict, much
beyond what was reasonable, their utilization by the people in the country
districts and hence the exchange could take place continuously excepting as
it might be disturbed on account of outside conditions. In a simple situation
people tend to act intelligently. They are not so likely to make the mistake
of creating a wage-price-profits-rental structure that is self-destructive. If a
change in conditions calls for reorganization it can be accomplished intelligently and without extreme delay.

Similarly there is an exchange of goods and services as between the people
of a great metropolitan center like New York and the farm people and
small townsmen in the rest of the country, but the process is more complex
and hence harder to understand. The New York carpenters and other
workers do not realize that they are exchanging services with remote farmers
and farm laborers. The exchange is mediated by so many in-betweens that
the essential nature of the exchange situation is obscured. Even if the situation were not further confused by the action of special-interest pressure-
groups it would be extremely difficult for people generally to understand the
situation well enough to accept any workable organization of wage-rates,
profits, and rentals that would work continuously. For example, the wages
of carpenters in the city of New York in 1929 were at the rate of $1.50 an
hour. At the same time American farm laborers who were employed by the
day and, hence, with some irregularity and who were not provided with their
board were paid, on the average, $2.42 for a day of ten or more hours or
at an hourly rate of less than 25 cents. Men who were employed steadily
by the month were paid less and those who were boarded by the employer,
still less. By 1931 the average rate of such farm workers had fallen to $1.89
a day or less than 19 cents an hour. But the New York carpenters undis-
mayed by the insufficiency of employment had secured a further advance
in their rates which were $1.65 an hour, or more than eight times the farm
wage rate. Even the comparatively low rate paid by farmers was higher
than the farmers could afford to pay in view of the prices of farm products.
High city wage rates, 1921–1929, had attracted farm laborers to the cities
and this raised farm wages so that they were inconsistent with the prices
of farm produce.

Associated with the inconsistencies in wage rates as between farm

The main point of the discussion up to this stage is that it is probable that in Hawaii there will be a more consistent and rapid development of communal morale than there will be in the more complex mainland situation. In a community of a simple economic organization where all enjoy full political rights and where there is a reasonably adequate provision for the education of all, the tendency is toward an organization of community affairs that is consistent with the reasonable interests of all. If, in the beginning, the existence of divergent mores creates a serious obstacle to the creation of a just organization it turns out to be less serious and less enduring than the obstacles inherent in a more complex social situation.

At best, social reorganization of the more fundamental sort, such as seems to be required in our time, involves some pretty hard problems. If there is to be political and intelligent social control, effective in the common interest, there must be sufficient intelligence to see how the common

laborers and New York carpenters, 1921–1929, was a whole system of inconsistencies involving profits and rentals as well as the wage rates of other classes of workers. The general effect was to put the farmers and farm laborers at a disadvantage in the exchange process and this disadvantage extended to the people of the smaller cities that served the farmers pretty directly. That is, the exchange ratios were such that there could not fail to be a reduction in trade sufficient to destroy the post-war structure of exchange as soon as farm credit was exhausted.

The fact that there was inconsistency in the ratio of exchange as between the goods and services of the metropolitan centers and those of the farming sections is not the most important thing. The most disconcerting feature of the situation is the apparent inability of the country to effect an intelligent readjustment now that the actual breakdown of the post-war structure of exchange is experienced. The people in the great metropolitan centers persist in producing goods in quantities far below capacity in order to maintain or to restore the inconsistent wage-price-profits-rentals structure of the Twenties. For the city workers this involves much unemployment and part time employment with incomes that are uncertain and too small on the average. For the farm people the tendency, aside from governmental action, is to produce abundantly and to suffer from adverse ratios of exchange. What makes the situation so nearly hopeless is the strength of economic, class or sectional sentiment opposed to any adjustment that would permit of a more nearly normal organization of exchange. Within certain special-interest groups there is a sense of loyalty, but what is lacking is communal morale on a national scale.

interest and the interests of various special groups are affected by any policy that may be used or contemplated.

The old group morale is weakened by social changes involving a modification of culture. This is easily seen in the experience of Hawaii. For example, the old country Chinese are notable for their dependability in the payment of debts. According to the Chinese way of thinking it is a moral question of very great importance and it rests on ancestor worship and the doctrine of filial piety. White business men testify to the extreme trustworthiness of Chinese in this respect. One such man, after relating incidents in his business experience to justify his high credit rating of the Chinese, suddenly checked himself to say, "I mean the *old* Chinese. You can't tell about these *young Americanized* Chinese." Since this moral trait rested on the most fundamental thing in the Chinese moral order it may be inferred that the change in moral sentiment involves something more than the mere payment of debts. There is a general weakening of Chinese morale so far as it rests on the things held sacred by their ancestors.

The Japanese have a traditional system of mutual aid known as *tanomoshiko*. A man in need of ready money organizes a group of his friends (thirty in number, commonly), who participate to the extent of paying, each a specified amount of money at stated intervals, usually monthly. The first month's payments are all loaned to the organizer to be repaid by installments at monthly intervals without interest. But the money paid in on each later date by investors and borrowers is loaned to the member who offers the highest premium or interest compensation. Since a man who desires the loan bids in the dark as to the other bids, there is an aleatory element in the bidding and in the rate of interest realized by the leaders. It is said that in Japan tanomoshiko is under a moral control so that it does not become, in a serious sense, an instrument of speculation and exploitation. But in Hawaii it tends to become a regular source of exploitative gains to shrewd promoters who have considerable money and the unfortunate borrowers may pay as high as thirty or forty per cent per annum for their borrowed money. The decay of morale that permits an old-country institution for the expression of mutual helpfulness to be used for exploitation does not stand alone. The Japanese are, more nearly than others, successful in maintaining old country standards, but still they are slipping.

The Portuguese in migrants as a Catholic people were not, in their native land, familiar with divorce as it is practiced in Hawaii or elsewhere in the United States. To them marriage was a sacrament. There was comparatively little divorce among those who came to Hawaii. Their children and grandchildren mainly profess the Catholic faith, but, among them, are considerable numbers who, in the language of the good priest, "hold sacred things lightly." More and more the divorce rate among the Portuguese tends to approximate that of the population in general. When there is a change in conduct that involves things that are traditionally of fundamental moral importance it is easy to infer that group morale, so far as it is based on the old traditions, is becoming weaker.

Instances could be multiplied. The point is, that under the contact conditions of a new social environment the special group morale of the various peoples cannot persist indefinitely. The earlier and more obvious consequences of this decadence of special group morale is an increase in anti-social conduct. In Hawaii as in many other parts of the United States it has become necessary to depend more on the police, the courts, the jails and the prison as the peoples have been emancipated from their traditional moral control.

But this decay of old special group morale is only one aspect of the situation. Not so easily seen or measured is the developing new communal morale. In the earlier stages the new forms of behavior do not represent morale at all. They are more or less intelligent devices for meeting the requirements of a situation involving the interests of the people generally. They are arrived at through deliberation and discussion and they are secular. If the devices work pretty well they are perfected and perpetuated. After a time they acquire the standing of custom and finally age gives them sanctity. At this point one may speak of them as representing the newly developing communal morale.

Communal morale develops somewhat in the way that boys playing baseball develop respect for the rules of the game. If, in the beginning, the boys are unenlightened and undisciplined in relation to the game they are pretty certain to refuse to be obedient to the rules and they will quarrel, thus spoiling their own fun. It is just the bad behavior and its outcome that serves to enlighten and discipline them. They have to reflect about the trouble and they come to see that obedience to rules is necessary. If any boy is too slow to see this, the penalty involved in the attitude of his mates is almost automatic. Finally, "Play ball," becomes a moral imperative. The team has morale.

In Hawaii one may see a development of communal morale in the field of party politics. There are a good many young voters who represent immigrant peoples who have never had any political experience. When the voters of any particular group first become sufficiently numerous to attract the attention of office seekers their votes are sought and the various sorts of inducements are used, some being in harmony with the public interest and others being designed to appeal to special persons or groups. When some of the men of the new voting group aspire to elective office their naive expectation is that the voters of their own racio-cultural group will stand by them. To a certain extent, they do get this support. But if a man has a disproportionate support from his own group it tends to put him in bad with his party associates. If the Chinese people vote pretty generally for the one Democratic candidate who is Chinese, and not for the rest of the ticket, the other candidates feel that he has not played fair with them and he suffers at the next election. Loyalty to the ticket as a whole is the condition of success. If a man wants to be supported by his party associates he must "play the game." If he is not bright enough to see that this is good politics from a personal point of view he is pretty certain to be eliminated as a politician. Eventually the control that at first grows out of a consideration of personal interest is generally accepted and after a while it comes to be supported by sentiment. That is, it becomes a moral standard underlying party politics. In a somewhat similar way the politician is forced to base his open campaign on a consideration of the general interest. To run for office as a representative of the special interest of some one racio-cultural group would be to insure defeat. More or less, candidates do represent special interests and sometimes they have a temporary success to the detriment of public interests. But this, too, is a means to education. The reaction of the public contributes to the development of communal morale, that is, it so contributes if the reaction is intelligent.

Perhaps it would go without saying that the schools,—the formal social agencies of education,—have a part in the creation of the new morale. But a few things will bear saying. Schools cannot be administered successfully unless there is, in reasonable measure, a school morale. The school is a community and the pupils are living as well as studying. In Hawaii the school people are consciously using the actual school situation as a means to the development of morale. School activities, not only on the playground, but those involved in study projects, are like the activities of the larger community in that they involve opportunities for conflict and accommodation, for insight and invention, and for the development of technique and standards. Children are encouraged to reflect about their school problems and sometimes on problems involving both home and school. That is, an effort is made to help them to entertain their

actual problems as intellectual problems and to develop
a technique for the intelligent solving of problems. Doubtless this is done elsewhere but the racio-cultural situation
in Hawaii makes the need of such procedure more clearly
evident and the school people are stimulated in ways that
result in insight.

The whole matter of communal morale belongs, broadly
speaking, to the field of education. That is, it is a matter of
social conditioning. If the habits and the sentiment of individuals are to be controlled adequately by society in the
interest of the common good there must be enlightenment
and discipline. When this control is being achieved the
emphasis is on enlightenment. The people need to see where
their true interests lie. But when it has been achieved it
manifests itself as discipline, that is, as morale.

The education whose outcome is morale is not precisely
like some other sorts of education. Morale cannot be discovered or measured in a laboratory and be handed on to
the community like knowledge relating to agricultural technique. It comes into existence through the efforts of people
to live together satisfactorily and through the conflicts
that arise inevitably when morale is inadequate. The in-
evitability of conflict is the best guarantee that the process
will go on, that is, that people will continue to seek a working arrangement of increasing success, that such working
arrangement will come to be valued, and that in time it
will acquire sanctity. While changing conditions tend to
weaken traditional moral standards there is always the
tendency to create new standards which in time acquire as
strong an influence over conduct.

There are periods in which the flood tide of social change
seems to endanger the whole structure of society. Since
the new morale is not in sight it may appear that the down-
fall of civilization is imminent. There may, indeed, be a
period of extreme disorganization involving genuine losses
of great importance. But then there comes a period in

which social relations become more stable in character and one in which a new morale gradually comes into existence. So far as Hawaii is concerned it is probable that a period of reduced social change is just ahead. Spacial mobility may be used as an index of social change. Where relatively large numbers of people change their place of residence and where they move frequently and far, the rate of social change runs high. In recent years there has been almost a complete cessation of immigration to Hawaii and the emigration from the Territory is reduced. The movement within the Territory is also greatly reduced. Doubtless there will be some acceleration of these movements when the world economic situation becomes more nearly normal, but it will not return to the level of the decade, 1920–1930, barring some unexpected influence from the outside. The outlook is for an unusually rapid development of communal morale in Hawaii the favoring conditions being the tradition of racial equality and the intelligible simplicity of its economic organization.

CHAPTER XXI

ASSIMILATION AND AMALGAMATION MUTUALLY
CONDITIONED

IN recent times people have migrated to many regions
mainly as individuals and small families and the movement
has been free and in response to personal incentives. Commonly the incentive has been a desire for economic advantage,—more or better land, better wages or profitable trade.
In a few cases there has been a cultural incentive, a desire
on the part of the members of a minority sect for freedom
to create institutions in harmony with their beliefs and
standards, but these also have desired economic advantage
in the new land. Commonly immigrants establish permanent
relations with the older inhabitants who are culturally and
sometimes racially different. In the course of time they and
their descendants and also the older inhabitants undergo
cultural changes as a result of living in a different sort of
social environment and, through intermarriage and otherwise, there may be an amalgamation so that in time the
descendants of the immigrants and those of the older inhabitants are one people, one in culture and in ancestry or
race. But in the beginning such acculturation and amalgamation are not desired. If it is thought about at all it serves
not as an incentive to migration but as a deterrent.

When immigrants have reached the land of their new
residence they are confronted with problems. They want
to make advantageous economic adjustments, but they desire to maintain their own traditions and to maintain themselves as a distinct people. But in order to make an advantageous economic adjustment it is necessary, commonly,

to modify their culture in some respects. Probably one will need to acquire at least a minimum facility in the use of a second language. Perhaps he will need to learn how to use new sorts of tools. If a farmer, the immigrant may be under the necessity of using new methods of cultivation, and he may find it advantageous to modify his diet and the style of clothing used when at work. New commercial relations are called for. What happens commonly is that a sort of compromise is worked out. The cultural modifications that are most obviously needful are of a technological character, mainly, and there is not much sentiment antagonistic to cultural change at this level. Acculturation in respect to such matters may take place rather promptly and without any obvious conflict. But in relation to the things that are important from the standpoint of social organization the aim is to maintain the old customs and standards unimpaired. The things that belong to technology are secular. One may be governed by a consideration of advantage. But the customs that pertain to marriage and the family and to religious ritual and the associated beliefs are sacred and one must observe them loyally, irrespective of seeming advantage.

One may find much evidence of this compromise wherever culture is undergoing considerable modification. Scandinavians and Germans in America when they pray use their respective native tongues but English serves better the purpose of the market place. A Quaker uses ordinary English for professional and business purposes, but in the family circle "thee" and "thou" come naturally to his lips. In Hawaii the Chinese immigrants are sufficiently alert to adopt modern mechanical devices and business methods, but when a man dies his bones are sent back to his old home village to be interred with ancient rites. The daughter of a Japanese man wears American style clothing on the street, but at her wedding she is dressed in a costume of old Japanese style. A traveler in Japan may see, at the bottom

312 INTERRACIAL MARRIAGE IN HAWAII

of a hill, a modern hydroelectric plant but, at the top, there is an ancient Shinto shrine. The Hawaiian Portuguese in relation to business affairs are much like the Americans of New England ancestry, but when they worship, they go mainly to the church of the old Portuguese tradition. Stated in more general terms, that part of the social heritage of a people that is not much affected with sentiment, the technological or secular part, is modified readily when the circumstances call for change. But the mores resist change. Their value lies below the level of ordinary reflective thought. One feels strongly and his thinking is dominated by sentiment. In matters of taste and of moral standards one is not free but is under the mores. On the side of technique one may be Americanized while on the side of loyalties he remains faithful to the old tradition. Immigrants and their descendants cannot be said to be assimilated to the American cultural pattern as long as they possess distinctive loyalties or other cultural traits of such a character as to prevent the development of full and free social relations outside of their own ancestral group.

Social relations tend to be on a similar compromise basis. At first all the more intimate sorts of contact including marriage are within the group. So far as the immigrants and the older inhabitants have contacts they are almost entirely economic. An employer is a source of income, and an employee, a means to profitable production. In an American farm community it has been possible for a foreign family to be almost completely isolated, since it could have its economic relations with town people outside the neighborhood. The writer has some interesting memories of how some such isolated families were finally brought into the economic and later the social life of the neighborhood by some sort of necessity. It was necessary to exchange work at threshing time or, in time of sickness, someone was needed to go for the doctor or to help in the home.

As long as the relations between immigrants and the older population are almost purely economic there is little or no intermarriage. This is true in America no matter whether the immigrants come from Europe or from Asia. It is true whether there is legal freedom to intermarry or whether such intermarriage is prohibited by law. It is true whether the immigrants profess the same or whether they profess different religious faiths. Only as there are social relations of a more intimate character do the peoples amalgamate through intermarriage. Accommodation at the first level of acculturation serves a purpose, but it does not serve the purpose of a complete assimilation nor does it permit of amalgamation.

This early compromise arrangement involving, for immigrants, acculturation at the technological level while, at the level of values and standards, there is a continuing loyalty to the old tradition is, for a time, possible and it is workable. It is hard to see how any other possible arrangement would work as well. But it never works perfectly or for long. Economic contacts lead inevitably to contacts of an increasingly intimate character. If, in the beginning, two men associated in an economic way regard each other merely as means to ends, they will in time get beyond this. In minor crises each gets new insights, he sees the other as a fellow human with fears and hatreds and hopes and loves and purposes and loyalties enough like his own to be understandable. There comes to be sympathy and, sometimes, antipathy and both alike are indicative of an approach toward relations of a more intimate character. How often one hears a man railing at some sort of people only to make an exception of one or a few with whom he is personally acquainted. For example, a Southern gentleman was telling of the generally untrustworthy character of Negroes, but a little later he told a story of an old family servant of his brother. The family was away from home till after midnight. Unexpectedly the daughter arrived home from col-

lege and occupied the plantation residence alone. An old
Negro servant placed himself on guard near the front door
where he remained till the folks came home. The story
closed with, "Nobody could have harmed that girl without
first passing over the dead body of that old nigger."

Such insights and aroused sympathies make possible
associations of a more intimate character and these result
in a further increase of understanding so that gradually and,
almost without observation, acculturation takes place at a
level that involves things greatly affected with sentiment.
This more advanced stage of acculturation necessitates accommodation in relation to standards. There is tolerance
toward conduct that conflicts with one's traditional standards. Such tolerance involves a subtle modification of
attitude in relation to one's own conduct. He comes to be
tolerant of himself. Old standards are not compulsory.
One considers them. They are useful under some circumstances but need not be observed in other cases. Decisions tend to be made from the standpoint of interest or
advantage. Sacred things become less sacred or even
secular. In short, a man is gradually emancipated from the
more distinctive part of his ancient mores so that he can
reflect about his behavior and choose what to do according
to his purpose.

This partial emancipation from the old mores is a condition precedent to the acceptance of new standards and to
the development of new loyalties. Sometimes individuals
make the transition from the old to the new without any
violent moral breakdown. They manage to organize their
activities in a fairly consistent way even at a time when
they are neither American nor old country men. It would
be of interest to consider how a successful and safe transition is made from one culture to another but that would
transcend the present purpose. But there is considerable
jeopardy at this point. The danger is that one escapes from
the influence of the old standards without achieving con-

trol under the new, or without achieving such control promptly. In many cases immigrant peoples become disorganized and a good many of the immigrants and their children are demoralized. If the immigrants are relatively numerous and influential so that there is, in considerable measure, a tendency for the old residents to be accultured to the immigrant pattern the social disorganization may extend to the whole community. This is true in some parts of the United States. But commonly the immigrant groups are minority groups or at least they are groups of inferior influence and authority and so it is the immigrant rather than the native who finds it necessary or advantageous to make the greater cultural change and who, therefore, suffers more from social disorganization.

There are always some disadvantages in being identified with a minority group. One may find certain satisfactions if he confines himself to the society of some group of inferior numbers and influence who are like-minded with himself, but there is always an advantage to be derived through contacts with the larger society and one wants to have a good status here also. Whether the members of a minority group do set about it to achieve such status in the larger society or not depends mainly on whether it seems to be attainable. If the more numerous or more powerful people are disposed to give recognition to members of the minority group on the basis of personal character and achievement there will be plenty of candidates. If, however, the dominant people draws a strict line admitting members of the minority group into economic and the less intimate sort of social relations only, and if it admits them in such a way as to imply inferiority of status, the minority finds it necessary to maintain its own distinctive organization or to create one.

If the larger social recognition is attainable on the basis of character and achievement the members of the minority group who seek such recognition find it necessary to conform to the standards of the society they would enter. Their previous partial emancipation from their own traditional mores makes this progressively possible and their ambition for recognition in the larger society makes it necessary. If, at first, their conformity is partly a matter of policy rather than sentiment it does not remain at that level permanently. New rituals, doctrines and standards lack the sacredness that comes with age, but in time the new become old.

But if such recognition in the larger society is impossible, the member of a minority group has no inducement to conform his conduct to the dominant standards and he does have an inducement to conform to the demands of his traditional mores. Since a good status cannot be acquired in the larger society he must depend for his personal status on his own group. If this group is to be able to create a secure and desirable status for its members it must maintain organization and this is possible only on the basis of its distinctive traditions. Under such conditions there may develop in the minority group a strong sentiment antagonistic to acculturation at the deeper level. There is loyalty to the old religion with its rituals, beliefs and moral standards, to nationalistic traditions and to family customs. Festivals of one sort or another serve to symbolize these loyalties and to keep alive memories of an older time when they were a separate people in every sense.

This is not to say that such a minority group can succeed in maintaining the old mores unimpaired. Doubtless, under the conditions of a changed environment, there will be important modifications but changes will not be of such a character as to make complete assimilation possible. They must be consistent with the maintenance of a distinctive social organization with its distinctive loyalties.

It turns out then that the problem of the assimilability in America of any particular immigrant group is primarily a problem relating to the attitude of the older Americans. If Americans are disposed to accept the immigrants and their descendants on the basis of personal character and achievement, the immigrants are assimilable. If Americans are not so disposed, the immigrants are not assimilable.

If one seeks for a test of the attitude of the Americans of the old stock he will find no other so significant as the marriage test. If intermarriage is permitted by law and public opinion it may be assumed that any existing obstacles to intimate social relations will turn out to be temporary and that acculturation will continue until the descendants of the old Americans and those of the new immigrants cannot be distinguished and that there will be, through intermarriage, a comparatively rapid amalgamation until the descendants are indistinguishable as to ancestry. In short, if intermarriage is legally permitted and socially approved as between two or more peoples they are sure to become one people, one in social inheritance and one in ancestry or race.

But if intermarriage is effectively prohibited by law and public opinion the outlook is for a much slower amalgamation. Since such slow amalgamation through extramarital relations is not sanctioned, it tends to be concealed or, if not concealed, there is a penalty of some sort involving a reduction of status for parents and their mixed-blood children. If intermarriage is to be prohibited effectively, the sort of social relations that naturally lead to marriage must be prohibited also. Where a familialism prevails or where the choice of mates is controlled directly by the parents or the family head this may be of little importance, but in a country in which young people are supposed to find their mates under the guidance of romantic love, a whole social code is involved.

A considerable part of American social life may be regarded as serving the purpose of marriageable young men and women. Dinners, dances, games, receptions, coming-out parties, outings, travel and even school attendance, churchgoing and some occupational activities serve the romantic interests of youth. They serve for meeting and getting acquainted, for the manifestation of interest and preference, for the display of charm and sentiment, for the paying of compliments, for the association in activities that more or less reveal personality traits. If parents do not directly control in the selection of mates, they may, nevertheless, limit the fields of choice by means of a social code. In effect, when the code permits young people to associate in such ways, freedom to marry according to personal choice is symbolized. Young people who may dine, dance and worship together without discrimination may intermarry.

So long as there is an effective sentiment against intermarriage between two peoples the social code may be expected to be discriminatory in such a way as to prevent full acculturation on the level of the things that are greatly affected with sentiment. If two peoples refuse to contemplate for their descendants a common ancestry they deny themselves the privilege of looking forward to a time when all will be bound together by common loyalties. An interesting side light on this is found in an observable difference between the Chinese of Hawaii and those of California. In both cases there has been a considerable time since there has been an important number of immigrants. When one meets middle-aged Chinese men and women in either California or Hawaii they are native-born American citizens and the children are mainly of the second and third generations of American birth. A considerable number of the early Chinese immigrants to Hawaii married native women and there is today a part-Chinese population nearly half as large as the pure Chinese. Associated with marriage freedom was a freedom of economic opportunity that has resulted in a diversification of Chinese occupational and business interests that is not characteristic of the Chinese in California. Moreover there was never in Hawaii a development of fighting tongs such as existed in San Francisco and other American cities. The fighting tong appears to have been an outcome of a sort of governmentally unrecognized extraterritoriality which was, in California, almost inevitable on account of the rigid exclusion of the Chinese from social relations with whites. The more nearly normal situation of the Hawaiian Chinese made such a development unnecessary. There is also a contrast in that, in Hawaii, the men of Chinese ancestry are taking an active part in politics, holding office and participating in the determination of public policy. Perhaps an even more important difference is found in connection with sports and social activities. In Hawaii the Chinese take an active part in baseball, swimming, tennis, golf and other sports and in such activities they are associated much with non-Chinese. While there is a degree of segregation in the more purely social activities there is, nevertheless, a sufficient enlargement of social opportunity to symbolize the existence of a status very different from that of the California Chinese.

As a result of all these and other differences there is an observable difference in the attitude of Chinese toward white people and others. When a white man of Hawaii goes to California and meets Chinese people he is impressed with a reserve on their part. Doubtless there are in San Francisco white men and women who are well known to some of the Chinese and who are trusted, but the normal attitude of Chinese toward an unintroduced white stranger with a friendly manner is one of distrust. The Hawaiian Chinese are, in the presence of whites, more given to laughter and when in sorrow they may weep. In an interracial group they act as if they have a sense of really belonging. In general the California Chinese speak a better type of English than most of those in Hawaii and in relation to some other matters they may be more fully Americanized, but they are under inhibitions of a sort that do not exist for the Hawaiian Chinese. The freedom from constraint of the Chinese in Hawaii is eloquent testimony as to the existence of a more satisfactory social status. Feeling that they are really members of the community not merely in relation to its economic activities but in relation to everything else, they are, more than the California Chinese, undergoing acculturation at the level of taste, mannerisms and loyalties.

In Hawaii there is a confident expectation that the descendants of all the present peoples, whether of European, Asiatic, or native Hawaiian ancestry, will be fully assimilated to one cultural pattern. The expectation is well founded since, through interracial marriage, all the peoples are participating in a general process of amalgamation. Now that immigration seems to be about at an end, one may expect the mixed-bloods to achieve a more important numerical position and that their interests and attitudes will influence social relations to an increasing extent. In the years 1931–33, excepting a few of unknown paternity, 24.5 per cent of the children born in the Territory of Hawaii were of mixed ancestry. But a forecast for the near future is found in the fact that in the same years, excepting a few cases not racially identified, 31.8 per cent of the marriages were of such a character that the children will be of mixed ancestry. While there is sentiment antagonistic to such marriages on the part of families and other groups too small to exercise control, the attitude of the peoples, each toward all the others, is affected by the fact that such marriage is lawful and that it is taking place in so great measure. While the original cultural differences among the peoples of Hawaii were very great they are steadily yielding to the influence of the social relations that exist in Hawaii. While there were very great differences in color and the other physical race traits, the peoples are intermarrying and, barring continuous immigration, a complete amalgamation may be expected.

There is, of course, considerable interest as to the pattern of the future culture to which all will be assimilated. It will not be precisely the American culture of the present, but neither will the American culture of the future be like the American culture of today. There will be change. The culture of Hawaii will never be just like that of New England, South Carolina or any other section of the United States, and, for that matter, all the main sections of the United States will, in all probability, maintain something distinctive in their customs and standards.

But Hawaii will not revert to a stone age culture. This would not happen even if all but the pure Hawaiians were to leave the Territory. When a cultural advance is made, it is retained because of the obvious advantages. The Hawaiians, if alone, would continue to use tools of iron and to write and read and to use money; and they would continue to prize a freedom unknown to their ancient ancestors. For a similar reason the future culture will not be a reversion to the ways of China or Japan. That would not happen even if the Chinese or the Japanese were left alone in the Territory. When Hawaiian-born Chinese go back to China they do not conform to the ancient Chinese mores but they try to remake China.

Some cultural trends are fairly clear and others are more a matter of speculation. Three fourths of the people speak English either as mother tongue or as a secondary language. Sometimes it is spoken in a very inadequate way but it is the chief means of communication in the Territory, and its position improves measurably each decade. Within fifty years English will be the common language of all but a few homes and the other languages now spoken by so many will survive merely among a few of the older people. With the passing of the various foreign tongues, the means of cultural contact with the various ancestral lands will be wanting and for lack of communication the various foreign traditions will tend to be forgotten. Distinctive cultural traits like the familialism of the Chinese and the Japanese will not long survive the languages in which their doctrines and ideals find expression. More and more the younger men and women of all races think in English and when they think in English the tendency is to be drawn into the current of the thought that is expressed in English. What about nationalistic sentiment? For a time and to the extent that there is an obvious advantage in the maintenance of organization on the part of the immigrant groups and their children the persistence of old country nationalistic sentiment may be expected. One need not look far to find evidence of such sentiment today. Probably the strongest manifestation of such sentiment in Hawaii is found among the Koreans who look forward hopefully to a time when they may assist in freeing Korea from Japanese control. For a long time there was, among the Chinese, an organization designed to abolish the Manchu dynasty and Sun Yat Sen received substantial financial aid from the Hawaiian Chinese. At the present time Chinese patriotic sentiment is strongly anti-Japanese. Some of the Hawaiian-born Chinese young men are serving the present Chinese government in positions of dignity. Likewise, some of the Hawaiian-born Japanese go back to Japan and render assistance in the creation of a greater Japan. So far as observed there is less tendency on the part of Japanese to make sacrifices in the old country interest. They seem to be more individualistic or, possibly, it is because Japan has less need than China. Among the Portuguese there is little manifestation of interest in the land of their ancestors, and the same may be said of the Spanish.

On the other hand, there is the fact that with the passage of time the practical interests of the immigrants and their descendants are more and more identified with Hawaii. A Japanese rice grower in Hawaii is in favor of the American tariff on rice and the Japanese business community in Honolulu discourages the investment in Japan of savings accumulated in Hawaii. The Hawaiian-born of all ancestries are participating in local political activities in increasing numbers. They are Republicans or Democrats and the party lines do not correspond to race lines but mainly to personal interests.

Commonly among the school children of Hawaii there has been a beginning of a development of American nationalistic sentiment. On the basis of their reading of American history and literature they become very proud of their American citizenship and some of them make eloquent speeches modeled on those of Patrick Henry, Daniel Webster and Abraham Lincoln. Those of Oriental ancestry, when they compare the customs maintained by their parents with the ideals of America, seem to be more keenly aware of the significance of American citizenship and of its demands on them than are mainland boys and girls commonly. The stories of American national greatness are read with keen interest and high resolve in the schools of Hawaii. Some of the young men when they go to the mainland experience much disillusionment and disappointment.

Schoolboy patriotism is a testimonial to the teaching and to the winning qualities of democratic ideals in school administration. But the sentiment developed in the schools undergoes some modification when school days are over. The earlier loyalties are tested, sometimes rudely tested, and not always do they meet the test successfully. Whether the early schoolboy loyalties develop into more mature loyalties in later life or whether they fail to do this depends mainly on the character of society. If, on the whole, the reasonable interests of the members of any class or group are provided for, if people of all classes or groups are able to participate reasonably in the making of decisions and if social recognition is on the basis of personal merit or if the actual social practice does not depart too far from this ideal, there will be, in general, a development of loyalty. But under other conditions the disloyalty of definite classes or peoples may be expected. Could a Berlin Jew be loyal to the present ruler of Germany?

In a country as large as the United States and with as great diversity of local interests, there is bound to be for each section a somewhat special development of tradition.

Each section has its own historic background and in addition to its national loyalty there is a sectional loyalty. It is a function of statesmanship, of education and of the press to strengthen national sentiment so that national interests shall not be neglected on account of sectional differences. It is also a function of government, more particularly, to further policies that take into consideration reasonably the special interests of the various sections. The constitutional division of powers as between the national and the state governments is such as to make it possible for the people of each state in large measure to govern themselves in harmony with local sentiment. As long as a suitable balance is maintained sectional sentiment may, in the main, supplement national sentiment, but, under other conditions, the sectional may conflict with national sentiment and, in an extreme case, this may involve serious conflict. There has been one civil war in the United States.

There is in Hawaii a considerable development of national sentiment and, under favoring conditions, it may be expected to become more general among the citizens and also stronger. With some exceptions, the conditions that have existed since the annexation of Hawaii in 1898 have been favoring conditions. Among the favoring conditions may be mentioned the trade relations and the intellectual contacts between the Territory and the States. Nearly all of Hawaii's trade is with continental United States. Educational policies in Hawaii march with those of the more progressive communities on the mainland. Hundreds of Hawaiian-born young men and young women are studying in colleges all the way from the Pacific Coast to New England. American books and periodicals are widely read. When the people of Hawaii travel they go, mainly, to the mainland and thousands of mainland people visit Hawaii each year.

Of great importance are governmental policies. Two deserve special mention: (1) Under a territorial form of government the people of Hawaii have been permitted to govern themselves in large measure. (2) The laws enacted by Congress, aside from a few unfortunate exceptions, have been applied to Hawaii as to the rest of the country, impartially. The elective legislature has been representative of the people of Hawaii in that local interests and local sentiment are reflected in the laws. The governors and other presidential appointees commonly have been men who had resided in the Territory and who were familiar with the local situation and responsive to local sentiment. United States governmental policies have been, at most times, of such a character as to facilitate the development of national sentiment.

But one must not make false claims. The citizens of Hawaii, no more than citizens elsewhere, are able to develop strong national sentiment when the appropriate conditions do not exist. It is a question of national policies. If in the future there shall be a failure in the development of national sentiment in Hawaii it will not be on account of the persistence of the ancient loyalties but on account of the adoption at Washington of less favorable policies than those that have been effective in the past.

The main purpose of this volume is to indicate the character of the social relations in Hawaii so far as they have been affected by the facts of cultural and racial difference among its peoples and so far as they are undergoing modification in consequence of the mutually conditioned processes of cultural assimilation and racial amalgamation. It is impossible to consider these processes without a constant reference to the outlook for the future. I have not hesitated to make forecasts where the indications have seemed to warrant them. Practical men are always making forecasts. Forecasts are implied in plans, and without reasonably adequate forecasting there can be no consistent organization of private behavior or of public activities. If, in relation to any field of interest, there is progress toward an adequate analysis, there is ability to make forecasts of increasing value. The adequacy of the analysis may, therefore, be tested by the dependability of the forecasts based on them. When a student, therefore, utilizes his analysis for the making of forecasts he submits his work to a very searching sort of test. If future events or trends are not according to expectation it is evidence of some deficiency of analysis or of factual information and this sets the requirement for further study.

It remains to be said that the forecasts of this volume are predicated on certain conditions, mainly on a reasonably stable economic and political situation. If there should be some violent modification of the economic situation through the action of the national government it might affect the population in such a way as to call for a revision of some of the forecasts. If a military government were to be set up in place of the territorial it is probable that in respect to race relations there would be a reversal of practice and with important local consequences. If there should be a war it would modify the character of social relations temporarily and, maybe, for a long time.

If it is granted that local sentiment will continue to be the most important factor in the situation, one may look forward to the amalgamation of all the races of Hawaii and to their complete assimilation. There will be common interests, common memories, and common loyalties. The peoples of Hawaii will become one people.

METHOD OF COMPUTING INDEXES OF IN–MARRIAGE PREFERENCE

IN Hawaii there is an organization of sentiment favorable to the marriage of the men and women of each racial group to each other. Or, otherwise stated, there is an organization of sentiment adverse to out-marriage. There is the sentiment of each group more or less adverse to intermarriage with members of each of the other groups and also the sentiment of each of the other groups. In relation to the marriage practice of any one group this organization of sentiment may be called in-marriage preference. The actual marriage choice of a man of any race is determined largely by personal attitudes or considerations and a good many do not make their choice in accordance with group sentiment. Nevertheless the group sentiment is there and its influence is great or small according to the character of a person's social relations.

The in-marriage preference in relation to one racial group such as the Japanese may be comparatively strong in which case there is only a little out-marriage. But in the case of the Hawaiian, preference is not so strong and hence a larger proportion marry out. The strength of preference is more or less measurable in terms of its results.

Indexes of in-marriage preference as affecting the rates of in-marriage and out-marriage of the men and women of the various groups are computed. The purpose is to determine the trend of sentiment favorable to in-marriage, that is, adverse to out-marriage, and also to permit of a ranking of the various groups according to the strength of such sentiment.

In the case of some racial groups, the Portuguese, for example, the rates of in-marriage *practice* are not seriously misleading if regarded as indicating the strength of sentiment. For these groups, opportunity has been such that practice has reflected sentiment pretty well. But in the case of some other groups, notably the Spanish and the Chinese, this has not been true. In both of these cases there was a defect on the side of opportunity. In the case of the Spanish, the numbers of both men and women were too small and in the case of the Chinese the principal defect came from the relative fewness of marriageable women.

The purpose of the computations is to eliminate, as nearly as may be, the effects of these opportunity factors so that one, by using the date of marriage *practice,* may draw valid inferences as to the strength of in-marriage *preference.*

The method of computation is as follows:

Part 1. An allowance for the difference in the size of the various racial groups.

Step 1. The purpose is to find the number of in-marriages for any group for the specified period on the assumption that there was no factor of preference associated with race.

First formula:
$$\frac{a}{b} \times \frac{c}{d} \times e = v$$

Where *a* is, for the period under consideration, the estimated average number of men eligible to marry, for the specified racial group;

b, the number of eligible men of all races;

c, similarly, the number of eligible women of the group;

d, the number of eligible women of all races;

e, the actual number of marriages,—all races,—for the period;

v, the hypothetical number of in-marriages, on the assumption of no racial preference.

Step 2. Preference is determined provisionally by comparing the actual with the hypothetical number of in-marriages. (Only so far as the actual exceeds the hypothetical number is preference indicated.)

Second formula:
$$\frac{\dfrac{m-v}{n-v} + \dfrac{m-v}{o-v}}{2} = x$$

Where *m* is the actual number of in-marriages for the specified group;

n, the total number of grooms of the group;

o, the total number of brides of the group;

x, the provisional index of in-marriage preference.

Part 2. An allowance for inequality of the sexes for the marriageable.[1]

Third formula: $1000 - \dfrac{1000 - x}{\sqrt{\dfrac{a}{c}}} = y$,

y being the index of preference affecting the rate of in-marriage.

The use of formulae may be illustrated by an application. The index of in-marriage preference for the Hawaiians is computed for the period, 1930–34. The data are as follows:

Average number of eligible Hawaiian men	1,499
Average number of eligible Hawaiian women	980
Average number of eligible men of all races	43,837
Average number of eligible women of all races	13,896
Number of Hawaiian in-marriages	258
Total number of Hawaiian grooms	546
Total number of Hawaiian brides	664
Total number of marriages—all races........	10,622

First formula: $\dfrac{1499}{43,837} \times \dfrac{980}{13,846} \times 10622 = 26$,

the number of Hawaiian in-marriages if there had been no racial factor of preference.

Second formula: $\dfrac{\dfrac{258' - 26}{546 - 26} + \dfrac{258 - 26}{664 - 26}}{2} = 405$,

the provisional index for in-marriage preference needing correction on account of the inequality in the number of eligible men and eligible women.

[1] In estimating the numbers of the marriageable it was necessary to use arbitrary definitions. Males, 20–44 years of age, were considered to be marriageable unless already married. Females, 18–44 years of age, marriageable unless already married. The status of enlisted men in the army and navy is doubtful. They are not prohibited from marrying but they are effectively discouraged so that for an equal number of eligibles there are only about a tenth as many marriages as in the case of civilians of the same race. One tenth of the legal eligibles among enlisted men are considered to be effectively eligible for the present purpose.

Third formula: $1000 - \dfrac{1000 - 405}{\sqrt{\dfrac{1499}{980}}} = 517,$

the index of in-marriage preference as affecting Hawaiians for the four years, 1930–34.

This index may be placed in a series so as to show the trend of sentiment.

Trend of in-marriage preference as relating to the Hawaiians:

1912–16	1920–24	1924–28	1930–34
722	659	574	517

If these indexes are compared with the figures representative of marriage practice it will be seen that they differ a little.

Number of Hawaiians in-married to 1000 brides and grooms:

1912–16	1920–24	1924–28	1930–34
688	603	588	426

In each case the index of in-marriage preference is higher than the rate of in-marriage. This means that the marriage practice of the Hawaiians did not, in full measure reflect sentiment in relation thereto.

This index together with the similar indexes for the other racial groups may be used to determine the rank of the Hawaiians with respect to the strength of in-marriage preference for the period, 1930–34. The order is as follows: Japanese, 955; Filipino, 954; Korean, 799; Chinese, 780; "Other Caucasian," 774; Porto Rican, 718; Portuguese, 634; part-Hawaiian, 545; Hawaiian, 517; Spanish, 287. See Tables XXIX and XXX for indexes of marriage practice and of marriage preference for all races for the four periods.

Appendix B

DISTRIBUTION OF POPULATION,
CITIES AND COUNTIES

THIS table is designed to show the territorial distribution of all the races by sex. While the racial groups are not quite evenly distributed through the various districts, they come surprisingly near to it except in the case of three groups, the Filipinos, who are not numerous in Honolulu, the Chinese, who are mainly in Honolulu and the "other Caucasians" who are mainly in Honolulu City and near-by rural districts. Females are relatively more numerous in Honolulu despite the presence of several thousand single enlisted men. They are least numerous in rural Oahu,—this on account of the presence of over eleven thousand enlisted men. Otherwise females are relatively fewest in the county of Kauai.

In the movement of young people from the country districts to Honolulu there has been a small excess of women. This is evident in the case of Hawaiians, part-Hawaiians and Portuguese and probably would be evident in the case of all Oriental groups except that the result is affected by movement into and out of the Territory.

Included in the population were enlisted men in the army and navy, 16,291,—15,862 "other Caucasians" and 429, all others. Of the 15,862, 4,431 were in the city of Honolulu and 11,431 in the rural part of Honolulu County. Besides the enlisted men there were nearly a thousand officers and, in the families of the officers, about three thousand women and children. Except for the enlisted men, the sex ratio of the "other Caucasians" is nearly normal.

331

TABLE XLVIII

The Population, Urban and Rural, Male and Female, by Race
(Census, 1930)

		URBAN		RURAL	
		City of Honolulu	City of Hilo	Honolulu County Exclusive of Honolulu City	Hawaii County Exclusive of Hilo City
Hawaiian . . .	Male	4,739	595	1,226	1,881
	Female	4,936	560	1,202	1,828
Caucasian-Hawaiian	Male	4,028	458	604	790
	Female	4,255	528	609	747
Asiatic-Hawaiian .	Male	2,885	442	472	860
	Female	3,074	453	432	793
Portuguese . . .	Male	6,081	1,260	1,084	1,902
	Female	6,216	1,207	1,054	1,801
Porto Rican . .	Male	1,160	80	446	857
	Female	1,051	78	372	633
Spanish	Male	272	24	132	46
	Female	302	27	87	32
Other Caucasian .	Male	14,171	591	13,407	761
	Female	9,790	539	2,077	520
Chinese	Male	11,146	577	1,916	813
	Female	8,188	320	818	388
Japanese . . .	Male	24,953	4,959	12,039	13,346
	Female	22,515	4,397	10,078	11,046
Korean	Male	1,442	167	979	608
	Female	1,162	121	566	235
Filipino	Male	3,337	1,539	12,264	12,535
	Female	1,439	516	3,350	1,366
All other . . .	Male	242	17	83	40
	Female	198	13	44	29
Total	Male	74,456	10,709	44,652	34,439
	Female	63,126	8,759	20,689	19,418

TABLE XLVIII (continued)

		RURAL (Continued)		TOTAL	
		Maui County	Kauai County	Urban	Rural
Hawaiian . . .	Male	2,184	686	5,334	5,977
	Female	2,122	677	5,496	5,829
Caucasian-Hawaiian	Male	1,373	507	4,486	3,274
	Female	1,244	489	4,783	3,089
Asiatic-Hawaiian .	Male	1,239	384	3,327	2,955
	Female	1,180	378	3,527	2,783
Portuguese . . .	Male	2,214	1,329	7,341	6,529
	Female	2,215	1,225	7,423	6,295
Porto Rican . .	Male	632	460	1,240	2,395
	Female	521	381	1,129	1,907
Spanish	Male	52	105	296	335
	Female	41	99	329	259
Other Caucasian .	Male	987	653	14,762	15,808
	Female	881	518	10,329	3,996
Chinese	Male	1,221	888	11,723	4,838
	Female	591	313	8,508	2,110
Japanese . . .	Male	12,220	7,491	29,912	45,096
	Female	10,173	6,414	26,912	37,711
Korean	Male	565	238	1,609	2,390
	Female	254	124	1,283	1,179
Filipino	Male	11,975	10,916	4,876	47,690
	Female	2,169	1,646	1,955	8,591
All other . . .	Male	50	15	259	188
	Female	43	6	211	122
Total	Male	34,712	23,672	85,165	137,475
	Female	21,434	12,270	71,885	73,811

Appendix C

DATA RELATING TO MARRIAGES

WHEN an application for a marriage license is made, it is necessary for the applicants to furnish personal information including their place of birth and that of their parents and also to their racial classification. Since the Bureau of Vital Statistics, which issues the license, has a birth record, with race, for most applicants it can and does check statements that seem to be doubtful. Under Hawaiian conditions there is not much tendency to misstate the facts except for some dark part-Hawaiians who prefer to be classified as pure Hawaiian.

There have been some minor shifts in the implied definitions of classificatory terms. Before 1930 the Bureau classified part-Hawaiians who had both Caucasian and Asiatic ancestry according to the classification of the mother. For example, if a child were reported as born to a Caucasian-Hawaiian woman, the father being Asiatic-Hawaiian, the classification, Caucasian-Hawaiian, would be given, while a child of precisely the same fractional three-way mixture would be classified as Asiatic-Hawaiian if the mother was Asiatic-Hawaiian and the father Caucasian-Hawaiian. Practically about half of the people of such three-way mixture were classified as Asiatic-Hawaiian and about half as Caucasian-Hawaiian. But according to the census definitions, all of these were Asiatic-Hawaiian, their Caucasian ancestry being ignored. Since June 30, 1930, the Bureau of Vital Statistics has followed the census method and hence the figures for these two groups are not quite comparable with those of earlier dates. For example, there were, 1930–34, 444 Asiatic-Hawaiian grooms and 690 Caucasian-Hawaiian. If classified in the former way the figures would have been about 420 and 714. Probably the rate of in-marriage for these two groups was affected a little by the change in classification. Similarly the number of Portuguese, Porto

334

Ricans and Spanish has been reduced by accepting the census definitions since 1930. Before 1930 the child of a Portuguese woman and an "other Caucasian" man was classified by the Bureau of Vital Statistics as Portuguese but now as "other Caucasian." It was in the first period, 1912–16, that Japanese brides were coming from their native land in largest numbers and this accounts for the comparatively large number of Japanese brides and grooms, the number being about twice as large as for the period, 1924–28.

In the period, 1920–24, a few hundred old Chinese husbands and wives were remarried. They had been living together, maybe for thirty or forty years, as married, but the courts held that ceremonies according to Chinese custom were not valid in Hawaii. I have not counted these remarriages since they were not relevant to the purpose.

The following tables are to show the racial distribution of the brides of the men of each racial group for five periods as specified.

TABLE XLIX

A Racial Classification of Brides and Grooms

Four Years, 1912–1916

RACES OF GROOMS	RACES OF BRIDES												Total
	Hawaiian	Caucasian-Hawaiian	Asiatic-Hawaiian	Portuguese	Porto Rican	Spanish	Other Caucasian	Chinese	Japanese	Korean	Filipino	All Other	
Hawaiian	821	98	56	24	1		8	3	2			6	1,018
Caucasian-Hawaiian	108	133	30	17		1	21		2			2	316
Asiatic-Hawaiian	71	38	17	7				6					139
Portuguese	36	26	11	828	2	13	14				1	12	943
Porto Rican	3			33	149	9	1				2		197
Spanish	4			15	4	154					1		180
Other Caucasian	100	140	16	185	16	16	674	6	1		6	13	1,174
Chinese	115	17	46	11	5	1		280	2		1	2	480
Japanese	20	3	4	6					6,364			1	6,395
Korean	40	1	2	7	2	9	1	1	3	196	3		267
Filipino	45	1		50	24	19	5	1	2		535	3	684
All other	3	5		16		1	5					3	33
Total	1,366	463	182	1,199	203	223	729	297	6,376	196	550	42	11,826

TABLE L

A Racial Classification of Brides and Grooms

Four Years, 1920-1924

RACES OF GROOMS	RACES OF BRIDES												
	Hawaiian	Caucasian-Hawaiian	Asiatic-Hawaiian	Portuguese	Porto Rican	Spanish	Other Caucasian	Chinese*	Japanese	Korean	Filipino	All Other	Total
Hawaiian	584	111	62	16	3		1	10	7			1	795
Caucasian-Hawaiian	126	256	68	42	4		15	8	3	1	1		524
Asiatic-Hawaiian	76	57	38	13		1	4	19	4				212
Portuguese	56	65	7	752	19	10	13	5	3			9	939
Porto Rican	5	1		23	236	8					2	1	276
Spanish	4	3	1	12	4	33	1					1	59
Other Caucasian	96	208	33	294	22	18	957	14	13	2	4	46	1,707
Chinese	47	29	35	8	3	2	3	455	7	1	2	3	595
Japanese	23	9	6	5		1	5	2	3,399				3,450
Korean	10	2	4	5	3		1		5	187	1	2	220
Filipino	105	22	13	72	70	16	4	5	16		1,018	3	1,344
All other	8	12	5	32	5	3	47					15	127
Total	1,140	775	272	1,274	369	92	1,051	518	3,457	191	1,028	81	10,248

* During this period there were several hundred remarriages of aged Chinese who had been married according to Chinese custom many years before. These remarriages were not included in the above table.

TABLE LI

A Racial Classification of Brides and Grooms

Four Years, 1924–1928

RACES OF GROOMS	RACES OF BRIDES												
	Hawaiian	Caucasian-Hawaiian	Asiatic-Hawaiian	Portuguese	Porto Rican	Spanish	Other Caucasian	Chinese	Japanese	Korean	Filipino	All Other	Total
Hawaiian	528	146	97	31	4		5	6	7		3	3	830
Caucasian-Hawaiian	134	314	78	52	4	8	44	20	16	1		5	676
Asiatic-Hawaiian	78	81	67	15	1	1	5	21	6	1	1	1	278
Portuguese	64	98	28	744	31	21	23	4	7			5	1,025
Porto Rican	7	7	1	42	245	8	1	3	1				315
Spanish	5	3	2	15	12	23	2		1				65
Other Caucasian	133	207	54	370	35	26	1,071	21	39	5	2	57	2,022
Chinese	46	42	36	11	1	1	1	506	16	1	4	2	663
Japanese	24	22	26	11	1		2	15	3,099	1	1	1	3,203
Korean	1	8	3		2		1	2	4	118	2	1	142
Filipino	117	35	28	58	70	8	3	5	30		1,030		1,384
All other	18	10	2	25	10	3	35	4	1			18	126
Total	1,155	973	422	1,374	416	99	1,193	607	3,227	127	1,043	93	10,729

TABLE LII

A Racial Classification of Brides and Grooms

Two Years, 1928-1930

RACES OF GROOMS	RACES OF BRIDES												
	Hawaiian	Caucasian-Hawaiian	Asiatic-Hawaiian	Portuguese	Porto Rican	Spanish	Other Caucasian	Chinese	Japanese	Korean	Filipino	All Other	Total
Hawaiian	204	62	39	14	4	2	4	10	6			2	347
Caucasian-Hawaiian	61	137	47	33	2	1	22	5	7			2	317
Asiatic-Hawaiian	34	50	37	10		1	3	17	3			2	157
Portuguese	28	38	13	361	13	9	16	7	7			6	498
Porto Rican	2	1		14	94	3	1						115
Spanish	1	1		6		7	1	1					17
Other Caucasian	39	100	28	181	15	17	545	12	21	4	3	4	969
Chinese	14	24	38	7	1		2	255	14	1		3	359
Japanese	10	25	9	8	1	2	2	6	1,544	1			1,608
Korean	6	3	6		1			1	4	60			81
Filipino	51	11	17	41	36	2	6	3	11		448	1	627
All other	3	3	2	3	1		1					5	18
Total	453	455	236	678	168	44	603	317	1,617	66	451	25	5,113

TABLE LIII

A Racial Classification of Brides and Grooms

Four Years, 1930–1934

RACES OF GROOMS	RACES OF BRIDES												
	Hawaiian	Caucasian-Hawaiian*	Asiatic-Hawaiian*	Portuguese	Porto Rican	Spanish	Other Caucasian	Chinese	Japanese	Korean	Filipino	All Other	Total
Hawaiian	258	95	130	22	4	1	8	9	9	4		6	546
Caucasian-Hawaii*	98	268	134	75	3	3	59	20	20	3	1	6	690
Asiatic-Hawaiian*	68	135	119	34	4	1	10	55	14	1		3	444
Portuguese	36	91	43	760	24	11	58	11	14	1	3	9	1,061
Porto Rican	7	7	1	21	175	3	8	1	1			3	227
Spanish	1	1		13		5	3	1					27
Other Caucasian	45	168	59	362	27	19	1,247	24	29	10	1	25	2,018
Chinese	22	31	69	11	3	3	6	495	24	3	3	4	672
Japanese	19	28	36	15		2	10	29	3,214	3	1	2	3,358
Korean	5	3	6	3				4	3	111		3	138
Filipino	100	41	74	83	52	4	23	5	46	7	922	13	1,370
All other	5	12	10	9	3	1	8	3	1		2	17	71
Total	664	880	681	1,408	297	53	1,440	657	3,375	143	933	91	10,622

* The statistical data of the preceding tables are based on the racial classifications used in Hawaii, there being nine racial and two mixed racial groups. Probably it would be of some interest to make a classification involving only five races and the two mixed racial groups. (1) The Chinese, Japanese and Koreans may be called "Mongolians." (2) The Filipinos are "Malay." (3) The people of white American or European ancestry are known as "Caucasian." (4) The people who are partly of Negro blood are classified as Negroes and with them are counted a very few others, who according to U. S. Census classifications, are "colored." (5) The Hawaiians are Polynesians. (6) The Caucasian-Hawaiians are "Caucasian-Polynesians" and the Asiatic-Hawaiians, "Mongolian-Polynesians." (Very few, if any, Filipino-Hawaiians are of marriageable age.)

TABLE LIV

Marriages, the Four Years, 1930–1934

(A Different Racial Classification)

RACES OF GROOMS	RACES OF BRIDES							
	Polynesian	Caucasian-Polynesian	Mongolian-Polynesian	Caucasian	Mongolian	Malay	Negro and All Other	Total
Polynesian	258	95	130	31	22		10	546
Caucasian-Polynesian . .	98	268	134	137	43	1	9	690
Mongolian-Polynesian . .	68	135	119	45	70		7	444
Caucasian	82	260	102	2,478	90	7	87	3,106
Mongolian	46	62	111	50	3,886	1	12	4,168
Malay	100	41	74	110	58	922	65	1,370
Negro and all other . .	12	19	11	50	6	2	198	298
Total	664	880	681	2,901	4,175	933	388	10,622

Table LV is to present the out-marriage rates of the brides and grooms of the eleven racial and mixed racial groups for the four four-year periods. Trends may be compared. The generally rising rates of out-marriage among the members of the pure racial groups may be compared with the high, but nearly constant, rates among the part-Hawaiians. Also, one may compare the fairly steady trend in one direction of the racial groups whose sex ratios are not very highly abnormal with the irregular trend of the Chinese and the Koreans as the sex ratio of the marriageable, highly abnormal in the first period, became more nearly normal.

TABLE LV

Number of Grooms and Brides Out–Married to 1000 Married

		Grooms	Brides	Brides and Grooms
Hawaiian	1912–16	194	399	311
	1920–24	265	487	396
	1924–28	364	542	468
	1930–34	527	611	573
Caucasian-Hawaiian	1912–16	579	712	658
	1920–24	511	669	607
	1924–28	535	677	619
	1930–34	612	695	659
Asiatic-Hawaiian	1912–16	877	905	894
	1920–24	820	860	843
	1924–28	759	841	808
	1930–34	732	825	788
Portuguese	1912–16	122	309	226
	1920–24	199	409	320
	1924–28	274	458	379
	1930–34	284	460	384
Porto Rican	1912–16	243	266	255
	1920–24	145	360	268
	1924–28	222	411	329
	1930–34	229	411	332
Spanish	1912–16	144	309	235
	1920–24	440	641	562
	1924–28	646	767	719
	1930–34	814	905	875
Other Caucasian	1912–16	425	75	291
	1920–24	439	89	306
	1924–28	470	102	333
	1930–34	382	134	278

344 INTERRACIAL MARRIAGE IN HAWAII

		Grooms	Brides	Brides and Grooms
Chinese	1912–16	416	57	279
	1920–24	235	121	182
	1924–28	236	166	203
	1930–34	263	246	255
Japanese	1912–16	5	2	3
	1920–24	14	16	15
	1924–28	32	39	36
	1930–34	42	47	45
Korean	1912–16	265		153
	1920–24	.150	21	90
	1924–28	169	71	122
	1930–34	195	223	208
Filipino	1912–16	217	27	132
	1920–24	242	10	141
	1924–28	256	12	151
	1930–34	327	12	242
All Races	1912–16	154	154	154
	1920–24	226	226	226
	1924–28	276	276	276
	1930–34 *	285	285	285

* If the short racial classification of Table LIV were used the rate of out-marriages, 1930–34, would be, instead of 285 to the 1000, only 234.

OUT-MARRIAGE IN HONOLULU CITY AND IN THE REST OF THE TERRITORY

In 1930, 37 per cent of the population of the Territory was enumerated in Honolulu. But of the female population, 43 per cent was in this city and of females, 20–29 years of age, 48 per cent. Over half of all marriages in the Territory in recent years have been in the city of Honolulu, the numbers being for the two years, 1932–34, 2722 for Honolulu, and 2679 for all other districts. It may be a matter of interest to compare the out-marriage rates of the city of Honolulu with those of the rest of the Territory which is mainly rural.

For certain racial groups there is a significant difference between the city and the rural districts. The Hawaiians, for example, marry out in higher proportions in the rural districts while the reverse is true of the Caucasian-Hawaiians. But for all groups together the rate of out-marriage was almost precisely the same as between Honolulu and the rest of the Territory.

TABLE LVI

Rates of Out-Marriage Urban and Rural, the Two Years, 1932–1934

| | NUMBER OUT-MARRIED TO THE 1000 MARRIED | | | | | |
| | Grooms | | Brides | | Brides and Grooms | |
	City of Honolulu	*All Other Districts*	*City of Honolulu*	*All Other Districts*	*City of Honolulu*	*All Other Districts*
Hawaiian .	622	461	663	598	644	539
Caucasian-Hawaiian	571	675	676	695	631	685
Asiatic-Hawaiian	772	677	843	819	814	768
Portuguese .	394	240	540	397	477	328
Porto Rican	250	239	263	436	256	345
Spanish . .	817	500	882	882	857	809
Other Caucasian	332	397	100	234	233	326
Chinese . .	201	440	234	371	218	407
Japanese .	43	51	38	67	40	59
Korean . .	116	419	208	307	164	368
Filipino . .	395	360	25	18	253	225
All Races	293	290	293	290	293	290

APPENDIX D

STATISTICALLY UNRECOGNIZED MIXED–BLOODS

WHEN the birth of a child of mixed racial ancestry is reported for registration the child is classified as of mixed-blood if he is part-Hawaiian, but all the mixtures of other sorts are classified as pure-bloods. There are data relative to the paternity and maternity of children available for only three years, 1930–31, 1931–32, and 1934–35. The number of children born in these three years, as reported, was 29,918. But, of this number there were 448, one or both of whose parents are classified racially as "unknown" or as "all others." Omitting these, there were 29,470 whose parents are racially classified. Those whose parents are both classified in the same racial group may be called pure-bloods if the group is not part-Hawaiian. All the rest are mixed-bloods.

Of the 29,470 children, 22,048 are pure-bloods, 74.9 per cent; 5,695 are part Hawaiians of various sorts, 19.3 per cent; and 1,727 are mixed-bloods of other sorts, 5.8 per cent; but in the statistical reports the latter are counted as pure-bloods.

These figures do not reveal the full extent of the statistically unrecognized mixture because some of the parents reported as pure-bloods are really mixed-bloods and the mixture is of Hawaiian origin. Probably there are about ten thousand such statistically unrecognized mixed-bloods in the Territory now.

Table LVII classifies the fathers and mothers of the 29,470 children and it gives some idea as to the number of types of first generation half-and-half mixture that are coming into existence. I am not familiar with any statistical device for indicating the complexity of the situation as it will be when the children of the following table intermarry with each other and with all the pure racial groups and produce offspring of more complex race mixture.

TABLE LVII

Births by the Race of Parents for the Three Years, 1931–1932, 1932–1933 and 1934–1935

RACES OF FATHERS	RACES OF MOTHERS											Total
	Hawaiian	Caucasian-Hawaiian	Asiatic-Hawaiian	Portuguese	Porto Rican	Spanish	Other Caucasian	Chinese	Japanese	Korean	Filipino	
Hawaiian	1,042	326	376	60	12	3	25	39	29	2	3	1,917
Caucasian-Hawaiian	305	651	313	141	8	14	85	41	41	5	6	1,610
Asiatic-Hawaiian	280	330	335	56	3	1	20	85	31	2	1	1,144
Portuguese	122	182	83	1,726	43	36	85	23	36	3	5	2,344
Porto Rican	12	10	6	68	607	10	37	5	5	1	3	764
Spanish	5	7	2	29	9	38	5	1	2			98
Other Caucasian	186	230	91	393	51	21	1,551	36	54	15	8	2,636
Chinese	88	89	174	32	3	3	4	1,533	41	15	1	1,983
Japanese	74	67	89	36	1		9	40	11,637	8	4	11,965
Korean	25	11	14	7	4	3	3	6	14	341		428
Filipino	292	85	122	183	159	17	36	18	89	7	3,573	4,581
Total	2,431	1,988	1,605	2,731	900	146	1,860	1,827	11,979	399	3,604	29,470

A GLOSSARY OF HAWAIIAN WORDS

Some of these words belong strictly to the old Hawaiian language but in some cases there has been a modification of meaning on account of the new experiences that followed the coming of foreigners. Other words were adopted from the vocabulary of foreigners, mainly the English speaking, and they were phonetically adapted to Hawaiian usage. Sometimes also the meanings were adapted to local needs.

1. *Ha-o-le,* (1) stranger; foreigner; (2) a white person, especially one of superior economic status.
2. *Ha-o-le el-e-el-e,* a black stranger (applied to Negroes).
3. *Ha-o-li-fied* (recent). Disposed to act like *haole.* Applied to Caucasian-Hawaiians or rarely to others who try to achieve *haole* status by acting like them.
4. *Ha-pa ha-o-le,* half white or part white.
5. *Ha-pa pa-ke,* half Chinese.
6. *Ka-ma-ai-na,* a child of the land; native born; sometimes graciously extended to old residents who are not native but who are sympathetic to the Hawaiian way of life.
7. *Ke-pa-ni,* the Hawaiianized pronunciation of Japanese.
8. *Ma-li-hi-ni,* a transient resident. A person who is not a *kamaaina.*
9. *Pa-ke,* Chinese. Probably the Hawaiianized pronunciation of the Chinese word *pak-ye,* meaning "uncle."
10. *Pil-i-pi-no,* the Hawaiianized pronunciation of "Filipino."
11. *Po-ko–Li-ko,* the Hawaiianized pronunciation of "Porto Rican."
12. *Po-ki-ki* and *Por-te-gee,* "Portuguese" as pronounced by Hawaiians.
13. *Pu-na-lu-a,* a term of relationship. A man called another husband of his wife his *punalua* and a woman called another wife of her husband her *punalua.*

INDEX

Abortion, 3, 14, 46, 47.

Acculturation, rate of, 185, 254; and in intermarriage, 199, 318; and group solidarity, 202; at two levels, 239–40, 311–14; incentives to, 252; obstacles to, 253, 279; and social disorganization, 278, 314–15; and conflict, 279–80; and plantation life, 284; and city life, 284–86; later stages of, 294–95; a compromise, 311, 313; and emancipation from the mores, 314–16; and social recognition, 315–16; and the social code, 317–20.

Agriculture, 2, 5, 7, 30–31.

Amalgamation, statistical data, 12–19, 20, 112–13, 346–47; through interracial marriage, 20; sex ratios and, 21–23, 192; the role of the mixed-blood liaison groups, 22, 199, 204; sectional aspects, 24–29; rate of, 107–08, 109; later stages of, 107–08; and size of minority groups, 198; the outlook, 204, 326; not desired at first, 310; and assimilation mutually conditioned, 310–26; and social relations, 313.

Americanization, and race attitude, 65, 138; and divorce, 207.

Ancestor worship and out-marriage, 144, 161.

Antipathy, racial, 45.

Asiatic-Hawaiians, statistical term, definition of, 12, 229; sectional distribution, 40, 89, 332–33; indexes of in-marriage preference, 103–04; marriage statistics, 111–12, 334–45; paternity of, 157.

Assimilation, problem of, 159; and social relations, 202, 315–17; and intermarriage, 203, 317–18; and intellectual parity, 250–73; and race,

279; and religion, 281; and sex ratio, 282; and numerical factors, 282; and length of residence, 282–83; and group morale, 289; and emancipation from the mores, 314; and the code of race relations, 317–20.

Attitude, of the British, 121; of Americans, 121, 165–66, 279; and the code of race relations, 167; follows behavior, 185; changeable, 195–96, 198.

Burgess, Ernest W., 274.

Cape colored, 183.

Caste, and the marriage code, 45, 52; has a religious sanction, 52.

Caucasians, 12–13. *See also* Portuguese, Porto Ricans, Spanish, "Other Caucasians."

Caucasian-Hawaiians, statistical term, definition of, 12; sectional distribution, 40, 332–33; traditions of the old families, 98–101; amalgamation of, 105–06; marriage statistics, 111–12, 334–45; superiority of, 230.

Censuses, dates of, 117–18.

Chinese, immigration of, 4–7, 31; sectional distribution, 28–29, 40, 332–33; occupational changes, 32–36; excite antagonistic sentiment, 58–60, 116; marriage practice, 142–43; betrothal by parents, 144; foot-binding and the immigration of women, 145–46; the four choices, 149–50; marital status, 150; social status, 151–52, 242–43; in Honolulu and in the rural districts, 152–54; attitude toward out-marriage, 153–56, 165; marriage of women, 154–55; probable future marriage trends, 156–57;

assimilation, 159; indexes of in-marriage preference, 194–96; and divorce, 214, 224; familiar with a commercial economy, 240; business ability of, 241–42; education of, 242, 264–66; personality traits of, 293.

Chinese-Hawaiians, a statistical group, 90; marginal position of, 90–93; traditions of, a beginning, 94–98; superiority, 96–97, 230–31; a liaison group, 97; marriage statistics, 97; social status, 104–05.

Chivalry among Filipinos, 176.

Code of race relations, symbolizes social equality, 43–44, 280; and opportunity, 68; and incentives, 255; and acculturation, 280; and assimilation, 281; and personality traits, 290–91.

Communal morale, and the general good, 296; and political control, 296–99; and regimentation, 299; and cultural differences, 299–301; and the situation in Hawaii, 300–03, 309; and social change, 304; schools, the role of, 307–08; and conflict, 308.

Crisis situation and interracial marriage, 132.

Cultural diffusion and intelligence, 250–73.

Cultural disorganization and personality traits, 246.

Cultural trends, 320–26.

Culture, a stone age, 2, 247.

Data, availability of, 20–21.

Death rates, of Hawaiians, 75, 248.

Definitions, of racial statistical terms, 12–18; terms of popular usage, 114–20.

Depopulation, 4, 7, 73, 75.

Divorce, racial and interracial character of, 205; grounds for, 205; and sex ratio, 206; and the decadence of tradition, 206, 215, 217, 219, 225; and the status of women, 207; and social disorganization, 207, 209, 225; rates and trends, 207, 213–15; and the recently immigrated, 208, 209, 212; and recently contracted marriages,

209, 218; and instability of residence, 210; urban and rural rates of, 217; and sex of libelants, 220–22; and minor children, 221; and remarriage, 221–23; of the in-married and of the out-married, 223–25.

Emancipation from the mores, and out-marriage, 123, 130; and assimilation, 314, 316.

Enlisted men in the army and navy, 13, 23, 27, 124–25, 128, 209–10, 220.

Equality, doctrine of, and code of, 43–44; and interracial marriage, 44–45; and opportunity, 68; meaning, 236–37.

Estates, landed, 48, 99.

Exploitation and the code of race relations, 50–52.

Family histories, 71.

Farmers, 33, 36, 37–38.

Fertility of Hawaiian and part-Hawaiian women, 3, 71–73.

Filipinos, immigration of, 32, 174; sectional distribution, 39–40, 332–33; numbers, 174; sex ratio, 174; the return movements of, 175, 178; social status, 175–76, 177–78; and unorganized group, 176, 178; religion and marriage, 176, 179–80; marriage in Honolulu and in rural districts, 176–78; race and marriage, 179–80; marriage statistics, 179, 334, 345; indexes of in-marriage preference, 195; divorce, 208–09, 214–24.

Forecasts, predicated on certain conditions, 326.

Foreigners, 4–7, 8, 21, 40.

Freedom in marriage and absence from home, 53.

Fur traders, 4, 21.

Genealogy, and family history, 70: Hawaiian, 70; part-Hawaiian, 99.

Haole, meaning derived from Hawaiian experience, 114–16; status, of, 115–16. See also "Other Caucasians."

Hawaiians, numbers, 2, 4, 8–9, 15;

352 INDEX

Migration, and social control, 87; and divorce, 213.

Minority peoples, and dominance, 181, 182–83; role of small groups, 181–82; decadence of morale of, 304–05; assimilability of, 316–20.

Missionaries and the code of race relations, 54–57.

Mixed-bloods, numbers of, 15–19, 78, 110–13, 227, 346–47; ancestry of, 18, 228–29; social status, 49, 236–39; family histories of, 71; racial trend, 73–74; role of, 85–113; fractional mixture of, 228–29, 232. See also Hybrids, Part-Hawaiians, Caucasian-Hawaiians, Asiatic-Hawaiians.

Morale of minorities and out-marriage, 88, 163–64.

Mores, of racial equality, 44; inhibitions of, 53, 60–61; emancipation from foreign, 424.

Movement of immigrants, 31–32.

Myth-making and group solidarity, 70, 95–97, 130–39.

Nationalistic sentiment, 200, 322–25.

Negroes, early immigrants, 5; called by another name, 24, 117–18; out-marriage of, 135, 138.

Nordic race, 247.

Occupations of immigrants, 32–41.

"Other Caucasians": a statistical term, 13; sectional distribution of, 40, 332–33; sentiment adverse to out-marriage, 43–53; marriage of women, 49, 129–31; marriage experience, 121–33; the role of the malihini, 127; marriage statistics of, 128, 131, 133, 332–45; indexes of in-marriage preference, 196; divorces of, 210–24.

Out-marriage, sentiment adverse to, 43, 53, 87–88; advantages of, 47–49; and social status, 48, 125–26, 129; trends of, 77, 79–83, 131, 155, 343–44; and being away from home, 122–25; and group solidarity, 201–03.

Pake, definition, 116–17. See also Chinese.

Park, Robert E., vi, 274.

Part-Hawaiians, number, 14–16; sectional distribution, 25–26, 29, 40, 332–33; social status, 49, 106–07, 238; paternity and maternity, 79, 347; indexes of in-marriage preference, 196; divorce of, 218–24; two groups, 229; racial passing, 229, 240; heterogeneity of, 232; education of, 232; intermediate, 232–33, 234, 247, 248; influences by Hawaiian tradition, 233, 239–40; personality traits, 249, 290–91; changing character, 247–48. See also Caucasians, Hawaiians, Asiatic-Hawaiians.

Personality, and opportunity, 106–07; definition, 274; socially conditioned, 274; and social disorganization, 274–95; types, 274–75; and social change, 275–76; and conflict of cultures, 277; marginal, 277, 279, 292–93, 280, 291, 294; and immigration, 278; and culture, 278; and race relations, 279.

Plantations and immigration, 5–7, 21.

Population, censuses and estimates, 1–2, 3, 4, 8, 9; foreign, 5–7; outlook, 9–10; racial composition of, 12–19; civilian, 13, 15, 16, 17, 18; sectional distribution, 28–29, 40, 331–33.

Portegee, popular term, definition of, 117; status of, 119–20. See also Portuguese.

Porteus, S. D., 233.

Porto Ricans, statistical term, definition of, 13; sectional distribution, 40, 332–33; attitude of Portuguese toward, 138, 187; a small group, 186; racial status, 187; social status, 187; indexes of in-marriage preference, 196; divorce, 214–24; marriage statistics, 336–45.

Portuguese, statistical term, definition, 13; numbers, 13–18; immigration of, 36, 134–35; sectional distribution, 36–37, 40, 139, 332–33; social status, 119, 136; a race, 119–20; occupational data, 134–36; sex ratio, 135, 193–94; eco-

PATTERSON SMITH REPRINT SERIES IN
CRIMINOLOGY, LAW ENFORCEMENT, AND SOCIAL PROBLEMS